THE
ART
OF
LOVING
WELL

A Character Education Curriculum
for Today's Teenagers

BOSTON
UNIVERSITY

School of Education
The Loving Well Project
Boston University
605 Commonwealth Avenue
Boston, Massachusetts 02215
617/353-4088

Boston University, Boston 02215
The Art of Loving Well: A Character Education Curriculum for Today's Teenagers
Copyright © 1993 Trustees of Boston University
Fourth printing, 1998

ISBN: 0-87270-079-8

This research-based curriculum was developed jointly over five years by the College of Communication and the School of Education at Boston University and funded in part by grant #APH000819 of the Office of Adolescent Pregnancy Programs, U.S. Department of Health and Human Services.

Project Staff:
    Dr. Stephan Ellenwood, *Project Director*
    Nancy McLaren, *Assistant Project Director*
    Dr. Ronald Goldman
    Dr. Kevin Ryan

In addition to the project staff, a number of individuals have been instrumental in making this project possible. These include: Dr. Richard Bishirjian, Errin Cecil, Anne Severson, Mary Ann Alexeeff, Shannon Kennedy, and the many teachers and students in Massachusetts, Maine, and South Carolina whose enthusiastic participation and thoughtful advice during field testing were invaluable.

TABLE OF CONTENTS

SECTION THREE: COMMITMENT AND MARRIAGE

Human beings derive fulfillment in several areas of life. Among these are work, artistic expression, and love. To achieve real fulfillment in each of these areas requires considerable knowledge and effort.

Typically, schools concentrate heavily on the world of work and teach the knowledge and skills necessary for success in a job or career. Schools also devote some resources and energy to developing artistic talents. Only rarely and awkwardly, however, do schools deal with the subjects of love, intimacy, and human sexuality even though these subjects are of enormous interest to adults and young adults alike. Perhaps one reason for this omission is that love is a difficult subject to talk about. It can be embarrassing to talk about a subject that is so confusing and so personal. Yet, if we are all to learn more about what it means to love well, it is important for older and younger generations to talk with each other. This book offers a way of gaining knowledge about love by reflecting on stories that reveal the full complexity of human relationships.

The premise of *The Art of Loving Well* is that the best way to gain knowledge about this most important part of life is by promoting conversation and reflection about our common human experience. Stories allow us to think and talk about profound emotional experiences without the embarrassment of talking directly about ourselves. Though experience may sometimes be the best teacher, in areas of love and sexuality experience can be painful, if not dangerous. Stories and conversations with parents, teachers, and friends about those stories enable us to learn important lessons from the experience of others. By reflecting on the actions and decisions of characters in literature, we can be better prepared as we face similar situations in our own lives.

Most people go through three stages on the journey toward real love and intimacy. This book has three sections, which correspond to these stages: 1) Early Loves and Losses; 2) Romance; and 3) Commitment and Marriage. Careful consideration of the stories in each of these sections should help readers make wiser choices as they set out on this adventurous journey with all its

5

ups and downs, its disappointments and pleasures.

Some common themes run through this book. One is that we learn to love from our families and communities. They have immense influence upon our attitudes and actions. Many of the stories in this book describe loves and losses that are connected with family life. Although it may be difficult for different generations to discuss these matters, parents and teachers have traveled some distance along the road to understanding and, therefore, can offer insights into the pitfalls, detours, and special attractions that exist along the way. The activities associated with each of the stories in this book are designed to make conversations about the art of loving somewhat easier.

Another central theme is that human relationships are complex and that it takes time to nurture true friendships and intimate partnerships. Love offers the potential for our greatest happiness but also renders us vulnerable to great pain. Genuine intimacy is not only a hedge against loneliness but a source of inspiration. When we love and feel loved, we are at our best. On the other hand, if we are disappointed by those we love or if we make harmful mistakes, we can suffer a tremendous sense of loss and pain. Therefore, because relationships are so complex, it takes time to understand the intricacies of our feelings and to learn how to deal with them wisely. It takes time to achieve the maturity necessary for genuine intimacy, but the reward is well worth the time invested.

The third theme is that sexual relationships *are* a big deal and should never be taken lightly. Momentary satisfaction outside the context of a mature and deeply intimate relationship usually results in someone getting hurt. The media are constantly barraging us with messages that the time for sexual activity is now and that nothing is gained by waiting. In addition, the pressure that it is somehow "cool" to be sexually experienced at an early age can overcome better judgment. Furthermore, people who feel lonely or unsure of themselves sometimes foolishly turn to sexual relationships as a way of soothing their loneliness and pain. However, unless they are in the context of a deeply intimate and committed partnership, sexual encounters usually complicate problems rather than solve them. These stories will guide students to see that premature sexual intimacy can bring with it severe consequences.

The fourth theme is that growth and change are possible if we are willing to take the time and trouble to learn all that is involved in loving well. Many of the stories in this collection offer the promise that people and conditions can improve even though at times we may feel that we are trapped and that nothing can ever change. The wisdom contained in good literature can empower us to make wise decisions about the course of our own lives. It is never too late to take a new direction.

Finally, this book is intended to enrich rather than to supplant the standard school curriculum. It was originally designed for English classes, and the literary selections and related activities provide an ideal vehicle for developing standard literary and language arts skills, However, *The Art of Loving Well* has been used successfully in a wide range of interdisciplinary settings. Whatever the context, we hope you enjoy your explorations into the pages that follow.

Section One:

EARLY

LOVES

AND

LOSSES

A NOTE ON SYMBOLISM

You have heard the phrase, "It means a lot to me." That is a good definition of a symbol.

Imagine discovering how you feel about someone during a romantic walk in the afternoon. You both want to remember this day. You see some wild daisies with tiny white flowers — and you each pick one.

At home you tape the wilting flower to your mirror. The daisy grows dry and colorless, but whenever you notice it, you remember that walk. No, you don't just remember — you live it again.

Now imagine that two of your friends see that tape holding what looks like a piece of straw to your mirror. One laughs; the other asks what's special about it.

Your second friend sees that the daisy is a symbol, but your first friend sees only the literal meaning — a dried-up flower.

You can read a story literally, memorizing the facts in case the teacher asks you what happened. Or you can read it as if it were happening to you, looking for the "daisies." If you search the stories for symbols, your own symbols, you will learn more about yourself than about the people in the story. The authors and editors of this book hope you'll do that.

LITTLE BRIAR-ROSE

by the Brothers Grimm

A long time ago there were a King and Queen who said every day: "Ah, if only we had a child!" but they never had one. But it happened that once when the Queen was bathing, a frog crept out of the water on to the land, and said to her: "Your wish shall be fulfilled; before a year has gone by, you shall have a daughter."

What the frog had said came true, and the Queen had a little girl who was so pretty that the King could not contain himself for joy, and ordered a great feast. He invited not only his kindred, friends and acquaintances, but also the Wise Women, in order that they might be kind and well-disposed towards the child. There were thirteen of them in his kingdom, but, as he had only twelve golden plates for them to eat out of, one of them had to be left at home.

The feast was held with all manner of splendor, and when it came to an end the Wise Women bestowed their magic gifts upon the baby: one gave virtue, another beauty, a third riches, and so on with everything in the world that one can wish for.

When eleven of them had made their promises, suddenly the thirteenth came in. She wished to avenge herself for not having been invited, and without greeting, or even looking at anyone, she cried with a loud voice: "The King's daughter shall in her fifteenth year prick herself with a spindle, and fall down dead." And, without saying a word more, she turned round and left the room.

They were all shocked; but the twelfth, whose good wish still remained unspoken, came forward, and as she could not undo the evil sentence, but only soften it, she said: "It shall not be death, but a deep sleep of a hundred years, into which the princess shall fall."

The King, who would fain keep his dear child from the misfortune, gave orders that every spindle in the whole kingdom should be burnt. Meanwhile the gifts of the Wise Women were plenteously fulfilled on the young girl, for she was so beautiful, modest, good-natured, and wise, that everyone who saw her was bound to love her.

It happened that on the very day when she was fifteen years old the King and Queen were not at home, and the maiden was left in the palace quite alone. So she went round into all sorts of places, looked into rooms and bed-chambers just as she liked, and at last came to an old tower. She climbed up the narrow, winding staircase and reached a little door. A rusty key was in the lock, and when she turned it the door sprang open, and there in a little room sat an old woman with a spindle, busily spinning her flax.

"Good day, old mother," said the King's daughter; "what are you doing there?" "I am spinning," said the old woman, and nodded her head. "What sort of thing is that, that rattles round so merrily?" said the girl, and she took the spindle and wanted to spin too. But scarcely had she touched the spindle when the magic decree was fulfilled, and she pricked her finger with it.

And, in the very moment when she felt the prick, she fell down upon the bed that stood there, and lay in a deep sleep. And this sleep extended over the whole palace; the King and Queen who had just come home, and had entered the great hall, began to go to sleep, and the whole of the court with them. The horses, too, went to sleep in the stable, the dogs in the yard, the pigeons upon the roof, the flies on the wall; even the fire that was flaming on the hearth became quiet and slept, the roast meat left off sizzling, and the cook, who was just going to pull the hair of the scullery boy, because he had forgotten something, let him go, and went to sleep. And the wind fell, and on the trees before the castle not a leaf moved again.

But round about the castle there began to grow a hedge of thorns which every year became higher, and at last grew close up round the castle and all over it, so that there was nothing of it to be seen, not even the flag upon the roof. But the story of the beautiful sleeping "Briar-rose," for so the princess was named, went about the country, so that from time to time kings' sons came and tried to get through the thorny hedge into the castle.

But they found it impossible, for the thorns held fast together, as if they had hands, and the youths were caught in them, could not get loose again, and died a miserable death.

After long, long years a king's son came again to that country, and heard an old man talking about the thorn-hedge, and that a castle was said to stand behind it in which a wonderfully beautiful princess, named Briar-rose, had been asleep for a hundred years; and that the King and Queen and the whole court were asleep likewise. He had heard, too, from his grandfather, that many kings' sons had already come, and had tried to get through the thorny hedge, but they had remained sticking fast in it, and had died a pitiful death. Then the youth said: "I am not afraid, I will go and see the beautiful Briar-rose." The good old man might dissuade him as he would, he did not listen to his words.

But by this time the hundred years had just passed, and the day had come when Briar-rose was to awake again. When the king's son came near to the thorn-hedge, it was nothing but large and beautiful flowers, which parted from each other of their own accord, and let him pass unhurt, then they closed again behind him like a hedge. In the castle yard he saw the horses and the spotted hounds lying asleep; on the roof sat the pigeons with their heads under their wings. And when he entered the house, the flies were asleep upon the wall, the cook in the kitchen was still holding out his hand to seize the boy, and the maid was sitting by the black hen which she was going to pluck.

He went on farther, and in the great hall he saw the whole of the court lying asleep, and up by the throne lay the King and Queen.

Then he went on still farther, and all was so quiet that a breath could be heard, and at last he came to the tower, and opened the door into the little room where Briar-rose was sleeping. There she lay, so beautiful that he could not turn his eyes away; and he stooped down and gave her a kiss. But as soon as he kissed her, Briar-rose opened her eyes and awoke, and looked at him quite sweetly.

Then they went down together, and the King awoke, and the Queen, and the whole court, and looked at each other in great astonishment. And the horses in the courtyard stood up and shook themselves; the hounds jumped up and wagged their tails; the pigeons upon the roof pulled out their heads from under their wings, looked round, and flew into the open country; the flies on the wall crept again, the fire in the kitchen burned up and flickered and cooked the meat; the joint began to turn and sizzle again, and the cook gave the boy such a box on the ear that he screamed, and the maid finished plucking the fowl.

And then the marriage of the King's son with Briar-rose was celebrated with all splendor, and they lived contented to the end of their days.

ACTIVITIES

FOR DISCUSSION

A. One of the ideas that will recur often in *Loving Well* is that love flourishes best when the time is right. It is worth waiting for that right time since we can be hurt if we try to rush things. Discuss the ways in which you think it is possible to "get caught on a hedge of thorns" if we give in to the desire to rush things.

What do we learn about timing from the following symbols?
• the prick of the finger
• the hedge of thorns and the hedge of flowers
• the hundred years of sleep (how might this be like a cocoon or hibernation?)

B. Because the King has only twelve golden plates, he leaves out one of the wise women. In her anger the thirteenth wise woman puts a curse on the King's daughter. Briar-rose was not at fault, but she must suffer. What situations are there in life when people who are not at fault suffer? How should human beings respond "when bad things happen to good people?"

C. We often have conflicting or confused feelings when it comes to issues of love and sexuality. What might the name Briar-rose reflect about the young princess? Imagine that the Prince and Briar-rose symbolize one person. What parts of the personality could they stand for?

D. In an attempt to protect their daughter from the curse, Briar-rose's parents try to destroy every spindle in the kingdom. But they fail. There is no way to keep her from turning fifteen, and there is no way they can guarantee her safety. In fact, the King and the Queen are not even home on her birthday. What is the symbolic significance of their absence? What limits are there to the security of home and family? On the other hand, what should adults do to protect their children?

CLASS ACTIVITY: Public Opinion Poll

The prick of a spindle is probably low on the list of today's fears, but all parents worry about their children. Though an infant may swallow a toy or a toddler may run into the street, physical safety is only one area of concern.

As a class, make a list of five things you think today's parents worry about the most when it comes to their children. Then for homework, see how accurate you were. Everybody must interview at least one parent. If possible, interview your own. Tell the parents about "Briar-rose" (or "Sleeping Beauty" as it is often called). Then ask them to list five of the biggest worries they have when they think about their children's lives now and in the future.

In class compare the lists. Are there some worries that appear on all the lists? Which worries have to do with loving well? Do fathers have different worries from mothers? Are the parents' fears what you thought they would be? Are they similar to yours?

A&P

by John Updike

In walks these three girls in nothing but bathing suits. I'm in the third checkout slot, with my back to the door, so I don't see them until they're over by the bread. The one that caught my eye first was the one in the plaid green two-piece. She was a chunky kid, with a good tan and a sweet broad soft-looking can with those two crescents of white just under it, where the sun never seems to hit, at the top of the backs of her legs. I stood there with my hand on a box of HiHo crackers trying to remember if I rang it up or not. I ring it up again and the customer starts giving me hell. She's one of those cash-register-watchers, a witch about fifty with rouge on her cheekbones and no eyebrows, and I know it made her day to trip me up. She'd been watching cash registers for fifty years and had probably never seen a mistake before.

By the time I got her feathers smoothed and her goodies into a bag— she gives me a little snort in passing, if she'd been born at the right time they would have burned her over in Salem—by the time I get her on her way the girls had circled around the bread and were coming back, without a pushcart, back my way along the counters, in the aisle between the check-outs and the special bins. They didn't even have shoes on. There was this chunky one, with the two-piece—it was bright green and the seams on the bra were still sharp and her belly was still pretty pale so I guessed she just got it (the suit)—there was this one, with one of those chubby berry-faces, the lips all bunched together under her nose, this one, and a tall one, with black hair that hadn't quite frizzed right, and one of these sunburns right across under the eyes, and a chin that was too long—you know, the kind of girl other girls think is very "striking" and "attractive" but never quite makes it, as they very well know, which is why they like her so much — and then the third one, that wasn't quite so tall.

She was the queen. She kind of led them, the other two peeking around and making their shoulders round. She didn't look around, not this queen, she just walked straight on slowly, on these long white primadonna legs. She came down a little hard on her heels, as if she didn't walk in her bare feet that much, putting down her heels and then letting the weight move along to her toes as if she was testing the floor with every step, putting a little deliberate extra action into it. You never know for sure how girls' minds work (do you really think it's a mind in there or just a little buzz like a bee in a glass jar?) but you got the idea she had talked the other two into coming in here with her, and now she was showing them how to do it, walk slow and hold yourself straight.

She had on a kind of dirty-pink — beige maybe, I don't know — bathing suit with a little nubble all over it and, what got me, the straps were down. They were off her shoulders looped loose around the cool tops of her arms, and I guess as a result the suit had slipped a little on her, so all around the top of the cloth there was this shining rim. If it hadn't been there you wouldn't have known there could have been anything whiter than those shoulders. With the straps pushed off, there was nothing between the top of the suit and the top of her head except just her, this clean bare plane of the top of her chest down from the shoulder bones like a dented sheet of metal tilted in the light. I mean, it was more than pretty.

She had sort of oaky hair that the sun and salt had bleached, done up in a bun that was unraveling, and a kind of prim face.

Walking into the A&P with your straps down, I suppose it's the only kind of face you can have. She held her head so high her neck, coming up out of those white shoulders, looked kind of stretched, but I didn't mind. The longer her neck was, the more of her there was.

She must have felt in the corner of her eye me and over my shoulder Stokesie in the second slot watching, but she didn't tip. Not this queen. She kept her eyes moving across the racks, and stopped, and turned so slow it made my stomach rub the inside of my apron, and buzzed to the other two, who kind of huddled against her for relief, and then they all three of them went up the cat-and-dog-food-breakfast-cereal-macaroni-rice-raisins-season-ings-spreads-spaghetti-soft-drinks-crackers-and-cookies aisle. From the third slot I look straight up this aisle to the meat counter, and I watched them all the way. The fat one with the tan sort of fumbled with the cookies, but on second thought she put the package back. The sheep pushing their carts down the aisle—the girls were walking against the usual traffic (not that we have one-way signs or anything)—were pretty hilarious. You could see them, when Queenie's white shoulders dawned on them, kind of jerk, or hop, or hiccup, but their eyes snapped back to their carts. The customers are just normal people in an A&P and they would by and large keep reaching and checking oatmeal off their lists and muttering "Let me see, there was a third thing, began with A, asparagus, no, ah, yes, applesauce!" or whatever it is they do mutter. But there was no doubt, this jiggled them. A few houseslaves in pin curlers even looked around after pushing their carts past to make sure what they had seen was correct.

You know, it's one thing to have a girl in a bathing suit down on the beach, where, what with the glare nobody can look at each other much anyway, and another thing in the cool of the A&P, under the fluorescent lights, against all those stacked packages, with her feet paddling along naked over our checkerboard green-and-cream rubber-tile floor.

"Oh Daddy," Stokesie said beside me. "I feel so faint."

"Darling," I said. "Hold me tight." Stokesie's married, with two babies chalked up on his fuselage already, but as far as I can tell that's the only difference. He's twenty-two, and I was nineteen this April.

"Is it done?" he asks, the responsible married man finding his voice. I forgot to say he thinks he's going to be manager some sunny day, maybe in 1990 when it's called the Great Alexandrov and Petrooshki Tea Company or something.

What he meant was, our town is five miles from a beach, with a big summer colony out on the Point, but we're right in the middle of town, and the women generally put on a shirt or shoes or something before they get out of the car into the street. And anyway these are usually women with six children and varicose veins mapping their legs and nobody, including them, could care less. As I say, we're right in the middle of town, and if you stand at our front doors you can see two banks and the Congregational church and the newspaper store and three real-estate offices and about twenty-seven old freeloaders tearing up Central Street because the sewer broke again. It's not as if we're on the Cape; we're north of Boston and there's people in this town haven't seen the ocean for twenty years.

The girls had reached the meat counter and were asking McMahon something. He pointed, they pointed, and they shuffled out of sight behind a pyramid of Diet Delight peaches. All that was left for us to see was old McMahon patting his mouth and looking after them sizing up their joints. Poor kids, I began to feel sorry for them, they couldn't help it.

Now here comes the sad part of the story, at least my family says it's sad, but I don't think it's so sad myself. The store's pretty empty, it being Thursday afternoon, so there was nothing much to do except lean on the register and wait for the girls to show up again. The whole store was like a pinball machine and I didn't know which tunnel they'd come out of. After a while they come around out of the far aisle, around the light bulbs, records at a discount of the Caribbean Six or Tony Martin Sings or some such gunk you wonder they waste the wax on, sixpacks of candy bars, and plastic toys done up in cellophane that fall apart when a kid looks at them anyway. Around they come, Queenie still leading the way, and holding a little gray jar in her hand. Slots Three through Seven are unmanned and I could see her wondering between Stokes and me, but Stokesie with his usual luck draws an old party in baggy gray pants who stumbles up with four giant cans of pineapple juice (what do these bums do with all that pineapple juice? I've often asked myself) so the girls come to me. Queenie puts down the jar and I take it into my fingers icy cold. Kingfish Fancy Herring Snacks in Pure Sour Cream: 49¢. Now her hands are empty, not a ring or a bracelet, bare as God made them, and I wonder where the money's coming from. Still with that prim look she lifts a folded dollar bill out of the hollow at the center of her nubbed pink top. The jar went heavy in my hand. Really, I thought that was so cute.

Then everybody's luck begins to run out. Lengel comes in from haggling with a truck full of cabbages on the lot and is about to scuttle into that door marked MANAGER behind which he hides all day when the girls touch his eye. Lengel's pretty dreary, teaches Sunday school and the rest, but he doesn't miss that much. He comes over and says, "Girls, this isn't the beach."

Queenie blushes, though maybe it's just a brush of sunburn I was noticing for the first time, now that she was so close. "My mother asked me to pick up a jar of herring snacks." Her voice kind of startled me, the way voices do when you see the people first, coming out so flat and dumb yet kind of tony, too, the way it ticked over "pick up" and "snacks." All of a sudden I slid right down her voice into her living room. Her father and the other men were standing around in ice-cream coats and bow ties and the women were in sandals picking up herring snacks on toothpicks off a big glass plate and they were all holding drinks the color of water with olives and sprigs of mint in them. When my parents have somebody over they get lemonade and if it's a real racy affair Schlitz in tall glasses with "They'll Do It Every Time" cartoons stenciled on.

"That's all right," Lengel said. "But this isn't the beach." His repeating this struck me as funny, as if it had just occurred to him, and he had been thinking all these years the A&P was a great big dune and he was the head lifeguard. He didn't like my smiling—as I say he doesn't miss much—but he concentrates on giving the girls that sad Sunday-school-superintendent stare.

Queenie's blush is no sunburn now, and the plump one in plaid, that I liked better from the back—a really sweet can—pipes up, "We weren't doing any shopping. We just came in for the one thing."

"That makes no difference," Lengel tells her, and I could see from the way his eyes went that he hadn't noticed she was wearing a two-piece before. "We want you decently dressed when you come in here."

"We are decent," Queenie says suddenly, her lower lip pushing, getting sore now that she remembers her place, a place from which the crowd that runs the A&P must look pretty crummy. Fancy Herring Snacks flashed in her very blue eyes.

"Girls, I don't want to argue with you. After this come in here with your shoulders covered. It's our policy." He turns his back. That's policy for you. Policy is what the kingpins want. What the others want is juvenile delinquency.

All this while, the customers had been showing up with their carts but, you know, sheep, seeing a scene, they had all bunched up on Stokesie, who shook open a paper bag as gently as peeling a peach, not wanting to miss a word. I could feel in the silence everybody getting nervous, most of all Lengel, who asks me, "Sammy, have you rung up their purchase?"

I thought and said "No" but it wasn't about that I was thinking. I go through the punches, 4, 9, GROC, TOT—it's more complicated than you think, and after you do it often enough, it begins to make a little song, that you hear words to, in my case "Hello (bing) there, you (gung) hap-py pee-pul (splat)!"—the splat being the drawer flying out. I uncrease the bill, tenderly as you may imagine, it just having come from between the two smoothest scoops of vanilla I had ever known were there, and pass a half and a penny into her narrow pink palm, and nestle the herring in a bag and twist its neck and hand it over, all the time thinking.

The girls, and who'd blame them, are in a hurry to get out, so I say "I quit" to Lengel quick enough for them to hear, hoping they'll stop and watch me, their unsuspected hero. They keep right on going, into the electric eye; the door flies open and they flicker across the lot to their car. Queenie and Plaid and Big Tall Goony-Goony (not that as raw material she was so bad), leaving me with Lengel and a kink in his eyebrow.

"Did you say something, Sammy?"

"I said I quit."

"I thought you did."

"You didn't have to embarrass them."

"It was they who were embarrassing us."

I started to say something that came out "Fiddle-de-doo." It's a saying of my grandmother's, and I know she would have been pleased.

"I don't think you know what you're saying," Lengel said.

"I know you don't," I said. "But I do." I pull the bow at the back of my apron and start shrugging it off my shoulders. A couple customers that had been heading for my slot begin to knock against each other like scared pigs in a chute.

Lengel sighs and begins to look very patient and old and gray. He's been a friend of my parents for years. "Sammy, you don't want to do this to your Mom and Dad," he tells me. It's true, I don't. But it seems to me that once you begin a gesture it's fatal not to go through with it. I fold the apron, "Sammy" stitched in red on the pocket, and put it on the counter, and drop the bow tie on top of it. The bow tie is theirs, if you've ever wondered. "You'll feel this for the rest of you life," Lengel says, and I know that's true, too, but remembering how he made that pretty girl blush makes me so scrunchy inside I punch the No Sale tab and the machine whirs "pee-pul" and the drawer splats out. One advantage to this scene taking place in summer, I can follow this up with a clean exit, there's no fumbling around getting your coat and galoshes, I just saunter into the electric eye in my white shirt that my mother ironed the night before, and the door heaves itself open, and outside the sunshine is skating around on the asphalt.

I look around for my girls, but they're gone, of course. There wasn't anybody but some young married screaming with her children about some candy they didn't get by the door of a powder-blue Falcon station wagon. Looking back in the big windows, over the bags of peat moss and aluminum lawn furniture stacked on the pavement, I could see Lengel in my place in the slot, checking the sheep through. His face was dark gray and his back stiff, as if he'd just had an injection of iron, and my stomach kind of fell as I felt how hard the world was going to be to me hereafter.

ACTIVITIES

VOCABULARY

A&P, n. — a market, one of the A&P chain of grocery stores

prima donna, n. — principal female singer in an opera; a vain or self-centered person

nubble, n. — small knobs or lumps

prim, adj. — very formal and precise

scuttle, v. — to scurry, to run in short swift steps

gesture, n. — something said or done merely for effect or as a formality

saunter, v. — to walk in an idle or leisurely manner, stroll

infatuation, n. — a foolish, extravagant love

chivalry, n. — the customs of medieval knighthood; the qualities such as bravery, honor and protection of the weak held to characterize an ideal knight

FOR DISCUSSION

A. Sammy may be a victim of his romantic ideas. Like a knight in shining armor he has charged in to protect his "Queenie" from the injustices of the world, but by the end of the story he has lost both Queenie and his job. Nonetheless, doesn't he deserve credit for courageously speaking out against what he considers to be unfair? He has acted on his beliefs. On a scale of 1 to 10 with 1 being FOOL and 10 being HERO, where would you place Sammy? Explain.

B. What details in the story reveal the setting to be several decades ago? Have times changed? What might a guy do today to act like a hero in front of a group of girls? How can one be a "prince" today? Can you think of ways guys and girls can act genuinely heroic with members of the opposite sex?

C. Sammy's attitude toward most of the women in his story is cynical. Find phrases that reflect his chauvinistic judgment of women. Is it possible that the women who are the objects of Sammy's scorn are "Queenies" to someone else? Can you imagine situations in which Sammy would come to regret his casual negative comments?

D. Sammy's family comes into his thoughts several times during this incident in the A&P. By reading between the lines, what can you guess about his relationship with them? In what way might they be similar to Briar-rose's parents?

E. Sammy's attempt at heroism doesn't work out the way it's supposed to according to all the romantic tales of chivalry. His story does not have a fairy tale ending. How might "A&P" be considered an *anti*-fairy tale? What precisely does Sammy mean at the end when he talks about feeling *"how hard the world was going to be to me hereafter?"* Can you think of anything to say to him to make him feel better?

CLASS ACTIVITY: Love at First Sight???

In *The Art of Loving*, Erich Fromm identifies the basic elements common to all forms of real love as CARE, RESPONSIBILITY, RESPECT, and KNOWL-EDGE. Pangs of love drive Sammy to great sacrifice in defense of his heroine, but he doesn't even know her name. All he knows is the way she looks and the way she walks.

The five senses do play an important part in love relationships. A baby bonds with its mother in response to the warmth and comfort of her touch, the sound of her voice, the smell of her skin, even her taste if she is nursing the child. Sight becomes increasingly more important as we grow older. We all make initial judgments about people on the basis of their appearance.

Sometimes our quick reaction is one of strong attraction, sometimes the opposite. Do you believe in "love at first sight?" The word "infatuation" refers to a foolish, extravagant love that is founded on physical attraction and romantic imagination. Is infatuation the same as love at first sight? What would Erich Fromm say about love at first sight?

As a class activity collect love stories. How did your parents, grandparents, neighbors, or other married friends meet? Do they believe in love at first sight or did their attraction grow slowly over time? Are there any stories similar to Sammy's that have a happy ending? Write a love story based on one from real life. Remember that the more detailed your descriptions, the more alive your story!

CLASS ACTIVITY: Truth in Advertising???

Sex appeal and romance sell. Whether they are for toothpaste, sports cars, or washing machines, advertisements frequently depend upon sex and romance to capture attention. At one time only the most glamorous and youthful lovers filled television screens and the pages of our magazines. But times are changing. In recent years there seems to be a broader range of people and values reflected in advertising. No longer are youth, beauty, and wealth the only standards. Male and female stereotypes are being reconsidered as well.

As a class project that will continue throughout the time spent on this curriculum, begin to collect ads that depict love relationships. For comparison, try to get old magazines as well as current ones. Consider how the men are depicted. The women? What is important in the relationship between them? Can you divide the pictures into two categories, those that demonstrate loving well, and those that demonstrate loving badly? What is the difference? Make a large poster for your classroom. Title it LOVING WELL: CARE–RESPONSIBILITY–RESPECT–KNOWLEDGE. The Loving Well staff recommends enriching Fromm's four basic elements by adding a fifth — GROWTH. Cover your poster as a collage, with the pictures that best demonstrate loving well.

PRESIDENT CLEVELAND, WHERE ARE YOU?

by Robert Cormier

A *uthor's Introduction:*

There's a sentence in "President Cleveland, Where Are You?" which is probably the most significant I have written in terms of my development as a writer. The sentence echoes back to a lost and half-forgotten story I wrote in the days when I was scribbling stories in pencil at the kitchen table. The story was about a boy from the poorer section of town who falls desperately in love with a girl from the other side of town where the people live, or so he thinks, grandly and affluently. The story was in the first person, the narrator was a twelve-year old boy.

The problem concerned description. The narrator (and I, the writer) faced the problem of describing the girl's house, a thing of grandeur and beauty, white and shining, alien to the three-story tenement building in which the boy lived. How to describe such a house? I knew little about architecture, next to nothing at all. The house had an aura of graceful antiquity—was it a relic of some earlier era? It seemed that I had seen such houses in books—but what books? I knew nothing about researching such a subject, and anyway, I didn't want to burden the narrative with a long description of the house. In fact, this would not only be fatal to the forward thrust of the story but would not be consistent with what a twelve-year-old boy would know about architecture. Yet, I wanted to describe it as more than just a big white house.

The problem brought the story to a complete halt. I walked my hometown streets, desolated by the thought of all the things I did not know. How could someone so ignorant about so much ever become a writer? Back home, chewing at the pencil, I read and reread the words I had written. The lean clean prose of Ernest Hemingway and the simplicity of William Saroyan had affected me deeply, and I always told myself: Keep it simple, don't get too technical. So, let's apply those principles to the girl's house. Forget architecture — what did the house look like? Not what did it really look like, but what did it look like to this twelve-year-old boy?

Yes, that was the key — the viewpoint of the boy and not the writer. And from somewhere the description came. It looks like a big white birthday cake of a house. I knew this was exactly the kind of image I had sought. I felt the way Columbus must have felt when he sighted land.

In that moment, I had discovered simile and metaphor, had learned that words were truly tools, that figures of speech were not just something fancy to dress up a piece of prose but words that could evoke scene and event and emotion. Until that discovery at the kitchen table, I had been intimidated by much of what I encountered in books of grammar, including the definitions of similes and metaphors. Suddenly, the definitions didn't matter. What mattered was using them to enrich my stories — not in a "Look, Ma, how clever I am" way, but to sharpen images, pin down emotions, create shocks of recognition in the reader.

At any rate, the story of the boy and the birthday cake of a house has been lost throughout the years. I doubt if it was ever published. In "President Cleveland, Where Are You?" I resurrected the description. It occurs in the second sentence of the third paragraph, a tribute to a marvelous moment in my hesitant journey toward becoming a writer.

That was the autumn of the cowboy cards — Buck Jones and Tom Tyler and Hoot Gibson and especially Ken Maynard. The cards were available in five-cent packages of gum; pink sticks, three together, covered with a sweet white powder. You couldn't blow bubbles with that particular gum, but it couldn't have mattered less. The cowboy cards were important — the pictures of those rock-faced men with eyes of blue steel.

On those wind-swept, leaf-tumbling afternoons we gathered after school on the sidewalk in front of Lemire's Drugstore, across from St. Jude's Parochial School, and we swapped and bargained and matched for the cards. Because a Ken Maynard serial was playing at the Globe every Saturday afternoon, he was the most popular cowboy of all, and one of his cards was worth at least ten of any other kind. Rollie Tremaine had a treasure of thirty or so, and he guarded them jealously. He'd match you for the other cards, but he risked his Ken Maynards only when the other kids threatened to leave him out of the competition altogether.

You could almost hate Rollie Tremaine. In the first place, he was the only son of Auguste Tremaine, who operated the Uptown Dry Goods Store, and he did not live in a tenement but in a big white birthday cake of a house on Laurel Street. He was too fat to be effective in the football games between the Frenchtown Tigers and the North Side Knights, and he made us constantly aware of the jingle of coins in his pockets. He was able to stroll into Lemire's and casually select a quarter's worth of cowboy cards while the rest of us watched, aching with envy.

Once in a while I earned a nickel or dime by running errands or washing windows for blind old Mrs. Belander, or by finding pieces of copper, brass, and other valuable metals at the dump and selling them to the junkman. The coins clutched in my hand, I would race to Lemire's to buy a cowboy card or two, hoping that Ken Maynard would stare boldly out at me as I opened the pack. At one time, before a disastrous matching session with Roger Lussier (my best friend, except where the cards were involved), I owned five Ken Maynards and considered myself a millionaire, of sorts.

One week I was particularly lucky; I had spent two afternoons washing floors for Mrs. Belander and received a quarter. Because my father had worked a full week at the shop, where a rush order for fancy combs had been received, he allotted my brothers and sisters and me an extra dime along with the usual ten cents for the Saturday-afternoon movie. Setting aside the movie fare, I found myself with a bonus of thirty-five cents, and I then planned to put Rollie Tremaine to shame the following Monday afternoon.

Monday was the best day to buy the cards because the candy man stopped at Lemire's every Monday morning to deliver the new assortments. There was nothing more exciting in the world than a fresh batch of card boxes. I rushed home from school that day and hurriedly changed my clothes, eager to set off for the store. As I burst through the doorway, letting the screen door slam behind me, my brother Armand blocked my way.

He was fourteen, three years older than I, and a freshman at Monument High School. He had recently become a stranger to me in many ways — indifferent to such matters as cowboy cards and the Frenchtown Tigers — and he carried himself with a mysterious dignity that was fractured now and then when his voice began shooting off in all directions like some kind of

27

vocal fireworks.

"Wait a minute, Jerry," he said. "I want to talk to you." He motioned me out of earshot of my mother, who was busy supervising the usual after-school skirmish in the kitchen.

I sighed with impatience. In recent months Armand had become a figure of authority, siding with my father and mother occasionally. As the oldest son he sometimes took advantage of his age and experience to issue rules and regulations.

"How much money have you got?" he whispered.

"You in some kind of trouble?" I asked, excitement rising in me as I remembered the blackmail plot of a movie at the Globe a month before.

He shook his head in annoyance. "Look," he said, "it's Pa's birthday tomorrow. I think we ought to chip in and buy him something . . ."

I reached into my pocket and caressed the coins. "Here," I said carefully, pulling out a nickel. "If we all give a nickel we should have enough to buy him something pretty nice."

He regarded me with contempt. "Rita already gave me fifteen cents, and I'm throwing in a quarter. Albert handed over a dime—all that's left of his birthday money. Is that all you can do—a nickel?"

"Aw, come on," I protested. "I haven't got a single Ken Maynard left, and I was going to buy some cards this afternoon."

"Ken Maynard!" he snorted, "Who's more important—him or your father?"

His question was unfair because he knew that there was no possible choice—"my father" had to be the only answer. My father was a huge man who believed in the things of the spirit, although my mother often maintained that the spirits he believed in came in bottles. He had worked at the Monument Comb Shop since the age of fourteen; his booming laugh—or grumble—greeted us each night when he returned from the factory. A steady worker when the shop had enough work, he quickened with gaiety on Friday nights and weekends, a bottle of beer at his elbow, and he was fond of making long speeches about the good things in life. In the middle of the Depression, for instance, he paid cash for a piano, of all things, and insisted that my twin sisters, Yolande and Yvette, take lessons once a week.

I took a dime from my pocket and handed it to Armand.

"Thanks, Jerry," he said. "I hate to take your last cent."

"That's all right," I replied, turning away and consoling myself with the thought that twenty cents was better than nothing at all.

When I arrived at Lemire's I sensed disaster in the air. Roger Lussier was kicking disconsolately at a tin can in the gutter, and Rollie Tremaine sat sullenly on the steps in front of the store.

"Save your money," Roger said. He had known about my plans to splurge on the cards.

"What's the matter?" I asked.

"There's no more cowboy cards," Rollie Tremaine said. "The company's not making anymore."

"They're going to have President cards," Roger said, his face twisting with disgust. He pointed to the store window. "Look!"

A placard in the window announced: "Attention, Boys. Watch for the New Series. Presidents of the United States. Free in Each 5-Cent Package of Caramel Chew."

"President cards?" I asked, dismayed.

I read on: "Collect a Complete Set and Receive an Official Imitation Major League Baseball Glove, Embossed with Lefty Grove's Autograph."

Glove or no glove, who could become excited about Presidents, of all things? Rollie Tremaine stared at the sign. "Benjamin Harrison, for crying out loud," he said. "Why would I want Benjamin Harrison when I've got twenty-two Ken Maynards?"

I felt the warmth of guilt creep over me. I jingled the coins in my pocket, but the sound was hollow. No more Ken Maynards to buy.

"I'm going to buy a Mr. Goodbar," Rollie Tremaine decided.

I was without appetite, indifferent even to a Baby Ruth, which was my favorite. I thought of how I had betrayed Armand and, worst of all, my father.

"I'll see you after supper," I called over my shoulder to Roger as I hurried away toward home. I took the shortcut behind the church, although it involved leaping over a tall wooden fence, and I zigzagged recklessly through Mr. Thibodeau's garden, trying to outrace my guilt. I pounded up the steps and into the house, only to learn that Armand had already taken Yolande and Yvette uptown to shop for the birthday present.

I pedalled my bike furiously through the streets, ignoring the indignant horns of automobiles as I sliced through the traffic. Finally I saw Armand and my sisters emerge from the Monument Men's Shop. My heart sank when I spied the long, slim package that Armand was holding.

"Did you buy the present yet?" I asked, although I knew it was too late.

"Just now. A blue tie," Armand said. "What's the matter?"

"Nothing" I replied, my chest hurting.

He looked at me for a long moment. At first his eyes were hard, but then they softened. He smiled at me, almost sadly, and touched my arm. I turned away from him because I felt naked and exposed.

"It's all right," he said gently. "Maybe you've learned something." The words were gentle, but they held a curious dignity, the dignity remaining even when his voice suddenly cracked on the last syllable.

I wondered what was happening to me, because I did not know whether to laugh or cry.

Sister Angela was amazed when, a week before Christmas vacation, everybody in the class submitted a history essay worthy of a high mark — in some cases as high as A-minus. (Sister Angela did not believe that anyone in the world ever deserved an A.) She never learned — or at least she never let on that she knew — we all had become experts on the Presidents because of the cards we purchased at Lemire's. Each card contained a picture of a President, and on the reverse side, a summary of his career. We looked at those cards so often that the biographies imprinted themselves on our minds without effort. Even our street-corner conversations were filled with such information as the fact that James Madison was called "The Father of the Constitution," or that John Adams had intended to become a minister.

The President cards were a roaring success and the cowboy cards were quickly forgotten. In the first place we did not receive gum with the cards, but a kind of chewy caramel. The caramel could be tucked into a corner of your mouth, bulging your cheek in much the same manner as wads of tobacco bulged the mouths of baseball stars. In the second place the competition for collecting the cards was fierce and frustrating — fierce because everyone was intent on being the first to send away for a baseball glove and frustrating because although there were only thirty-two Presidents, including Franklin Delano Roosevelt, the variety at Lemire's was at a minimum. When the delivery-man left the boxes of cards at the store each Monday, we often discovered that one entire box was devoted to a single President — two weeks in a row the boxes contained nothing but Abraham Lincolns. One week Roger Lussier and I were the heroes of Frenchtown. We journeyed on our bicycles to the North Side, engaged three boys in a matching bout and returned with five new Presidents, including Chester Alan Arthur, who up to that time had been missing.

Perhaps to sharpen our desire, the card company sent a sample glove to Mr. Lemire, and it dangled, orange and sleek, in the window. I was half sick with longing, thinking of my old glove at home, which I had inherited from Armand. But Rollie Tremaine's desire for the glove outdistanced my own. He even got Mr. Lemire to agree to give the glove in the window to the first person to get a complete set of cards, so that precious time wouldn't be wasted waiting for the postman.

We were delighted at Rollie Tremaine's frustration, especially since he was only a substitute player for the Tigers. Once after spending fifty cents on cards—all of which turned out to be Calvin Coolidge—he threw them to the ground, pulled some dollar bills out of his pocket and said, "The heck with it. I'm going to buy a glove!"

"Not that glove," Roger Lussier said. "Not a glove with Lefty Grove's autograph. Look what it says at the bottom of the sign."

We all looked, although we know the words by heart: "This Glove Is Not For Sale Anywhere."

Rollie Tremaine scrambled to pick up the cards from the sidewalk, pouting more than ever. After that he was quietly obsessed with the Presidents, hugging the cards close to his chest and refusing to tell us how many more he needed to complete his set.

I too was obsessed with the cards, because they had become things of comfort in a world that had suddenly grown dismal. After Christmas a layoff at the shop had thrown my father out of work. He received no paycheck for four weeks, and the only income we had was from Armand's after-school job at the Blue and White Grocery Store—a job he lost finally when business dwindled as the layoff continued.

Although we had enough food and clothing—my father's credit had always been good, a matter of pride with him—the inactivity made my father restless and irritable. He did not drink any beer at all, and laughed loudly, but not convincingly, after gulping down a glass of water and saying, "Lent came early this year." The twins fell sick and went to the hospital to have their tonsils removed. My father was confident that he would return to work eventually and pay off his debts, but he seemed to age before our eyes.

When orders again were received at the comb shop and he returned to work, another disaster occurred, although I was the only one aware of it. Armand fell in love.

I discovered his situation by accident, when I happened to pick up a piece of paper that had fallen to the floor in the bedroom he and I shared. I frowned at the paper, puzzled.

"Dear Sally, When I look into your eyes the world stands still . . ."

The letter was snatched from my hands before I finished reading it.

"What's the big idea, snooping around?" Armand asked, his face crimson. "Can't a guy have any privacy?"

He had never mentioned privacy before. "It was on the floor," I said. "I didn't know it was a letter. Who's Sally?"

He flung himself across the bed. "You tell anybody and I'll muckalize you," he threatened. "Sally Knowlton."

Nobody in Frenchtown had a name like Knowlton.

"A girl from the North Side?" I asked, incredulous.

He rolled over and faced me, anger in his eyes, and a kind of despair too.

"What's the matter with that? Think she's too good for me?" he asked. "I'm warning you, Jerry, if you tell anybody . . ."

"Don't worry," I said. Love had no particular place in my life; it seemed an unnecessary waste of time. And a girl from the North Side was so remote that for all practical purposes she did not exist. But I was curious. "What are you writing her a letter for? Did she leave town, or something?"

"She hasn't left town," he answered, "I wasn't going to send it. I just felt like writing to her."

I was glad that I had never become involved with love — love that brought desperation to your eyes, that caused you to write letters you did not plan to send. Shrugging with indifference, I began to search in the closet for the old baseball glove. I found it on the shelf, under some old sneakers. The webbing was torn and the padding gone. I thought of the sting I would feel when a sharp grounder slapped into the glove, and I winced.

"You tell anybody about me and Sally and I'll — "

"I know. You'll muckalize me."

I did not divulge his secret and often shared his agony, particularly when he sat at the supper table and left my mother's special butterscotch pie untouched. I had never realized before how terrible love could be. But my compassion was short-lived because I had other things to worry about: report cards due at Eastertime; the loss of income from old Mrs. Belander, who had gone to live with a daughter in Boston; and, of course, the Presidents.

Because a stalemate had been reached, the President cards were the dominant force in our lives — mine, Roger Lussier's and Rollie Tremaine's.

For three weeks, as the baseball season approached, each of us had a complete set—complete except for one President, Grover Cleveland. Each time a box of cards arrived at the store we hurriedly bought them (as hurriedly as our funds allowed) and tore off the wrappers, only to be confronted by James Monroe or Martin Van Buren or someone else. But never Grover Cleveland, never the man who had been the twenty-second and the twenty-fourth President of the United States. We argued about Grover Cleveland. Should he be placed between Chester Alan Arthur and Benjamin Harrison as the twenty-second President or did he belong between Benjamin Harrison and William McKinley as the twenty-fourth President? Was the card company playing fair? Roger Lussier brought up a horrifying possibility—did we need two Grover Clevelands to complete the set?

Indignant, we stormed Lemire's and protested to the harassed storeowner, who had long since vowed never to stock a new series. Muttering angrily, he searched his bills and receipts for a list of rules.

"All right," he announced. "Says here you only need one Grover Cleveland to finish the set. Now get out, all of you, unless you've got money to spend."

Outside the store, Rollie Tremaine picked up an empty tobacco tin and scaled it across the street. "Boy," he said. "I'd give five dollars for a Grover Cleveland."

When I returned home I found Armand sitting on the piazza steps, his chin in his hands. His mood of dejection mirrored my own, and I sat down beside him. We did not say anything for a while.

"Want to throw the ball around?" I asked.

He sighed, not bothering to answer.

"You sick?" I asked.

He stood up and hitched up his trousers, pulled at his ear and finally told me what the matter was—there was a big dance next week at the high school, the Spring Promenade, and Sally had asked him to be her escort.

I shook my head at the folly of love. "Well, what's so bad about that?"

"How can I take Sally to a fancy dance?" he asked desperately. "I'd have to buy her a corsage . . . And my shoes are practically falling apart. Pa's got too many worries now to buy me new shoes or give me money for flowers for a girl."

I nodded in sympathy. "Yeah," I said. "Look at me. Baseball time is almost here, and all I've got is that old glove. And no Grover Cleveland card yet . . ."

"Grover Cleveland?" he asked. "They've got some of those up on the North Side. Some kid was telling me there's a store that's got them. He says they're looking for Warren G. Harding."

"Holy Smoke!" I said. "I've got an extra Warren G. Harding!" Pure joy sang in my veins. I ran to my bicycle, swung into the seat—and found that the front tire was flat.

"I'll help you fix it," Armand said.

Within half an hour I was at the North Side Drugstore, where several boys were matching cards on the sidewalk. Silently but blissfully I shouted: President Grover Cleveland, here I come!

After Armand had left for the dance, all dressed up as if it were Sunday, the small green box containing the corsage under his arm, I sat on the railing of the piazza, letting my feet dangle. The neighborhood was quiet because the Frenchtown Tigers were at Daggett's Field, practicing for the first baseball game of the season.

I thought of Armand and the ridiculous expression on his face when he'd stood before the mirror in the bedroom. I'd avoided looking at his new black shoes. "Love," I muttered.

Spring had arrived in a sudden stampede of apple blossoms and fragrant breezes. Windows had been thrown open and dust mops had banged on the sills all day long as the women busied themselves with housecleaning. I was puzzled by my lethargy. Wasn't spring supposed to make everything bright and gay?

I turned at the sound of footsteps on the stairs. Roger Lussier greeted me with a sour face.

"I thought you were practicing with the Tigers," I said.

"Rollie Tremaine," he said. "I just couldn't stand him."

He slammed his fist against the railing. "Jeez, why did he have to be the one to get a Grover Cleveland? You should see him showing off. He won't let anybody even touch that glove . . ."

I felt like Benedict Arnold and knew that I had to confess what I had done.

"Roger," I said, "I got a Grover Cleveland card up on the North Side. I sold it to Rollie Tremaine for five dollars."

"Are you crazy?" he asked.

"I needed that five dollars. It was an—an emergency."

"Boy!" he said, looking down at the ground and shaking his head. "What did you have to do a thing like that for?"

I watched him as he turned away and began walking down the stairs.

"Hey, Roger!" I called.

He squinted up at me as if I were a stranger, someone he'd never seen before.

"What?" he asked, his voice flat.

"I had to do it," I said. "Honest."

He didn't answer. He headed toward the fence, searching for the board we had loosened to give us a secret passage.

I thought of my father and Armand and Rollie Tremaine and Grover Cleveland and wished that I could go away someplace far away. But there was no place to go.

Roger found the loose slat in the fence and slipped through. I felt betrayed: weren't you supposed to feel good when you did something fine and noble?

A moment later two hands gripped the top of the fence and Roger's face appeared.

"Was it a real emergency?" he yelled.

"A real one!" I called. "Something important!"

His face dropped from sight and his voice reached me across the yard: "All right."

"See you tomorrow!" I yelled.

I swung my legs over the railing again. The gathering dusk began to soften the sharp edges of the fence, the rooftops, the distant church steeple. I sat there a long time, waiting for the good feeling to come.

ACTIVITIES

VOCABULARY

tenement, n. — apartment building, esp. for poorer families
spirit, n. — life giving force, soul; an alcoholic liquor
disconsolate, adj. — hopelessly sad
stalemate, n. — deadlock, position where no one can move
indignant, adj. — angered from unfair treatment

dejection, n. — gloom, lack of energy caused by disappointment
lethargy, n. — abnormal drowsiness; the state of being lazy
   or uninterested

FOR DISCUSSION

A. In the course of his narration, 11-year-old Jerry describes a series of emotional ups and downs. Explain where each of the following quotations occurs and how it fits into the plot of the story. Then consider how each one is related to the topic of love. What kind of love is involved: love for a family member, for a friend, for a member of the opposite sex, self-love? How are the feelings similar, and how are they different?

1. *"I was without appetite, indifferent even to a Baby Ruth, which was my favorite. I thought of how I had betrayed Armand and, worst of all, my father."*

2. *". . . the inactivity made my father restless and irritable . . . he seemed to age before our eyes."*

3. *"I did not divulge his secret and often shared his agony, particularly when he sat at the supper table and left my mother's special butterscotch pie untouched. I had never realized before how terrible love could be."*

4. *"Pure joy sang in my veins. I ran to my bicycle, swung into the seat — and found that the front tire was flat."*

5. *"I felt like Benedict Arnold and knew that I had to confess what I had done."*

6. *"I swung my legs over the railing again. The gathering dusk began to soften the sharp edges of the fence, the rooftops, the distant church steeple. I sat there a long time, waiting for the good feeling to come."*

B. Armand and Jerry seem to be friends as well as brothers. In fact, there seems to be a great deal of love evident in the way the members of this closely knit family treat each other. Find examples of the CARE, RESPONSIBILITY, RESPECT, KNOWLEDGE, and GROWTH that are important qualities of good loving relationships.

CLASS ASSIGNMENT: Falling in Love . . .

In the introduction to "President Cleveland, Where Are You?" author Robert Cormier talks about his problem describing the architecture of an elegant, white house in terms a young person could understand. The image of a *"big, white birthday cake"* said it all.

Jerry does not understand the feelings and seemingly foolish behavior of his lovestruck older brother. How might Armand be able to give Jerry a good, clear image of what it feels like to fall in love? As a class, search for an image that captures the feeling. You can ask older, more experienced friends, family members, teachers, or neighbors. You can go to books. You can use your own imagination. Collect all the entries. Is there a clear winner? Can you find a single image that reflects the complex feelings of falling in love? You may wish to duplicate a list of the entries and get votes from people outside as well as inside the class.

Perhaps the similes offered by a group of eighth graders in Newton, Massachusetts, will stimulate your own brainstorming:

FALLING IN LOVE IS LIKE . . .

"jumping off the high dive without testing the water first."
"eating a lemon for the first time."
"driving on a road without a map."
"playing in the seventh game of the world championship."
"getting into a warm bed on a cold night."
"trying to score a goal when you don't know which goalpost is which."

IF ONLY

(Anonymous)

ately I take long walks by myself. I think about life and death — things everyone wonders about, I suppose. Sometimes I walk for hours, but I always end up at the same place.

Today it was a crisp November afternoon. Not one person was in sight when I arrived. My feet moved toward the little mound of dirt, just as they had yesterday, and the day before and the day before, every day for the past month.

I took my usual kneeling position beside the small stone inscribed with these sad tidings: "Here lies Timmy Langdon — Born May 23, 1957, Died October 14, 1965." The words sent new shocks up my spine, just as I knew they would. For even after a month I still could not believe it. When I thought of Timmy, I thought of a golden-haired boy hurrying off to school or baseball practice, not a cold form here with all these strangers.

Something else troubled me, and I don't think I will ever forget it. I had come home from school after a long and hectic day. Mrs. Trimble had decided our reports were due tomorrow instead of next Friday. Mr. Johnson was kind enough to warn us of a history test on the last five chapters to be given tomorrow. Anyway, dotted here and there among these big headaches was my usual homework — algebra and bookkeeping. I had come draggin' into the house with my "it's been a hard day" look. Mom knew better than to ask about my day.

As I headed for my bedroom I heard two small voices laughing. I opened the door, and there sat Timmy and a little neighbor friend at my desk looking at my lipstick. They weren't making a mess. In fact, they were being very careful not to. Anyway, this was the straw that broke the camel's back, and I lost my temper. I told them to get out and never to come back into my room when I'm not home and to "stay out of my stuff, you little pest!" I must have called him a pest four or five times. How could I have been so crude?

Tim's face turned beet red, and I know he was sorry and ashamed. He even apologized; but oh, no, I couldn't let him get away with it. I had to be firm.

At the dinner table Tim was unusually quiet and didn't eat much, but I guess I was the only one who noticed, because Mom and Dad were talking about so-and-so and should they go to the reception two hundred miles away. After supper I excused myself and got to work. While I was working, I felt someone watching me. I turned, and there stood Timmy in the doorway.

"Please close the door," I said curtly.

He hesitated, then slowly closed it, with a hurt, puzzled look.

"I'll make it up to him," I thought, then turned my thoughts back to my work.

The next morning was warm, and I felt fatigue as I climbed out of bed. I hurriedly dressed and dashed out to the breakfast table, I had five minutes to eat. Timmy was the only one at the table. Mom was cooking eggs in the kitchen. As I sat down, I felt his warm, brown eyes on me, and I met his imploring gaze with a cool stare.

"Are you still mad at me?" he asked.

"I suppose so." I really wasn't, but I felt he hadn't learned his lesson yet.

"I'm sorry, I won't do it again."

"We'll see," I said cuttingly. Then hurriedly gulping the last of my breakfast, I grabbed my books and ran for the bus stop, purposely ignoring him. But as I hurried out the door, something about the sadness in his eyes brought a guilty feeling, and I remember thinking, "I'll make it up to him later." That was my trouble. I was always in too much of a hurry to get close to him. I was too busy with my debate to go to his baseball game for an hour. I was too busy with algebra to go to his school play. I was always too busy for him, and I could have made time so very easily.

That was the last time I saw him alive — at the breakfast table.

The next time I saw him, he was lying under a white sheet.

I had come home from school as usual with my mind full of my usual thoughts. I noticed my brother's badly twisted bike on the lawn. I suddenly felt panic sweeping over me. I ran for the house, my heart beating in my throat. The kitchen was quiet. There was no dinner cooking. It was too quiet. The living room door was shut, and I was terrified of the circumstances that were happening on the other side; but the silence of the kitchen was too much to bear and I found myself pushing the door open.

My mother was sitting in the rocking chair with Father kneeling by her side, holding her shaking hand. Their faces wore identical expressions — very pale with eyes staring straight ahead. When Mom saw me she stood up and took me in her shaking arms. I expected the worst from that action, and my fears were confirmed as Dad related the events of the last half hour.

Timmy had been in a hurry to get home and start on the new model airplane Mom had bought him. He must not have been looking as he came racing across the street. The driver of the car did not see him till it was too late. I had read of this type of thing many times in the newspaper; but it happened to other people, not to me, not to my family.

The next few days were full of tears, I cried until my eyes were dry and red and tears just wouldn't come anymore. I couldn't eat for days. I couldn't sleep very long. I would always have the same dream of coming home from school that day.

I remember so many small things he had done for me — things like getting me a glass of water while I was studying, polishing my shoes when I was in a hurry, bringing me dandelions, showing me his new baseball bat (which I thought was a bore). I am sure everyone has thought "If only I could do it again. If only I had one more chance."

Suddenly I wished more than anything to talk with him if for just five minutes. And when he would ask me, "Are you still mad at me?" with his brown eyes studying my face, I would take him in my arms and say, "No, my darling, I'm not mad anymore, and I'll never be mad at you again."

I slowly got to my feet from the misty grass. My legs were cramped and stiff from kneeling so long. I pulled my coat tighter, because November gets chilly in the late afternoon. Then I started for home.

ACTIVITIES

A. Summarize the main idea of "If Only" in one sentence.

B. At the end of both "President Cleveland, Where Are You?" and "If Only," the narrator telling the story is depressed. The momentary feelings of loss and sadness may be similar, but the causes and outlook for the future are quite different. Compare and contrast the two situations.

C. "If Only" begins with the lines *"Lately I take long walks by myself. I think about life and death—things everyone wonders about, I suppose."* Thinking about death sounds rather morbid and gloomy, but the effect can be the opposite. As a class, brainstorm on how thinking about death might help us lead richer and happier lives. How might our relationships with friends, family, and even strangers change for the better?

D. G.K. Chesterton wrote, "The way to love anything is to realize that it might be lost." The story "If Only" shows how it often takes misfortune to reveal our true feelings. Too often we fail to say important things when we have the opportunity. It is much easier to say thank you for little things than for the big ones. Sometimes we want to apologize but aren't sure how. Hardest of all may be to tell someone when we love them. Write a letter to someone important to you. Tell them what you'd want to say if you knew it were the last chance you'd have. (This letter never has to be delivered, and it definitely will *not* be read or graded by your teacher; but it should help you think about your own feelings).

ANCESTOR

by Jimmy Santiago Baca

I t was a time when they were afraid of him.
My father, a bare man, a gypsy, a horse
with broken knees no one would shoot.
Then again, he was like the orange tree,
and young women plucked from him sweet fruit.   5
To meet him, you must be in the right place,
even his sons and daughter, we wondered
where was papa now and what was he doing.
He held the mystique of travelers
that pass your backyard and disappear into the trees.   10
Then, when you follow, you find nothing,
not a stir, not a twig displaced from its bough.
And then he would appear one night.
Half covered in shadows and half in light,
his voice quiet, absorbing our unspoken thoughts.   15
When his hands lay on the table at breakfast,
they were hands that had not fixed our crumbling home,
hands that had not taken us into them
and the fingers did not gently rub along our lips.
They were hands of a gypsy that filled our home   20
with love and safety, for a moment;
with all the shambles of boards and empty stomachs,
they filled us because of the love in them.
Beyond the ordinary love, beyond the coordinated life,

beyond the sponging of broken hearts,   25
came the untimely word, the fallen smile, the quiet tear,
that made us grow up quick and romantic.
Papa gave us something: when we paused from work,
my sister fourteen years old working the cotton fields,
my brother and I running like deer,   30
we would pause, because we had a papa no one could catch,
who spoke when he spoke and bragged and drank,
he bragged about us: he did not say we were smart,
nor did he say we were strong and were going to be rich someday.
He said we were good. He held us up to the world for it to see,   35
three children that were good, who understood love in a quiet way,
who owned nothing but calloused hands and true freedom,
and that is how he made us: he offered us to the wind,
to the mountains, to the skies of autumn and spring.
He said, "Here are my children! Care for them!"   40
And he left again, going somewhere like a child
with a warrior's heart, nothing could stop him.
My grandmother would look at him for a long time,
and then she would say nothing.
She chose to remain silent, praying each night,   45
guiding down like a root in the heart of earth,
clutching sunlight and rains to her ancient breast.
And I am the blossom of many nights.
A threefold blossom: my sister is as she is,
my brother is as he is, and I am as I am.   50
Through sacred ceremony of living, daily living,
arose three distinct hopes, three loves,
out of the long felt nights and days of yesterday.

ACTIVITIES

VOCABULARY

mystique, n. — a distinctive set of beliefs and attitudes associated with a group

bough, n. — a branch of a tree

calloused, adj. — thickened and hardened

"Ancestor" is like a patchwork quilt of memories. Though individual pieces or individual recollections may be far from pretty, interwoven they become warm and attractive. The poem itself reflects the puzzling complexities and contradictions of life. Many details hint at a troubled family life, but essentially the poem is a loving son's tender tribute to his loving father. Here is a father who seems negligent, irresponsible, and even hurtful at times. Yet the son has learned a great deal about loving well from his father. It may even be that the son's poetic gift, his skill in communicating delicate emotions, is a valued legacy from his father.

CLASS ACTIVITY: A Day in Court

For the sake of analysis, put the father on trial. Is he guilty or innocent of faulty fathering? Cut up as many squares of paper as there are members of the class. On one piece write JUDGE and on six other pieces write JUROR. Divide the remaining pieces in half, labeling those in one pile D for DEFENSE and the remaining pieces P for PROSECUTION. Everyone then picks an assignment for the courtroom scene. Unfortunately, the father cannot appear for cross examination because his whereabouts are unknown.

While the jurors and judge are deliberating about the courtroom procedure and analyzing the evidence (the poem) themselves, the prosecution and the defense have about fifteen minutes to prepare their presentations. The prosecution's charge is to find as much detailed evidence as they can to prove that the father should be found guilty of bad fathering. At the same time, the defense team must collect as much evidence to the contrary as they can find. Both cases will depend on specific references to lines and quotations from the poem.

When the judge signals that it is time for the trial to begin, the jurors take their seats in chairs along the side of the room, and a speaker for the prosecution has five minutes to present the prosecution's argument. Then the defense has five minutes to provide its own evidence of good parenting and to counter the previous argument. If needed, each side can have an additional two minutes for rebuttal. The jurors should feel free to take notes during the proceedings.

After both sides have been given equal opportunity to persuade the jury, the jurors begin their deliberations. Although deliberations in an actual court are always private, it will be more interesting for the class if the rest of the courtroom participants are allowed to be silent observers. When the jury has finished its deliberations, each member is polled for a vote of GUILTY or NOT GUILTY. If the majority vote GUILTY, the jurors must decide on a recommended sentence.

THE OLD GRANDFATHER AND HIS LITTLE GRANDSON

by Leo Tolstoy

T he grandfather had become very old. His legs would not carry him, his eyes could not see, his ears could not hear, and he was toothless. When he ate, bits of food sometimes dropped out of his mouth. His son and his son's wife no longer allowed him to eat with them at the table. He had to eat his meals in the corner near the stove.

One day they gave him his food in a bowl. He tried to move the bowl closer, it fell to the floor and broke. His daughter-in-law scolded him. She told him that he spoiled everything in the house and broke their dishes, and she said that from now on he would get his food in a wooden dish. The old man sighed and said nothing.

A few days later, the old man's son and his wife were sitting in their hut, resting and watching their little boy playing on the floor. They saw him putting together something out of small pieces of wood. His father asked him, "What are you making, Misha?"

The little grandson said, "I'm making a wooden bucket. When you and Mamma get old, I'll feed you out of this wooden dish."

The young peasant and his wife looked at each other and tears filled their eyes. They were ashamed because they had treated the old grandfather so meanly, and from that day they again let the old man eat with them at the table and took better care of him.

ACTIVITIES

This story was originally written in Russian many generations ago, but its central conflict is equally familiar in America today. Whatever the setting, relationships among children, parents, and grandparents are often complex emotionally, particularly as they change over time. Both "The Old Grandfather and His Little Grandson" and "A Distant Bell" reflect how family relationships and bonds of love change throughout the different stages of our lives.

WRITING ASSIGNMENT: As Time Goes By . . .

Think of your relationship with your parents. How has it changed over the past few years? Speculate! How do you believe it will change if you marry? If you become a parent? Spend 10 minutes answering these questions. Then begin your discussion of the story and how family relationships change.

QUESTIONS FOR DISCUSSION

A. Is it possible that the son and daughter-in-law could love the old man yet treat him badly? If love is gone, what holds them together?

B. Why do you suppose it is the grandson who is most sensitive to the old man's needs?

C. Anne Frank, a Jewish girl forced into hiding and eventually sent to a concentration camp and killed by Nazi soldiers in World War II, was writing about her grandmother when she wrote, *"A person can be lonely even if he is loved by many people, because he is still not the 'One and Only' to anyone." (The*

Diary of Anne Frank, (Pocket Books, NYC, 1958, p. 112). How does this quotation fit the grandfather's situation? Is there a solution for the grandfather?

CLASS ACTIVITY: Lights, Camera, Action!

It's Valentine's Day and television station WXOX has scheduled a feature story on the topic of LOVE. Reporters have already questioned the "experts"—psychiatrists, poets, and professors—but the producer wants some first hand, on-the-street interviews. Television crews have been dispatched to Lovers' Lane, to the local florist, and to random homes throughout the community. One crew arrives at the cottage of the family of our story.

In preparation for the taping, the class should divide into five groups with a separate group for each character:

A. the TV reporter   **D.** the daughter-in-law
B. the grandson   **E.** the grandfather
C. the son

One member of each group is to act the part. The other members of the group are drama coaches who will help interpret the role. For example, how would a reporter introduce this feature story? What questions should the reporter ask about love? What experiences and feelings are each of the other characters likely to describe? What tone should be in their voices? What gestures would be appropriate? What messages about love will each of the family members wish to communicate? Take ten or fifteen minutes to prepare, then let the imaginary cameras roll.

A DISTANT BELL

by Elizabeth Enright

T he year after my father and mother were divorced, my father, who got me in the summers, took me to a town on the Cape called Harbor Landing. It was a fish-smelling, gull-squeaking, heterogeneous sort of town heaped up on the hills and bluffs that commanded a view of the harbor with its fringe of docks and shanties. Artists swarmed there in the summertime.

The name of our hotel was "The Nippanoggin Inn." The name was the jauntiest thing about it; indeed it was the only jaunty thing. The clapboarded building was painted egg-yolk yellow and had a mansard roof. The tiers of porches on the harbor side were stocked with wooden rocking chairs that rocked untenanted when the east wind blew, and that summer they rocked often.

"All right, Susie, this is yours, right next to mine," my father said, as if his hearty tone could liven up the room he led me into. Through the two windows facing me I saw the gray, littered harbor. The scrim curtains were limp and blotched with liver spots of rust, and looped on a hook beside the right-hand window there was a coil of knotted rope.

"What's that thing for?" I said, unbuttoning my coat.

"Well, not to hang yourself with, Sue! Quite the opposite. That's your own personal fire escape. But I'm certain you won't need to use it unless you're planning to elope."

My father, I sensed, was trying hard. I smiled obligingly, though I thought he could not know much about me if he didn't know I loathed most boys and planned never to marry; and it was no joking matter. I was eleven years old, with straight red hair, and skinny knees that jutted out above my socks. I felt uncomfortable with my father, and I think he did with me. We did not know each other very well, having lost track of each other, rather, in the years just past.

"Well, I hope you're going to be comfortable here, Susie. It's not what I'd call . . . it's not a luxurious bower exactly. But then we'll be outdoors a lot," he said, brightening. "Now why don't you unpack, get settled? I will, too, and then we'll go out and explore the town, shall we?"

"All right," I said.

When he had gone I went to the iron bedstand and sat down. The mattress felt as if it had been stuffed with the unclaimed laundry of former guests. I examined my new furniture: bureau, washstand, small lamp table by the window. There were two chairs; my father had put my suitcase on one of them, and instead of a closet there was a cretonne curtain that hung from a rod at one side of the room. I supposed that by the time I returned to the city all these things would have become familiar and accepted, a sort of home, but it was hard to believe just then.

I got up and opened my suitcase and took out the reading material that lay on my folded clothes: a copy of John Martin's *Book*, a copy of the *Atlantic Monthly*. One by one I lifted out my dresses and hung them on the jangling hangers behind the curtain. When I was putting my underclothes into a bureau drawer I caught sight of my face in the mirror.

"Hideous mule," I said to it, and then leaned forward with interest to watch as a tear rolled slowly down one cheek.

There was a knock at the door. I hastily disposed of the tear with a pair of socks, and turned to face my father.

He looked greatly refreshed, and there was a whiff of something new about him: a whiff of something to drink, I thought. I was glad. If he felt better, then I felt better, too.

The town was remarkably ugly, I remember that. Ugly in spite of the elms, in spite of the fine old houses, in spite of the harbor. It was ugly with people. At that time of day the trippers from Boston, with their celluloid visors and boat-burned faces and paper bags and cameras and children, poured into the main street. All their faces were in motion as they talked, laughed, ogled, jeered, and, dipping things out of the brown paper bags, chewed, gobbled, sucked, and spat out pits. All their eyes roved and darted eagerly, looking for artists, for the outlandish (and perhaps scandalous?) artists they had come to see; and the artists obliged. Not only had they left their traces everywhere, palette-knife scrapings on elm bark and curbstone and fence picket, but they were themselves boldly in evidence. Sporting sandals and beards, Navajo necklaces and earrings like buckets, they walked along the street in loud groups or sat at their easels in full view, together or alone, painting the same outpainted wharves, boats, and old characters that had been their subjects for years; but painting them, now, with a difference.

"Don't look like no boat to me, looks more like my gram-mother's flatiron," remarked an onlooker, ramming peanuts into his mouth, as his boiled-red wife shook with laughter and shifted the baby to her other hip.

More and more people clogged the street.

"Let's get out of this. They may stampede," my father said. He took my hand and tucked it in his arm and we plowed a course through the crowd, turned down a side street, and came to the harbor. It was low tide, and the exposed marly sand was studded with shells and bits of interesting trash. I picked up an old tin fork and a piece of green bottle glass.

"We'll find the bathing beach tomorrow," my father promised.

That night after dinner he produced a parcheesi board and we had a long satisfying game which I won. Afterward when I lay down on my remarkable mattress I fell asleep almost at once and slept for eleven hours, and when I woke up the windows were full of sun.

My father and I were alike in this way; we didn't care for talk at breakfast time. My mother was the opposite; she would begin to burble like a house wren the moment she opened her eyes. But now, alone with my father, I sat in silence reading while I ate, a habit I was never allowed to indulge at home. My father allowed it because he wanted to read himself; the arrangement suited us both.

During the morning he worked in his room, and I would sit at my little lame table painting pictures of sorceresses and queens. When I looked out the window I saw the harbor, the fussy boats, the swinging gulls. Next door I could hear the clacking of the typewriter, sometimes hurried and voluble; sometimes hesitant. There would be a long exasperated pause, a tentative tap and tap-tap, another pause, then sometimes the sound of an exclamation and the dry crumpling of paper.

At noon he would knock on my door and we went off to swim at the bathing beach where the water was clean and dazzling. He was an excellent swimmer, my father, and liked to swim well out and away from the shore. I used to watch with real anxiety as his head and rhythmically flailing arms grew more and more distant, were nearly lost to view. I could not settle down to my enjoyment until he had returned from that first long sortie into the blue.

"Don't worry about me, Sue," he said. "I always turn back as soon as I see Spain."

He told me of the creatures he had met along the way: the plaice fish who gave him tips on the horses, "Sea horses, that is," he said; and the jellyfish named Mrs. Cadwallader, "a Main Line jellyfish. But she can't find a corset to fit her."

He made short shrift of my formless side stroke and spent hours teaching me the crawl and the truden: accomplishments I cherish to this day.

It was always rather late when we returned to the inn. Sometimes they had run out of corn on the cob. The other occupants of the dining room, mostly in aging pairs, bowed chewing above their plates. The stained-glass clerestory above sent down a churchly light, and imposed a churchly hush. We spoke in low tones.

"Southern fried chicken," grumbled my father, sawing away at a drumstick. "Southern fried buzzard, more likely. Southern fried emu."

Besides the chicken there was always roast beef au jus on the menu, and Boston scrod. The beef was served in green-gray slices chilled at the edges, and I could never bring myself to try anything called scrod. The vegetables came in little extra dishes: succotash awash in milk, potatoes mashed with water and flung onto the dish with a ladle.

"Thank God for catsup," my father used to say; but I did not care for catsup. I was perfectly happy, though, on my diet of bread and butter and milk and ice cream.

"I don't suppose I ought to allow it," my father said helplessly. "Don't they . . . doesn't your mother make you eat everything at home?"

"Oh, they can't make me, Daddy," I assured him. "I have the appetite of a bird."

When he didn't go back to work we spent the afternoons together; going on expeditions in the little roadster he had hired, walking along the ocean shore where surf gnawed the beaches, or searching in the pine woods for Indian pipes. When he played golf I walked the course with him and was his caddy.

And I had found a friend for the days when he was busy: a girl named

Avalon Bray, who lived near the beach. She was two years older than I was, and in certain ways seemed older than that; I noticed that she looked at any boys we saw with a worried, wistful glance. As yet the boys did not respond. Avalon wore braces on her teeth that looked like lead, her hair was a mess, and she had not "filled out;" instead she looked pulled out, as if she had just recently been stretched from something smaller.

Still, she was a companion, and we spent hours playing in the sea together, wandering on the tide flats that smelled of chowder and crackled with the occupations of crabs.

"Gee, Sue, I think your father's cute!" she startled me by saying, one day.

"Cute? Men can't be cute," I said.

"Sure they can. Some. He is. He's good-looking."

I know that. It was strange. I could not tell whether my mother was pretty or not; her face was simply Mother's face. But I knew my father was handsome, and could see it.

At night, after dinner, he and I played our games, parcheesi or dominoes, and sometimes, if I begged him, he would tell me a story as he had often done when I was younger. He was very good at this and could spin a story out to last for hours. I went to bed late those nights, and often the last thing I heard before I slept was the irregular castanet-note of his typewriter.

All those days were fair. I remember them as being fair. The weather changed when Mrs. Fenwick came: the morning of the day she came.

When I woke up that day the east wind was blowing; the window curtains tossed listlessly, and the noise of gulls was sharp in the room. At breakfast my father was even more silent than usual. Perhaps the weather and the constant companionship of an eleven-year-old daughter were beginning to chafe his spirits.

His work went badly that morning; I could tell by the silences. The rain began to spit at ten; and I upset a jar of crimson madder on the rug.

At lunch he was morose. The vegetable was spinach. "Or is it kelp?" he wondered; and he said his coffee tasted as if there were limpets in it.

Afterward he returned to work, and I went to Avalon's house, which was wracked with the noise of younger brothers. We locked ourselves in her room with a supply of graham crackers and peanut butter, and she told me the facts of life.

"My heavens, Sue, you mean you honestly didn't know?"

"Not quite. Not exactly," I admitted, fascinated and appalled. Could I believe her, or was she crazy?

"Oh, my heavens, you're such a baby!" she cried, suddenly exasperated by my youth. With this beginning we managed a quarrel, and soon I left the house, upset on several counts.

At the inn I found my father in the lobby reading the paper.

"Couldn't stand that damned room another second," he said. "And I think the typewriter has rabies. It bit me. Where's what's-her-name? Avalon?"

"Oh, we're mad."

"What about?"

"Oh, nothing much," I said, glad of a sudden stir at the outer entrance of the lobby.

Calvin, the elderly bellboy, hobbled in with a load of Vuitton luggage. Behind him came two women, two new guests. One of them was old, stooped and tremulous, but the other, on whose arm she was leaning, was tall and commanding. She gave an immediate effect of confidence, perhaps accentuated by the contrast between herself and her companion. She also gave an effect of luxury, of well-being; all her appurtenances seemed exactly right for her: the fur scarf, the large hat with a veil, the big pearls on her ear lobes, and most of all the soft expensive aura of perfume that breathed from her.

"You sit down here, Auntie," she said to the older woman. "I'll sign the register." Her voice was rich and confident, too. I thought of the word contralto, although I was not certain of its meaning.

"Daddy," I said. "It's stopped raining. Can we go over to the surge now? Daddy? Can we?"

Though he stood facing me, my father was looking intently from the corners of his eyes at the tall woman signing the register. He did not answer.

"Daddy!" I repeated sharply.

At this the tall woman turned suddenly and looked over her shoulder at me, at him. She smiled a warm, friendly smile at me, at him. The fur stole slipped from her shoulders to the floor, and my father sprang forward.

"Oh, thank you so much! How clumsy of me!"

My father bowed and smiled, then turned to me lightheartedly. "All right, Mrs. Murphy, what do you say we go for a spin?" This was a name he called me when he was feeling cheerful.

In the dining room that evening, we saw that the newcomers had a table near the door. The tall one greeted us as we went by, and I noticed that my father glanced in her direction more than once during the meal.

Afterward, though the air was gray and damp, we went through the lounge to the veranda, as we did every evening. My father liked to smoke there after dinner.

He took a cigar from his pocket and clipped the end; absently he lopped the cigar band off and handed it to me. "Here's the ring you ordered, Mrs. Murphy."

I took it but did not put it on my finger. Cigar-band rings were for people of seven or less; I had finished with them years ago.

There was a sound of women's voices in the lounge, and I knew who was coming because of the smell of perfume that came first.

The tall woman held the screen door open for her aunt.

"I hope we're not disturbing you?"

"Of course not!" said my father quickly, standing up. He moved two rockers to the rail near ours, then introduced himself and me.

"And I am Meta Fenwick," she said. "Mrs. Abel Fenwick. And this is my aunt, Miss Currier."

We all sat down, Miss Currier taking a while to settle, cocooning herself against the damp; requiring a cushion from the lounge. Her niece opened a beaded bag and took out a cigarette case. Gold. And in it were flat little cigarettes with golden tips.

"I didn't think they'd care to have me smoking in the lounge!" she confided, smiling at my father. "But I simply must have my cigarette after dinner. I am an addict!"

My father held a light for her; and soon there was another smoke to mingle with his: light, musky, rather sweet. I left my rocker and sat on the rail so I could watch her better.

"Honey, don't you fall," said Mrs. Fenwick, but not as if she were really worried; just to be polite.

She was an ample woman, not fat or plump, but ample. She was tall, as I have said, with a large bosom, and creamy skin. Her gray eyes were large and luminous, her glossy hair was marcelled under a hair net, and there was a deep dimple in her chin. She laughed as often as she did, I suspect, because her teeth were flawless; and how well I remember that laugh! It had an easy, gratified quality. Everything about her was smooth, luxurious, unhurried.

Examining my memory of her I can see, now, that she was dead ripe: a woman at the last perfect moment before the gray begins in the hair and the soft flesh becomes a little too soft . . . It surprises me that I hated her so soon. She did her best to win me; she was kind, and I was not often given to hatred.

After that evening nothing was the same again. On the few days when we could swim, Mrs. Fenwick swam with us. She was a good golfer, too, so most of my father's afternoons were spent with her on the course; and now when we played our evening games there were three of us; sometimes four, though Miss Currier had become, as such old ladies often do, a background type.

("Poor Auntie, she's had so little. I'm all the family she has left. And she is all that I have . . . now."

"Your husband?" murmured my father.

"I've been a widow for three years," she told him gently.)

So I spent more and more time with Avalon. We had patched our quarrel up as we patched up many others. Our quarrels were not important; but neither was our friendship. We were nothing to each other but a means of killing time. Avalon, especially, was restive; she longed to be off and away in the next exciting part of her life. All of her was ready for it but her looks, poor thing. My childishness must have been a constant reminder and goad to her.

One day we took a picnic (with Mrs. Fenwick) to a place called Kettle Cove. Avalon went with us. All of us swam, but she and I kept on till we were sodden, as we always did. It was noon when we came out. Mrs. Fenwick and my father lay propped on their elbows on the sand, talking in low voices.

"Look at them," whispered Avalon, giving me a jab. "Your father's got a case on her, they've got a case on each other. Anyone can tell." She giggled, and suddenly, against my will, I thought of the things she had told me in her room that day.

"Oh, they have not. You're disgusting! Go to hell!" I whispered furiously. But we had to sacrifice that quarrel; after all, we were stuck there for the day, and with them.

As we got out of the car at the inn I heard Mrs. Fenwick murmur to my father: "We don't care what the tabbies in the rocking chairs are saying, do we?"

That evening she came out on the veranda to smoke her cigarette, wrapped in a pale-blue cashmere coat.

"Autumn is in the air," my father said.

"Yes, too soon . . . It always comes too soon." She looked at me perched on the railing, trying not to shiver. "Why, Susie dear, your teeth are chattering. Come here, come under my wing."

She held out the edges of her coat and a warm gust of perfume came from her. Half fascinated, half repelled, I allowed myself to be drawn into this shelter and stood there rigidly, conscious of the soft bosom and the breath behind it, and the perfume. Her arms and her coat were warm around me. For some reason I thought suddenly and longingly of a boy at home named Raymond Trout, who could walk on his hands, and spit like a man. I remembered his voice in the twilight shouting, "All-ee, all-ee in free!"

"Relax, you little giraffe," Mrs. Fenwick said teasingly. "Really, Howard—" ("Howard!" I thought.) "Your daughter feels just as bony and on guard as a little captured giraffe."

I hated her for that, too; for the first time I felt as Avalon must feel: that I was an unfinished product, ridiculous for this reason, as goslings, half-grown cats, and colts are, having lost their infancy's appeal and not yet having gained the authority of being grown.

So for this, and for calling my father "Howard," I knew at last how much I hated Mrs. Fenwick, and freed myself from her embrace.

"I'd rather go and get my sweater," I said brusquely.

"You'd better go and get in bed if you can't be more polite," my father chided.

But now it was impossible to be polite to Mrs. Fenwick. When she begged me not to chew the stalks of beach grass because she had heard of a child who had died of anthrax from doing this, I skipped before her along the path, pulling stalks and chewing them defiantly. When she invited me to go to the movies I said that movies gave me a headache, and when she offered me candy I said I wasn't hungry. Both lies. Sometimes she brought me presents, and while I accepted them (they were good presents), it was all I could do to thank her.

"She is a lovely person," my father said, and though the words weren't spoken as a question, I know that he desired an answer, and I gave none.

They were always together, and I tagged along. In the evenings they sat on the veranda long after I had gone to bed. I never heard the typewriter now, as I went off to sleep. Sometimes we would go down to the deserted "ballroom" in the basement where there was a piano. It was afflicted with a seaside twang, but she would play on it and sing in German or English. When she sang in English she pronounced the words as trained singers do; to me they sounded elegant, distorted, and embarrassing. But my father looked as though he could not hear enough, or watch enough.

Summer was nearly over. We were to leave Harbor Landing on the last day of August, while Mrs. Fenwick and her aunt planned to stay through Labor Day. "It will only be a week," she said to my father, and he said: "That week will have too many days in it."

But on the twenty-ninth Mrs. Fenwick had an unexpected visitor: a gentleman who arrived in a white Wills-St. Clair roadster with the top down. He had a red-bronze sunburn, and in the gray hair that rippled back from his forehead there was a glimpse of red-bronze bald spot. His gray mustache was twisted with wax into a little quill at each corner.

"Why, Carroll!" cried Mrs. Fenwick, when she saw him. "How on earth — why didn't you let me know? You never said — "

"I wanted to surprise you! I'm on my way to Bar Harbor" — "Bah Habbah," he called it — "to stop with the Murrays for Labor Day. So I thought, I'll just take a detour" — "daytew," he called it — "and spend a few days with Meta."

I saw the way his fingers slid up and down the inside of her smooth arm; and I saw her draw the arm away.

"Aren't you glad to see me?"

"Of course, Carroll. Surprised, that's all. You startled me."

I didn't think she cared for her surprise, and when she introduced the man, Mr. Bailey, to my father, it was the first time I had ever seen her look uncomfortable, not in command. My father must have noticed it. I saw his eyes go from her face to Mr. Bailey's and back to hers. After a minute of talking he put his hand on my shoulder.

"Beach time, Sue. Go get your things."

Mrs. Fenwick and her friend were not in the dining room for lunch that day. They were not there for dinner. Alone at the table, Miss Currier picked daintily and ravenously at her food.

My father and I sat in the lounge to play our evening games, and every time someone entered or went past the door he looked up quickly. "Daddy, you're not paying attention!" I said. I was winning all the games, but it was not fun to win them this way.

Mr. Bailey did not stay for his "few days" after all. He left early the next morning, and no one saw him off. Calvin the bellboy told me that.

My father had promised, on this last day, to take Avalon and me for a picnic at a lighthouse twenty miles away.

"But isn't Mrs. Fenwick coming?" I asked him.

"No," he said, and slammed the car door firmly. That day was flawless, and at the end of it Avalon and I had our good-byes. "You write me now, Susie!"

"Oh, I will, and you write me! Promise?"

"I promise."

We knew that we would never write.

As we went in to dinner that night I noticed that though my father smiled and greeted Mrs. Fenwick and her aunt, he did not stop to speak to them as he usually did. I skipped gaily to my place and ate an enormous dinner.

Afterward we had the veranda to ourselves; it was too damp for everyone but us. Fog had come smoking in from the sea, milky, and so dense that it collected on the eaves and dripped from them. Far, far away the harbor buoy tolled on the lifting tide.

"It's the last time," I said mournfully, for though I was fond of that veranda I had a superstitious regard for leave-takings. My father did not reply. He smoked in silence, and I forbore to rock my chair.

Behind us the screen door opened, closed. There was a smell of perfume in the air. My father stood up.

"Good evening," he said, severely.

She came and stood before him wearing her blue cashmere coat. She did not need to touch him with her hand; she used her voice.

"Howard," she said. "Howard?"

I understood her tone. It was one I sometimes used myself, pleading for something I wanted very badly. Hoping for something.

"Susie, it's your bedtime," my father said.

I was outraged. "It is not!"

"You have packing to do, I think."

"I have not. It's done."

Mrs. Fenwick took my hand in hers, a full, smooth hand; I snatched my own away.

"Susie, dear. Honey. Forgive me, will you? I want to talk to your father, may I? Alone? Just for a little while?"

"Scat, Susie," said my father, and then, more kindly: "I'm sure you have some things to do. We won't be long."

I wasn't a baby. I couldn't howl and clutch the railing. I left without a word. As I went through the lounge I looked back and saw his arm come up around her shoulders.

My father was wrong; I had no "things to do." My suitcase was packed; my traveling clothes were ready. The room was bare and tidy, home no longer, and through the window came the sound of the far bell.

I told myself they wouldn't mind if I went back to the lounge, where there were magazines to read. How could they mind that? Still, I tiptoed as I crossed the varnished floor to the magazine table. The lounge was deserted except for an old man in a chair, asleep and puffing softly.

Fog muffled the town noises, but the bell came clear, and the voices of the two on the veranda were a steady murmur. Hers, then his, then hers again. I turned the pages of a National Geographic and studied the pictures of a Dyak family, all with large stomachs.

"No!" said my father loudly from the porch.

Her voice rose, too. "But, Howard, honestly! What did you think . . . what can you expect? . . . I am not a nun!"

"But that fellow . . . how could you bring yourself—"

Her voice murmured and murmured, then rose again: "I thought we could be honest with each other. I really did. I thought we should be . . ."

"But that fellow. That tin-plate Percy Million-bucks. My God!"

Murmur, murmur, from her; then his voice gruff and abrupt. I had heard voices like these before, in my own house, when they thought I was asleep. Hers came up again.

". . . didn't suppose that you'd be pleased, but this boorish jealousy . . . I never would have imagined, I never would have dreamed—"

"Very well. All right. I'm a boor. But there's a name I could call you, too, you know, Meta!"

I heard her gasp, and I knew she stood up suddenly: her rocker banged to and fro with an agitated sound.

"Enough!" she cried. "That will be enough!"

Her footsteps came ringing on the boards, and I shrank back as she sailed through the door. Her anger went by me like a ship on fire: I swear I felt its heat.

The rocker on the porch soon stopped its noise. There was the dripping fog, the harbor bell; nothing else. After a while I tiptoed to the door. My father stood with his back to me, staring out at the blank night.

"Daddy?"

He turned on me. "For Christ's sake, Susie! What are you doing lurking there! I told you to get to bed!" He had never spoken to me in such a tone in all my life, and I began to cry.

"Oh, my God!" he said. "Tears, now! Tears!" He left me and strode through the lounge. The old man never stirred.

My father apologized the next morning; he was really sorry and concerned. And he told me that I was not to worry about what I'd heard; that he and Mrs. Fenwick had become very fond of one another, that she had caused him pain and he'd reacted badly — "hurt her feelings," he put it — but that everything would be "all right," because he was going to explain to her and tell her he was sorry.

"Grownups aren't always as grown up as they'd like to be," he said. "Years haven't much to do with it, unfortunately. You'll find that out."

I was finding it out. And everything was not "all right" with Mrs. Fenwick. She would not see my father. She would not speak to him.

"But she'd see you, Susie," he said, shameless with anxiety as the morning wore on; we were to leave at noon. "You go see her, you ought to, anyway. Knock on the door and when she hears your voice . . . tell her . . . no, wait, I'll send a note with you."

With his letter in my hand I walked slowly down the stuffy hall and around the corner to her door. Number 33. I knocked on it, then called her name, but there was no answer. I tried the handle; the door was not locked and I opened it gently, planning to leave the letter on her bureau. I was curious, too. I had never seen her room.

She was lying on the bed asleep.

I stood and looked at her. She had taken the pins out of her hair; they lay in a small heap on the bedside table with her earrings and a wrinkled handkerchief. Her hair covered her shoulders in a silky fall. Her eyelashes were dark and long. She slept gracefully, with her mouth closed, and the room was full of her perfume.

I looked at her for a minute, or a second; long enough, anyway, to remember her asleep forever, and then I went out of the room and closed the door as quietly as I could. I tore the letter up and dropped the pieces into one of the red fire buckets that hung on a hook by the stairs. Then I leaned against the wall and waited for my heart to quiet down; it was banging like the rockers on the porch.

When I turned the corner I saw my father waiting in his doorway.

"Did you give it to her, Sue? What did she say?"

"She tore it up," I said. "She never opened it. She just stood there and tore it up."

"Oh," he said, and his face turned dull. "Well, I guess she's . . . well, never mind. Never mind . . . Are you all ready?"

Indeed I was ready, and more than ready.

"Hurry, Daddy, come on, let's go!"

"Yes, all right . . . oh, here's Calvin. These two Calvin; I'll take the others . . ." And then as I waited nervously snapping my hat elastic under my chin, he turned away, turned to the window, and put his hand to his forehead just for a moment as if his head ached, and something about that simple gesture showed me how unhappy he was. I was appalled. I must tell him. Could I tell him? But I thought I could not. I thought I had gone too far, and was afraid.

"Daddy, let's go!"

"Yes. All right. Right now."

He didn't even turn his head as we went by the door, and I was perfectly miserable all the way home. I suppose I knew then that by my action I had lost my father just as truly as Mrs. Fenwick had.

ACTIVITIES

VOCABULARY

heterogeneous, adj. — mixed, having dissimilar qualities
jaunty, adj. — lively, merry
bower, n. — a place for rest, a retreat
ogle, v. — to look at in a flirting way
voluble, adj. — talkative
sortie, n. — an excursion, a rushing forth
chafe, v. — to irritate
morose, adj. — gloomy
kelp, n. — a kind of seaweed
appalled, adj. — shocked, horrified

aura, n.—a distinctive atmosphere or impression
gosling, n.—a young goose
boor, n.—a rude or insensitive person

QUESTIONS FOR REVIEW

1. Why don't Susie and her father know each other very well?

2. Susie says she was glad to smell alcohol on her father's breath. Why?

3. What kind of work does her father do?

4. Find evidence that Susie's father still thinks of his daughter as a little girl.

5. How is Susie's attitude toward boys different from Avalon's attitude toward them?

6. Susie walked out *"upset on several counts"* after Avalon called her *"such a baby!"* What has she just learned that she finds so upsetting?

7. Why does Susie come to hate Mrs. Fenwick so quickly?

8. Susie's emotions are very complex at times. What conflicting feelings do you suppose Susie might have had for Raymond? Why do you think her feelings about Mrs. Fenwick remind her of Raymond Trout?

9. After Mrs. Fenwick calls her a *"little giraffe,"* Susie goes on to compare herself to *"goslings, half-grown cats, and colts."* What is the basis of the comparison?

10. How does Carroll Bailey's surprise visit change things?

11. Why does Susie's father say, *"Grownups aren't always as grown up as they'd like to be?"*

12. Throughout the story Susie has wanted her father's full attention, and she hates sharing him with Mrs. Fenwick. Why, then, isn't she happy at the end? In what way has she damaged both her relationship with her father and her self-respect?

FOR DISCUSSION

A. "A Distant Bell" comes from a book titled *Early Sorrow*, a collection of short stories about the grief involved in growing up. Grief is the experience of sorrow after any loss. Our first thoughts may be of old age and death whenever grief is mentioned, but we face losses throughout our lives.

We grieve when we leave the security of childhood, when we end a friendship, when we have to give up our first love or our tenth, when we go away from home for the first time, when we lose a job, when we move from a comfortable community, when divorce or serious illness disrupts our family. We grieve as we leave each stage of life. We grieve at the loss of innocence whenever we learn things we'd rather not know. We grieve if we compromise our integrity and lose our self-respect.

Because Susie is the narrator of "A Distant Bell," we learn more about her than about any of the other characters. But she is not alone in her sorrow and grief. She is not the only one dealing with past, present, or future losses. How many examples of loss can you find? Take about ten minutes to look through the story and make your own list. Then work jointly as a class to compile a master list.

B. *"Each loss conditions us, for better or worse, for the next. Our happiness in maturity depends upon the ways we have learned to handle our losses."* (Rev. John Hay Nichols, *The Minns Lectures*, 1985).

Susie is hurting. It has been a painful summer and now she has to return to her mother's home and to school. Although she is going to need a friend, she may be reluctant to get too close to anyone. Why do you think this might be the case?

Do you believe Susie's experience as an eleven-year-old will affect her happiness as an adult? Explain. Susie longs for the love and security she apparently had before her parents' divorce. How might someone in her situation handle her grief and sense of loss in a more productive, positive way?

C. Both Sammy, the narrator of "A&P," and Susie of "A Distant Bell" learn all too well that spur-of-the-moment decisions can have long-term consequences. Sammy's words at the end of his story could just as well have come from Susie: "... *my stomach kind of fell as I felt how hard the world was going to be to me hereafter.*"

The lessons of life are often painful. One of the benefits of literature is that we can expand our experiences far beyond what is possible in our limited worlds, and we can learn from the experiences of others without suffering real consequences. No matter how many tears we may shed over the plight of our favorite character, we can always close the book. We still have the opportunity to change the endings in our own lives.

Both Sammy and Susie find themselves in situations they don't like. Sammy's reaction is heroic, at least he intends it to be. In quitting his job he is standing up for what he believes is right, and he pays a heavy price. He loses both the job and the girl and must face the fact that his idealism doesn't work very well in today's world. Susie, on the other hand, takes the easy way out, or so it seems at first. She knows what she is doing is wrong, but by tearing up her father's note she is essentially able to make Mrs. Fenwick disappear from her life. Susie has already begun by the end of the story to pay the painful price for her hasty action.

Use your imagination to picture Sammy and Susie twenty years after they told us their stories. How have their decisions affected their lives, their self-respect? Has either one paid a higher price? What have they learned from hindsight? How could such experiences as these enrich their lives and lead to greater happiness in the long run? You may wish to tell the two stories to an adult and get some help with these questions.

WELCOME

by Ouida Sebestyen

y father's Aunt Dessie peered through the windshield at a road sign. "Slow up a little bit, Mary," she told my mother. "The last time I tried to find kinfolks I hadn't visited for a while, I got the house number and the street perfect, but I was in the wrong town." She turned to me in the back seat. "I ran across this yard yelling, 'Guess who's here, Annabelle,' and burst right in on a white lady. Perfect stranger."

I caught my mother's eyes in the rearview mirror and made a pretend smile for Aunt Dessie, thinking how I would describe her to my friend Sharon when I got home. *Picture this eighty-year-old drill sergeant? In drag? With this head of corn-row hair she must have made with a real hoe?* Sharon would double up. At least as far as she could double, now.

My mother slowed to a creep. Yesterday evening, bowling along through Texas on her way to see her parents, she had swerved off the interstate toward a dismal little town. Before I could figure what in blazes she was doing, we were spending the night on Aunt Dessie's let-down couch between two whatnots crammed with spinster junk. I had hissed, "What is this—I hate changes." But my mother just lay with her back to me, pretending to be asleep, while strange summer things from the piney woods tapped against the screens.

Aunt Dessie said, "Noella's going to be as surprised as I was. I still can't believe I'm riding along beside you, Mary. After seventeen years."

"Is it that long?" my mother said.

Aunt Dessie turned back to me. "And to finally get to see you, pretty thing. The image of your daddy."

"Are you sure this is the road?" my mother said sharply. "We've really got to keep this visit brief."

"Then why don't you stop at that little place up there and let me ask. Some of this backwoods is hazy in my mind."

We stopped. Aunt Dessie unfolded out of the car like a carpenter's ruler, and yanked open the screen door of a little grocery that had been waiting for a customer since the Depression.

I murmured, "Lordy mercy, as they say down here. Are we talking hazy or crazy?"

"That's enough smart lip," my mother warned me. "You be nice to her. She took us in like royalty. She didn't have to."

"If she tells me one more time I look like my daddy—"

"You do."

"I look like me." It mattered that I was my own special leg of the proud unsteady tripod my mother and father and I had always made. "I feel very guess-who's-here- Annabelle."

"Me too, a little. But suddenly I just wanted to see her and your great-aunt Noella again. I've never forgotten how they took me into the family. No questions. No testing. Just welcome." She was silent, remembering. "I guess I needed their blessing, or something. But I can't tell if Dessie knows."

She lifted the hot hair off her coffee-and-cream neck. She had always worn her hair long and straightened, to please my father. Reverse perm after reverse perm. But now the newest inch of it had its own natural crinkle, recording almost to the day, I guess, when they stopped loving each other. Old fears began to press me like fingers finding the deep secret acupressure points of pain. "What do you mean, *if she knows?* What's to know? You're going to patch all this up. Like the other times, and everything's going to be fine again."

She put her hands on the wheel as if she needed to be driving.

"You are," I said.

"Tina, sometimes things—"

"No. You are."

Aunt Dessie came striding out, carrying a piece of paper in one hand and a bright canvas bag in the other.

"Lady in there makes these totes," she announced, handing it to me. "A souvenir."

I took it, surprised. "Thanks," I said, actually smiling in my confusion.

Her old eyes studied me so long that I said too loudly, "Hey, I could embroider YUCK! on it and give it to Sharon for a diaper bag."

"Who's Sharon?" Aunt Dessie asked.

My mother started off with a jerk. "A bubble-headed little blond Tina knows back home."

"Just my best friend," I said.

Aunt Dessie studied the scrap of paper someone had drawn a map on. "Ah," she nodded. "I see."

"Actually," my mother said, her voice accelerating with the car, "she's a strange little person who keeps trying to saddle Tina with all her problems. I hoped this trip would give them a vacation from each other."

Lie, I said to get her back. *You'd rather run from that empty-feeling house than face up to your life.*

"She didn't saddle me," I told Aunt Dessie. "Somebody has to look after Sharon, she's so casual, so inconceivably —" I began to giggle crazily and couldn't stop. "I have to remind her what the doctor says to do, or she'll eat like she wants a French-fried baby with diet-cola blood."

"I think we can spare Aunt Dessie the details."

"Hey, all I did was ask if she could stay with us till the baby comes. And you went off like a ton of dynamite — rip, mangle, roar." My mother's eyes tried to grab mine in the mirror, but I wouldn't look. I wanted to give the details. Hadn't she driven miles out of her way to give her side of things to my father's aunts before he did? Okay, I wanted to tell about my friend who wasn't afraid to gulp down whole chunks of life I hadn't even dared to taste.

She said, "The last thing I need is a tenth-grade drop-out with a fatherless child on the way."

"There's always a father," I objected. "She just doesn't want him around." I tried to think what the slang had been in my mother's day. "He's a creep. She doesn't really like him."

"Turn left," Aunt Dessie said. My mother swerved.

"It's the baby that's important," I said. "Sharon's going to have something really truly her very own. She's glad about it."

"My God," my mother said. She bore through a tunnel of pines riddled with sunlight shafts. "But not in my house."

I braced myself carefully. "But she *is* in our house. I gave her the key before we left."

The car lurched to a stop. My mother swung around in her seat. "Tina!

You knew perfectly well how I felt about that."

"Where else could she go?"

"Good heavens, she has parents."

"Oh, sure, her mother's in Florida with four stepchildren and her dad got an ultimatum from his girlfriend. Who's she supposed to turn to besides us? I'm her friend. I thought you were, too, the way you were always nice to her and laughed when she did weird things—"

Aunt Dessie said firmly, "Left again up there at that tree."

My mother started the car and drove past a field of sunflowers all staring at us with little happy faces. Slowly tears as hard as hailstones filled my throat. "I thought I could depend on you," I said, bumping along like the car. "To help her. But you slide out of things like a plate of noodles."

Aunt Dessie said, "I gather your daddy's away from home."

"He still travels, you know," my mother answered for me. "In his kind of work he has to, a great deal."

She slowed as the rutted road dipped for a creek. A little boy in overalls stood expectantly beside a mailbox. Suddenly I knew how my father had looked, growing up in those piney woods. Waiting for the mail carrier to come with something wonderful. I snapped my eyes shut to block him off. I didn't want to think about my father. I didn't even know how to think about him anymore. I just wanted everything to stand still, frozen like that little boy, so that nothing would ever have to arrive.

"How long has he been dead?" I heard my mother say. I jerked to attention, but she added, "Noella's husband."

"I guess two years now," Aunt Dessie said. "Bless her heart, it must be hard for her." She turned around in the seat, raising her voice in case I had gone deaf. "Noella's husband was your Granddaddy Mayhew's brother, you see, and I'm from your grandmother's side, so Noella and I aren't anything like blood kin."

My mother said, "Why have you kept up with each other all these years?"

Aunt Dessie craned to read the name of a small wooden church we were passing. "I guess we just feel related." She turned back to me. "Your daddy stayed with me four years, so he could be close to a better school. I loved that boy."

I gazed at the crooked rows of her gray hair, wondering what age she had been when she stared into a mirror at her horse face and rawboned body and knew no man was ever going to love her.

We passed a square unpainted house smothering under a trumpet vine. "Whoa!" Aunt Dessie commanded. "It says Mayhew on the mailbox."

"This is it?" My mother stopped and backed up. At the side of a barn two pigs lay in a juicy wallow. Some little granny in clodhopper shoes just had to be around the corner, stewing the wash in a black pot. "Good heavens," she murmured, "I wouldn't live out here all alone for the world."

"Well, Noella's not alone, you remember. She's still got Arley with her." Aunt Dessie flipped her stiff old hand at a hill nearby. "And the old Mayhew cemetery's up there. There's family around."

We stopped in front of the house. The screen opened and a little dried-apple woman came to the edge of the porch. Aunt Dessie unfolded and strode up the steps into her arms.

"Who do you think I brought to see you, Noella?" she demanded. "Here's Jimmie's wife. Mary."

"Jimmie?" I thought. My father could never have been anyone but James. Cool upwardly mobile James.

"Of course it's Mary," Noella said in a quavery voice as tender as cake. "You precious thing. I'm so thankful to see you again." She wound her arms around my mother like roots.

Aunt Dessie said, "And this is Jimmie's daughter. This is Tina." Then I was inside that root-hold, as helpless as a rock being broken by long gentle pressure.

"I would have known you," Noella said. I braced myself. "You have his face, your daddy's face. I always hoped I'd get to see you." She looked beyond me at the empty car.

My mother looked, too, as if she had just recalled the trips we used to take when my father would wake up in the back seat, yelling, "Hey, we've *arrived*—why didn't you tell me?" while we laughed. "James would have liked to come, I'm sure. But he's a busy man these days."

Noella took her arm. "Tell him I miss him."

"Yes," my mother said, glancing sharply at me to make sure I didn't blurt out, *How can she tell him when he moved out a month ago?*

We sat in Noella's cramped little living room while she slushed around in her slippers, bringing us iced tea. She and Aunt Dessie took big breaths and brought each other up-to-date on who had died since they last visited. They made me nervous, reminding me how life changes and the people we love fall away.

I stared out the window through a bouquet of plastic flowers that was never going to die. All at once I realized that a man's bearded face was staring in at me.

I screamed, giving a start that filled my lap with iced tea.

Noella said calmly, "It's just Arley, precious. He wants to see who you are, but he's shy." The face scowled, punctured by a gaping mouth, and disappeared. She patted my skirt with everyone's pink paper napkins and sent me out into the sun to dry.

Aunt Dessie strolled out behind me. "Who's Arley?" I whispered, afraid I'd see that face again peeking through the beanpoles of the garden.

"Noella's son," Aunt Dessie said.

"But he's middle-aged." It sounded stupid, but I couldn't recall ever seeing a retarded adult. I guess I thought they stayed children.

"Of course he is. We grow, whether we're ready or not. We do the best we can." She picked a skinny red-pepper pod and bit off the end. "Mercy! Jalapeño." She fanned her tongue.

We walked along the garden rows while my skirt dried. Behind a hedge a bear-shaped shadow stayed even with us.

"Your mother seems very sad." Aunt Dessie said.

I shrugged. "Really?" Suddenly it would have been a relief to pour out the whole They've-split-again-and-it's-awful-and-I'm-scared story.

"Trouble at home?"

I kept shrugging. "Not exactly. Well, maybe a little, but they'll work it out. They always do."

"Ah," Aunt Dessie said.

When we went into the kitchen, my mother was setting plates around a table that practically sagged under bowls of macaroni and cheese and sliced tomatoes and fried okra and chowchow and peaches that perfumed the room. All at once I was famished.

Noella piled food on a tray and took it to the door, saying, "Arley wants to eat on the porch. It takes him a little while to get used to new people."

I stuffed myself. Aunt Dessie kept right up with me, begging her gall bladder to forgive and forget. My mother ate in silence, watching the two old faces opposite her like a play.

Noella said, "The last time Dessie came for a visit she brought me the most beautiful crocheted bedspread you ever set eyes on. I'll show it to you. Are you still doing bedspreads?"

"Can't afford the thread anymore," Aunt Dessie said. "Now it's bootees and little sacques and caps. I sell some for baby showers and give the rest away to whoever's expecting."

Noella asked, "What kind of projects keep you busy, Mary?"

My mother opened her mouth and nothing came out. I waited with them, curious. *Tell them your hobby is collecting little keys that lock out the things in your life that scare you. And lock you in.*

A glass shattered out on the porch. We jumped again as something crashed against the wall. A blubbering growl rose and faded as footsteps pounded off the porch and away.

Noella took a broom and went out. We waited. My mother pressed a careful furrow in her food and we all studied it like a divination. She asked, "Who will take care of him when she dies?"

Aunt Dessie nodded, musing. "Yes. When he's alone. She worries terribly about that."

Unexpectedly my mother reached across the table and laid her hand on Aunt Dessie's. Aunt Dessie put her other hand on top of theirs and we all looked at the funny fragile layers of hands until Noella came back with the tray full of spilled food and broken glass.

In the hurting silence I found myself offering to do the dishes while they visited, but Noella shooed us out, saying she could do dishes when she didn't have us. I hung at the kitchen door, feeling somehow drawn to her, as she put up the food. "I'm sorry I screamed," I said. "I didn't know."

"Of course you didn't, sugar." She took a dozen gorgeous peaches off the windowsill and put them in a sack. "When Arley was little and I finally knew he was never going to be right, I screamed too. Screamed and screamed." She put the sack into my hands. "Take these with you. Your mother said you're on your way to see her folks."

I wished she hadn't reminded me. "She never did this before." As if I had taken the bottom piece of fruit out of the pyramid at the market, everything began to tumble. "Left home, I mean. To go talk to her folks about it. Like this time it was — it was — " I felt silly tripping over a simple word like *serious*.

"Bless your heart," Noella said.

When we went into the living room, Aunt Dessie asked us, "We do have time to go up to the cemetery a minute, don't we?"

My mother shook her head. "I'm afraid it's getting — "

"We have time," I said. I offered my arm to Noella and we went out past my mother's surprised face.

She and Aunt Dessie followed us up a shade-spattered road to the top of the hill. Noella opened a gate in a wire fence and let us into the little graveyard filled with dark cedars. "Used to be a church here, at the beginning," she said. I looked around, wondering why I had wanted so suddenly and urgently, back at the house, to stand up there with my kin.

Noella led us through the high weeds to a grave with a neat concrete cover. A jar with the stem of a rose in it stood beside the nameplate. Dried petals lay around it. "Arley comes," Noella said.

Aunt Dessie pulled two weeds and brushed the nameplate with their leafy tops. "He was a good kind man, Noella." They looked down in silence. "You were fortunate."

"Oh, yes," Noella said, and put her thin arm through Aunt Dessie's bony one.

My mother walked slowly away toward a worn stone. Years of wind had scoured off all the inscription except one line. It said, *beloved wife of.*

She began to cry, with the loud surprised sound of an animal in pain.

"Oh, precious," Noella exclaimed. "Are you sick?"

My mother pivoted blindly into Aunt Dessie's arms. A sob broke through her fingers. They both caught her tight, not understanding. But I knew.

Fear froze me. My voice made a long arc. "Nooo — you can fix it, you can work it out, you're adults!"

My mother's head rocked back and forth, her long hair sliding.

"Oh, Mary," Aunt Dessie said. "No hope at all?"

"No hope," my mother sobbed.

"What?" Noella asked. "What?"

"The marriage," Aunt Dessie said. "Over."

I whirled and ran. Before the fact could touch me. Over the humps of graves lost in the weeds. "No!" I insisted, with every gasp of breath.

But I knew the fact was right behind me, riding piggy-back the way it always had, and there was no way I could ever run fast enough. My father had escaped. Oh, God, I knew it wasn't his fault that he had to keep growing. Out of the piney woods. Out of a marriage with somebody who was growing at a different speed. But I wished I could have hunted for that little boy he had been once, and coaxed him out, and made friends with him.

The fence loomed up. I grabbed the rusty wire and hung over it, listening to myself gulping air as though nothing in me had died.

When I lifted my head, a hand was reaching toward me from behind a gravestone. I recoiled into the weeds before I saw that it was holding out a yellow flower.

Arley peeped out. "I'm nice," he whispered. "Don't cry." His soft wet mouth crumpled with anxiety. "I don't scare you." He pushed the flower closer.

I cringed away before I could stop myself. He did scare me. All the things I didn't understand scared me. Losing the people I had belonged to. Letting a special person change my life someday. Or mess it up, the way Sharon had let someone mess up hers. I had collected as many keys as my mother to lock the changes out.

Carefully, Arley sniffed the flower to show me what he wanted me to do. He held it out again, smiling, with pollen on his nose.

"Don't cry," he begged. "I'm nice." He had my father's deep eyes. The family face. Mine.

"I know," I said shakily. I could see he was. A big, bearded man-child distressed to see me sad. "It's not you." A year's collection of tears tried to burst out, sweeping my breath away again. I pointed up the hill. "It's that."

He looked up and nodded solemnly, as if he knew all about divorces, and all about the key I'd given Sharon so she'd hang out at our house like always and teach me to be brave. He smiled as if he could explain why people kept rearranging themselves into families so they could take care of each other.

I looked up the slope. My mother was walking toward me, between Aunt Dessie and Noella. Her face was calm. She held their hands. She would cut her hair, I thought. She would let it go natural.

Slowly I reached out and took Arley's flower.

I wondered if he would nod if I suddenly said that, in spite of everything, I knew I was lucky. Lucky to be able to go on from this, without too much to handle like Sharon, or starting from scratch like my mother.

Noella came to me and held me close in her root arms. She gave me a brisk pat. "I don't have a brain cell working. I forgot to show you Dessie's bedspread."

We went through the gate and down the road again. Behind me, my mother said, "Tina?" I felt the tips of her fingers brush my back. "If you're giving Sharon the diaper bag, maybe I could give her some bootees."

I stumbled around to look at her. My voice wiggled as I said, "Would you? It would mean a lot."

Aunt Dessie smiled. "What color shall they be, for this modern little mother? Purple, with orange ribbons?"

"Just a nice traditional white, I would think," my mother said. "Some things don't change."

ACTIVITIES

VOCABULARY

spinster, n. — an unmarried woman or one who seems unlikely to marry
lurch, v. — to stagger or move with a sudden swaying or tipping
ultimatum, n. — a final condition or demand
wallow, n. — an area of deep mud in which animals roll
famished, adj. — suffering from extreme hunger
furrow, n. — a trench or a groove as made by a plow
divination, n. — unusual insight or intuitive perception
scour, v. — to scrub or wear away

FOR DISCUSSION

A. Many a parent seeks advice from the experts when the "terrible twos" or the tumultuous teens at least momentarily obscure the joys of family life. The reassuring advice is typically that these are perfectly normal stages in the growth toward independence and maturity. But children are not the only ones to pass through stages. The term "mid-life crisis" has become as familiar a term as the "terrible twos." In fact, our preoccupations and our needs continue to change throughout all the decades of our lives. What insight does Tina have into her parents' behavior? Why can't they live together any longer?

B. Life has taken a nasty turn for Tina and her mother, and both are hurting. Tina has felt pain, fear, and anger since the separation of her parents a month ago, and she blames her mother. Are there other feelings you would add to this list? How are anger and love related? How does Tina change over the course of the story?

CLASS ACTIVITY: Help Wanted — Mother

Imagine an ad for MOTHER placed in the classified section of a newspaper by an unborn child. List all the requirements that would go into the job description. What qualities and conditions are basic to a healthy family life?

Then think about filling the job. Would Mary, Tina's mother, be a strong candidate? What about Sharon? What would she need to do to improve her chances? Can you argue that Sharon might actually be a better mother if she gave up her child for adoption?

WRITING ASSIGNMENT: A Friend in Need Indeed

Tina's family history has had its share of sadness and tragedy, but support has always been available for those in need. When her father leaves home, Tina learns about an expanded sense of the word "family." Her people have a tradition of "rearranging themselves into families so they could take care of each other." The welcome mat has always been out.

But life is harder for some people than for others. In contrast to Tina, Sharon has had many doors shut in her face. Just as a child grabs for a favorite teddy bear in moments of loneliness or fear, Sharon wants her baby as "something really truly her very own." Tina, however, recognizes that Sharon's pregnancy is not a simple answer to a complicated problem. Sharon is certain to end up "with too much to handle."

Given her difficult family circumstances, what better choices could Sharon have made? Go back to a time just before her pregnancy and write Sharon a letter. Gently try to convince her that sexual intimacy is likely to cause problems rather than solve them. What else could she do to satisfy her craving for love and support? To whom could she turn for help? How might she take control of her life in a constructive rather than a destructive way? After everybody has finished, compare letters and make a list of the best advice the class has for Sharon.

FIFTEEN

by Bob Greene

T his would be excellent, to go in the ocean with this thing," says Dave Gembutis, fifteen.

He is looking at a $170 Sea Cruiser raft.

"Great," says his companion, Dan Holmes, also fifteen.

This is at Herman's World of Sporting Goods, in the middle of the Woodfield Mall in Schaumburg, Illinois.

The two of them keep staring at the raft. It is unlikely that they will purchase it. For one thing, Dan has only twenty dollars in his pocket, Dave five dollars. For another thing—ocean voyages aside—neither of them is even old enough to drive. Dave's older sister, Kim, has dropped them off at the mall. They will be taking the bus home.

Fifteen. What a weird age to be male. Most of us have forgotten about it, or have idealized it. But when you are fifteen . . . well, things tend to be less perfect.

You can't drive. You are only a freshman in high school. The girls your age look older than you and go out with upperclassmen who have cars. You probably don't shave. You have nothing to do on the weekends.

So how do you spend your time? In the 1980s, most likely at a mall. Woodfield is an enclosed shopping center sprawling over 2.25 million square feet in northern Illinois. There are 230 stores at Woodfield, and on a given Saturday those stores are cruised in and out by thousands of teenagers killing time. Today two of those teenagers are Dave Gembutis and Dan Holmes.

Dave is wearing a purple Rolling Meadows High School Mustangs windbreaker over a gray M*A*S*H T-shirt, jeans, and Nike running shoes. He has a red plastic spoon in his mouth, and will keep it there for most of the afternoon. Dan is wearing a white Ohio State Buckeyes T-shirt, jeans, and Nike running shoes.

We are in the Video Forum store. Paul Simon and Art Garfunkel are singing "Wake Up Little Susie" from their Central Park concert on four television screens. Dave and Dan have already been wandering around Woodfield for an hour.

"There's not too much to do at my house," Dan says to me.

"Here we can at least look around," Dave says. "At home I don't know what we'd do."

"Play catch or something," Dan says. "Here there's lots of things to see."

"See some girls or something, start talking," Dave says.

I ask them how they would start a conversation with girls they had never met.

"Ask them what school they're from," Dan says. "Then if they say Arlington Heights High School or something, you can say, 'Oh, I know somebody from there.'"

I ask them how important meeting girls is to their lives.

"About forty-five percent," Dan says.

"About half your life," Dave says.

"Half is girls," Dan says. "Half is going out for sports."

An hour later, Dave and Dan have yet to meet any girls. They have seen a girl from their own class at Rolling Meadows High, but she is walking with an older boy, holding his hand. Now we are in the Woodfield McDonald's. Dave is eating a McRib sandwich, a small fries, and a small Coke. Dan is eating a cheeseburger, a small fries, and a medium root beer.

In here, the dilemma is obvious. The McDonald's is filled with girls who are precisely as old as Dave and Dan. The girls are wearing eye shadow, are fully developed, and generally look as if they could be dating the Green Bay Packers. Dave and Dan, on the other hand . . . well, when you're a fifteen-year-old boy, you look like a fifteen-year-old boy.

"They go with the older guys who have cars," Dan says.

"It makes them more popular," Dave says.

"My ex-girlfriend is seeing a junior," Dan says. I ask him what happened.

"Well, I was in Florida over spring vacation," he says. "And when I got back I heard that she was at Cinderella Rockafella one night, and she was dancing with this guy, and she liked him, and he drove her home and stuff."

"She two-timed him," Dave says.

"The guy's on the basketball team," Dan says.

I ask Dan what he did about it.

"I broke up with her," he says, as if I had asked the stupidest question in the world.

I asked him how he did it.

"Well, she was at her locker," he says. "She was working the combination. And I said, 'Hey, Linda, I want to break up.' And she was opening her locker door and she just nodded her head yes. And I said, 'I hear you had a good time while I was gone, but I had a better time in Florida.'"

I ask him if he feels bad about it.

"Well, I feel bad," he says. "But a lot of guys told me, 'I heard you broke up with her. Way to be.'"

"It's too bad the Puppy Palace isn't open," Dan says.

"They're remodeling," Dave says.

We are walking around the upper level of Woodfield. I ask them why they would want to go to the Puppy Palace.

"The dogs are real cute and you feel sorry for them," Dan says. We are in a fast-food restaurant called the Orange Bowl. Dave is eating a frozen concoction called an O-Joy. They still have not met any girls.

"I feel like I'd be wasting my time if I sat at home," Dan says. "If it's Friday or Saturday and you sit home, it's considered . . . low."

"Coming to the mall is about all there is," Dave says. "Until we can drive."

"Then I'll cruise," Dan says. "Look for action a little farther away from my house, instead of just riding my bike around."

"When you're sixteen, you can do anything," Dave says. "You can go all the way across town."

"When you have to ride your bike . . ." Dan says. "When it rains, it ruins everything."

In the J.C. Penney store, the Penney Fashion Carnival is under way. Wally the Clown is handing out favors to children, but Dave and Dan are watching the young female models parade onto a stage in bathing suits.

"Just looking is enough for me," Dan says.

Dave suggests that they head out back into the mall and pick out some girls to wave to. I ask why.

"Well, see, even if they don't wave back, you might see them later in the day." Dan says. "And then they might remember that you waved at them, and you can meet them."

We are at the Cookie Factory. These guys eat approximately every twenty minutes.

It is clear that Dan is attracted to the girl behind the counter. He walks up, and his voice is slower and about half an octave lower than before.

The tone of voice is going to have to carry the day, because the words are not all that romantic:

"Can I have a chocolate-chip cookie?"

The girl does not even look up as she wraps the cookie in tissue paper.

Dan persists. The voice might be Clark Gable's:

"What do they cost?"

The girl is still looking down.

"Forty-seven," she says and takes his money, still looking away, and we move on.

Dave and Dan tell me that there are lots of girls at Woodfield's indoor ice-skating rink. It costs money to get inside, but they lead me to an exit door, and when a woman walks out we slip into the rink. It is chilly in here, but only three people are on the ice.

"It's not time for open skating yet," Dan says. "This is all private lessons."

"Not much in here," Dave says.

We sit on benches. I ask them if they wish they were older.

"Well," Dan says, "when you get there, you look back and you remember. Like I'm glad that I'm not in the fourth or fifth grade now. But I'm glad I'm not twenty-five either."

"Once in a while I'm sorry I'm not twenty-one," Dave says. "There's not much you can do when you're fifteen. This summer I'm going to caddy and try to save some money."

"Yeah," Dan says. "I want to save up for a dirt bike."

"Right now, being fifteen is starting to bother me a little bit," Dave says. "Like when you have to get your parents to drive you to Homecoming with a girl."

I ask him how that works.

"Well, your mom is in the front seat driving," he says. "And you're in the back seat with your date."

I ask him how he feels about that.

"It's embarrassing," he says. "Your date understands that there's nothing you can do about it, but it's still embarrassing."

Dave says he wants to go to Pet World.

"I think they closed it down," Dan says, but we head in that direction anyway.

I ask them what the difference is between Pet World and the Puppy Palace.

"They've got snakes and fish and another assortment of dogs," Dan says. "But not as much as the Puppy Palace."

When we arrive, Pet World is, indeed, boarded up.

We are on the upper level of the mall. Dave and Dan have spotted two girls sitting on a bench directly below them, on the mall's main level.

"Whistle," Dan says. Dave whistles, but the girls keep talking.

"Dave, wave to them and see if they look," Dan says.

"They aren't looking," Dave says.

"There's another one over there," Dan says.

"Where?" Dave says.

"Oh, that's a mother," Dan says. "She's got her kid with her."

They return their attention to the two downstairs.

Dan calls to them: "Would you girls get the dollar I just dropped?"

The girls look up.

"Just kidding," Dan says.

The girls resume their conversation.

"I think they're laughing," Dan says.

"What are you going to do when the dumb girls won't respond," Dave says.

"At least we tried," Dan says.

I ask him what response would have satisfied him.

"The way we would have known that we succeeded," he says, "they'd have looked up here and started laughing."

The boys keep staring at the two girls.

"Ask her to look up," Dan says. "Ask her what school they go to."

"I did," Dave says. "I did."

The two boys lean over the railing.

"Bye, girls," Dave yells.

"See you later," Dan yells.

The girls do not look up.

"Too hard," Dan says. "Some girls are stuck on themselves, if you know what I mean by that."

We go to a store called the Foot Locker, where all the salespeople are dressed in striped referee's shirts.

"Dave!" Dan says. "Look at this! Seventy bucks!" He holds up a pair of New Balance running shoes. Both boys shake their heads.

We move on to a store called Passage to China. A huge stuffed tiger is placed by the doorway. There is a PLEASE DO NOT TOUCH sign attached to it. Dan rubs his hand over the tiger's back. "This would look so great in my room," he says.

We head over to Alan's TV and Stereo. Two salesmen ask the boys if they are interested in buying anything, so they go back outside and look at the store's window. A color television set is tuned to a baseball game between the Chicago Cubs and the Pittsburgh Pirates.

They watch for five minutes. The sound is muted, so they cannot hear the announcers.

"I wish they'd show the score," Dave says.

They watch for five minutes more.

"Hey, Dave," Dan says. "You want to go home?"

"I guess so," Dave says.

They do. We wave goodbye. I watch them walk out of the mall toward the bus stop. I wish them girls, dirt bikes, puppies, and happiness.

ACTIVITIES

Bob Greene is a columnist who has worked for the Chicago Times-Sun, the Chicago Tribune, and *Esquire* magazine. "Fifteen" comes from *American Beat*, a collection of columns he wrote for these publications. Whereas a reporter's job is to report news as factually and objectively as possible, a columnist can interpret the world he sees. But insight and truth remain common goals. How truthful, how accurate, is Bob Greene's description of fifteen-year-olds? Does his description apply to you, or do you know guys like Dan and Dave? In what way is Greene's portrait accurate? Where does he miss the mark?

HOMEWORK ASSIGNMENT: The TV Teen

Teenagers come in all shapes, sizes, and colors, and they vary greatly in interests, abilities, and personalities. Many television series feature teenagers as major characters. Choose a character who rings true to you and explain, in one page or less, what it is about the character that seems authentic. In what way do you identify with that fictional character?

BOY MEETS GIRL

by Peter Stone and Carl Reiner

To perform this skit you will need two volunteers to come to the front of the class, one to read in a mock deep voice, the other to read in a high voice. Improvise some props like baby bonnets or blankets if you can, but no pink or blue stereotypes please!

DEEP VOICE: Hi!

HIGH VOICE: Hi!

DEEP VOICE: I'm a baby.

HIGH VOICE: What do you think I am, a loaf of bread?

DEEP VOICE: You could be — what do I know? I'm just born. I'm a baby. I don't even know if I'm under a tree or in a hospital or what. I'm just glad to be here.

HIGH VOICE: Well, I'm a baby, too.

DEEP VOICE: Have it your own way. I don't want to fight about it.

HIGH VOICE: What are you, scared?

DEEP VOICE: Yes, I am. I'm a little scared. I'll tell you why. See, I don't know if I'm a boy or girl yet.

HIGH VOICE: What's that got to do with it?

DEEP VOICE: Well, if you're a boy and I'm a girl you can beat me up. Do you think I want to lose a tooth my first day alive?

HIGH VOICE: What's a tooth?

DEEP VOICE: Search me. I'm just born. I'm a baby. I don't know nothing yet.

HIGH VOICE: Do you think you're a girl?

DEEP VOICE: I don't know. I might be. I think I am. I've never been anything before. Let me see. Let me take a little look around. Hmm. Cute feet. Small, dainty. Yup, yup, I'm a girl. That's it. Girltime.

HIGH VOICE: What do you think I am?

DEEP VOICE: You? That's easy—you're a boy.

HIGH VOICE: Are you sure?

DEEP VOICE: Of course I'm sure. I'm alive, already four, five minutes and I haven't been wrong yet.

HIGH VOICE: Gee, I don't feel like a boy.

DEEP VOICE: That's because you can't see yourself.

HIGH VOICE: Why? What do I look like?

DEEP VOICE: Bald. You're a bald fellow. Bald, bald, bald. You're bald as a pingpong ball. Are you bald!

HIGH VOICE: So?

DEEP VOICE: So, boys are bald and girls have hair.

HIGH VOICE: Are you sure?

DEEP VOICE: Of course, I'm sure. Who's bald, your mother or your father?

HIGH VOICE: My father.

DEEP VOICE: I rest my case.

HIGH VOICE: Hmm. You're bald, too.

DEEP VOICE: You're kidding!

HIGH VOICE: No, I'm not.

DEEP VOICE: Don't look!

HIGH VOICE: Why?

DEEP VOICE: A bald girl—blech—disgusting!

HIGH VOICE: Maybe you're a boy and I'm a girl.

DEEP VOICE: There you go again. I told you—I'm a girl. I know it. I know it. I'm a girl, and you're a boy.

HIGH VOICE: I think you're wrong.

DEEP VOICE: I am never wrong! What about shaving?

HIGH VOICE: What about it?

DEEP VOICE: You just shaved, right?

HIGH VOICE: Wrong.

DEEP VOICE: Exactly! And you know why? Because everyone's born with a clean shave. It's just that girls keep theirs and boys don't.

HIGH VOICE: So, what does that prove?

DEEP VOICE: Tomorrow morning, the one that needs a shave, he's a boy.

HIGH VOICE: I can't wait until tomorrow morning.

DEEP VOICE: See? That proves it. Girls are patient, boys are impatient.

HIGH VOICE: Yeh? What else?

DEEP VOICE: Can you keep a secret?

HIGH VOICE: Absolutely.

DEEP VOICE: There you go—boys keep secrets, girls don't.

HIGH VOICE: Go on.

DEEP VOICE: Are you afraid of mice?

HIGH VOICE: No.

DEEP VOICE: I am. I'm terrified of them. I hate them. Squeak. Squeak. Squeak. What do you want to be when you grow up?

HIGH VOICE: A fireman.

DEEP VOICE: What'd I tell you?

HIGH VOICE: How about you?

DEEP VOICE: A cocktail waitress. Does that prove anything to you?

HIGH VOICE: You must be right.

DEEP VOICE: I told you—I'm always right. You're a boy and I'm the girl.

HIGH VOICE: I guess so. Oh, wait—here comes the nurse to change our diapers.

DEEP VOICE: About time, too—I have never been so uncomfortable in my life.

HIGH VOICE: Hey—look at that!

DEEP VOICE: What?

HIGH VOICE: You see that? I AM a girl — and you're a boy!

DEEP VOICE: Hey—it sure looks like it.

HIGH VOICE: What do you think of that?

DEEP VOICE: I can't understand it.

HIGH VOICE: Well, it sure goes to show you.

DEEP VOICE: What?

HIGH VOICE: You can't judge a book by its cover.

DEEP VOICE: Ha. Ha. Ha. What does that mean?

HIGH VOICE: How should I know? I'm only a baby.

DEEP VOICE: So am I. Goo.

HIGH VOICE: Goo.

ACTIVITIES

FOR DISCUSSION

For decades we have been hearing about the women's liberation movement, but recently there has been talk about a men's liberation movement as well. In what ways are both sexes struggling to free themselves from restrictive stereotypes? Does television programming reflect changing attitudes toward what it means to be male or female? Which TV reruns give us a look at romance and marriage in past decades? Do they differ in any significant ways from today's productions? Also consider advertising. Do the men and women in today's television advertisements reflect new attitudes toward masculinity and feminity?

STUDENT POETRY

s a fourteen-year-old, Anne Frank talks to her diary about herself and also about her seventeen-year-old friend Peter, as she struggles to understand puberty and just what is happening to them. Anne agrees with a book she has read that says:

> "... *a girl in the years of puberty becomes quiet within and begins to think about the wonders that are happening to her body ... girls of this age don't feel quite certain of themselves, and discover that they themselves are individuals with ideas, thoughts, and habits.*"

Anne writes *"what is happening to me is so wonderful, and not only what can be seen on my body, but all that is taking place inside"* and senses that Peter is experiencing the same mixture of confusion, uncertainty, and excitement. Anne longs to share her own feelings with someone else, someone who would understand.

> *"It gave me a queer feeling each time I looked into his deep blue eyes, and he sat there with that mysterious laugh playing round his lips. I was able to read his inward thoughts. I could see on his face that look of helplessness and uncertainty as to how to behave, and, at the same time, a trace of his sense of manhood. I noticed his shy manner and it made me feel very gentle; I couldn't refrain from meeting those dark eyes again and again, and with my whole heart I almost beseeched*

*him: oh, tell me, what is going on inside you, oh, can't you look beyond
this ridiculous chatter."*
The Diary of Anne Frank, (Doubleday and Co., 1958, pp. 115–117)

The following poems are by young writers who are also struggling to define
what it means to be a boy or girl, man or woman, masculine or feminine.
These young poets are courageous enough to question "what people have
always been telling me" or what "they say." What new definitions or concepts
of identity and individuality do they suggest? Can you add any? What advertisements in magazines or on television reflect today's attitudes toward what
it means to be male or female?

BEING MALE

Someone might say being male,
a man
a rough-hearted
guy
is just like being
an animal
a boar
a vulture
that flies in the sky.
Up high he flies
then soars down low
to pick at the bones of all the animals he disposes of.
But guys, we're not like that
cruel,
mean,
harsh.
We're sensitive
caring,
and kind . . .
And if you look further,
just that little bit further,
You might even find
Someone that loves,
And someone that cares,
And maybe he's just a guy . . .

(from the Lawrence School, Brookline, MA)

DO YOU THINK

Do you think
that being a woman
is pretty, prim, and precise?
Showing off your body,
flirting with the guys
Putting on mascara
So it covers your beautiful eyes
Driving around with your rich boyfriend

That's all very well
Are you all trying to impress us?
Well you're not doing so well . . .

(from the Lawrence School, Brookline, MA)

UNCERTAINTY

My relatives tell me to act ladylike.
I can't
swear
punch people
wear jeans with rips or
get a crew cut (not like I wanted one).
I must
wear dresses
drink tea, with one lump of sugar
sew
cook
act dainty.
Some of my friends tell me to act like a girl.
I can't
beat up my enemies
sit with boys at lunch (without getting teased)
laugh at things boys think are funny.
I must
giggle when a guy talks to me
be boy-crazy
talk about boys, not horses
eat salad to maintain my slim figure (huh?).
Why can't I be
Me?

(Cathy Holland, Williamstown, MA, grade 8)

ACTIVITIES

CLASS ACTIVITY: Create!

Write your own poem about what it means to you to be male or female, a boy or girl, man or woman.

EARLY LOVES AND LOSSES: *FINALE*

A s our lives become richer, we become more vulnerable to loss. The more we have to lose, the greater the risk. In the story "A Distant Bell," we see no emotion in the farewell between Susie and Avalon at the end of the summer because *"We were nothing to each other but a means of killing time."* They promise to write each other, but both know they'll never bother. On the other hand, the loss of her father is devastating to Susie.

Life's greatest joys do make us vulnerable to life's greatest sorrows, yet one of the best known quotations about love is: *"Tis better to have loved and lost than never to have loved at all."* How is the image of the Catskill eagle related to this idea?

> *"And there is a Catskill eagle in some souls that can alike dive down into the blackest gorges, and soar out of them again and become invisible in the sunny spaces. And even if he for ever flies within the gorge, that gorge is in the mountains; so that even in his lowest swoop the mountain eagle is still higher than other birds upon the plain, even though they soar."*
>
> (from *Moby Dick* by Herman Melville)

Divide the class into groups of four or five and help each other understand Melville's quotation. Melville died in 1891, but if he were able to visit your classroom today, what advice would he be likely to give you about living and loving well. About loves and losses? Translate his ideas into two or three bits of practical advice. What kind of risks might he recommend taking? What risks would be considered foolish?

Section Two:

—

ROMANCE

PREFACE TO THE CINDERELLA STORIES

Nearly everyone knows some version of the Cinderella story. There are over 700 known versions, and some form of it seems to exist in every culture. How much of the Cinderella story can you recall? As a class reconstruct as many of the details as you can before beginning to read. Are your memories similar to Perrault's version?

CINDERELLA

by Charles Perrault

O nce there was a gentleman who married, for his second wife, the proudest and haughtiest woman ever seen. By her former husband she had two daughters who were exactly like her. Her new husband had a daughter, too, by an earlier marriage, but this child was the sweetest and best creature one could imagine.

As soon as the wedding ceremony was over, the wife began to show her true nature. She could not bear it that her husband's pretty daughter with all her goodness made her own daughters appear the more hateful. She began to use her for the meanest housework. She ordered her to scour the pots and scrub the tables and the floors. She gave her a wretched straw pallet for a bed in the garret while her own daughters lay below upon soft new beds and had full-length mirrors in which to admire themselves.

The poor girl bore all this with patience and dared not tell her father, for she saw that he was ruled completely by his new wife. When the child had done her tasks, she would go to the chimney corner, to sit amid the ashes. This caused her to be called Cinderella. In spite of her poor appearance, however, Cinderella appeared a hundred times handsomer than did her sisters in their rich gowns.

Now it happened that the King's son was giving a ball and invited to it all his fashionable friends. Thus the two sisters of Cinderella received invitations and were filled with delight. At once they set about choosing gowns, petticoats, and head-dresses which would best suit them for the occasion. Cinderella had still more work to do now, for she was the one to iron their linen and plait their ruffles; and all day long she had to listen to their chatter about how they should be dressed.

The eldest girl said, "I shall wear my red velvet with the French trimming."

"And I," said the younger of the two, "shall wear my gold-flowered mantle and my diamond stomacher—which is far from ordinary."

Next they sent for the very best hairdresser to do up their hair.

Cinderella also had to be consulted about the hairdressing, for the sisters knew she had excellent ideas. While she was helping them, they asked her, "Cinderella, would not you be glad also to go to the ball."

"Ah, but you only joke," said Cinderella. "It is not for one such as I am to go to a ball."

"You are right," they replied. "People would laugh to see a Cinderella at a ball."

Anyone but Cinderella would have dealt roughly with them now, but she was so patient that she went on dressing them with the greatest care.

For almost two days the sisters were so transported by their joy that they could not bother to eat. They worked so hard trying to make their waists appear slender that they broke more than a dozen laces. And they paraded continually before their long mirrors.

At last the happy day arrived and they rode off to court. Cinderella looked after them as long as she could, and when they had gone out of sight she fell to crying.

Luckily, Cinderella had a fairy godmother who came to her and was moved by her tears. "What is the matter?" she asked.

"I wish I could—I wish I could—" Cinderella was not able to go on, but her godmother understood and asked, "You wish you could go to the ball. Is that not so?"

"Y-yes," cried Cinderella, with a great sigh.

"Well now," said her godmother, "be but a good girl, and I shall see that you go."

She ordered Cinderella to run into the garden and get her a pumpkin.

Cinderella went at once to gather the finest pumpkin there was, though she could not imagine that this would enable her to go to the ball.

Her godmother took the pumpkin and scooped out the inside, leaving nothing but the shell. Then she struck it with her wand. Instantly it turned into an elegant coach, gilded all over with shining gold!

Now she went to a mouse-trap where she found six live mice. She ordered Cinderella to lift the door to the trap and as each mouse ran out she tapped it with her wand. Lo, each became a fine horse — all of them together a matched set in a beautiful, mouse-colour dapple-grey. They lacked only a coachman.

Cinderella had an idea. "I shall see if there is a rat in the rat-trap. We might make a coachman of him."

"You are right," replied her godmother. "Do go and look."

When Cinderella brought the rat-trap, there was indeed not one rat, but there were three huge ones! Her fairy godmother chose the one with the finest whiskers and touched him with her wand, whereupon there stood before them a fat, jolly coachman with the smartest beard ever beheld.

Now the fairy godmother ordered Cinderella to go into the garden once more, to find six lizards behind the watering-pot.

Cinderella had no sooner returned with the lizards than these were turned into six footmen. They skipped behind the coach, their liveries shining with gold and silver, and they stayed in one line as if they had always been footmen.

The fairy godmother now turned to Cinderella. "Well, you see here a carriage fit to take you to the ball. Are you not pleased?"

"Oh, yes, indeed," she cried. "But must I go in these horrid rags?"

Now it was Cinderella's turn to be tapped by the magic wand. At once her dingy rags became a gown of gold set with jewels, and her feet were shod with sparkling glass slippers.

Thus decked out, Cinderella climbed into her golden coach and was ready to set off. But before this was allowed, the godmother commanded her not to stay one moment after midnight. If she did, the coach would turn back into a pumpkin, her horses into mice, her coachman a rat, her footmen lizards, and her apparel again would be rags.

Cinderella promised her godmother that she would not fail to leave the ball before midnight. She drove off then, scarcely able to contain her joy.

At court, when the King's son was told that a great princess whom nobody recognized had come, he ran out to meet Cinderella. He gave her his hand as she alighted and with all ceremony led her into the hall among his guests. Everyone stopped dancing; the musicians ceased to play; each guest had to admire the extraordinary beauty of the unknown newcomer.

The King himself, old as he was, could not help watching her. He told his Queen that it had been a long time since he had beheld so lovely a creature.

All the ladies began to study her gown and head-dress, planning to have them copied the next day, if they could find such exquisite materials and so able a seamstress.

The Prince led Cinderella to a special seat and then took her to dance with him. So gracefully did she step and bow that they admired her all the more. When refreshments were served the Prince was so intent on gazing at her that he ate not a morsel himself.

Cinderella sat down by her sisters and even shared with them the special fruits and sweetmeats that the Prince had brought her. This surprised them indeed.

While Cinderella was thus amusing her sisters, suddenly she heard the clock strike eleven hours and three quarters. She got to her feet immediately, curtsied to the guests, and hastened away as fast as she could.

At home again, Cinderella sought out her godmother. After thanking her, she said she wished she might go next day to another ball, to which the Prince had invited her.

While she was telling her godmother all that had happened at the ball, Cinderella's two sisters knocked at the door.

"How long you have stayed," cried Cinderella as she opened the door, and she rubbed her eyes as if she had just awakened.

"Ah, but if you had been at the ball," said one of the sisters, "you would not have tired of it. There came to it the most beautiful princess ever seen. And she was kind to us, and generous, too. She shared her fruit and sweetmeats with us."

Cinderella asked them for the name of that princess. But she learned that they did not know and also that the King's son was anxious about the princess and would give everything to know her name.

At this, Cinderella smiled and replied, "She must be most beautiful, indeed. How happy you have been! Could I not see her, too? Ah, Charlotte, could not you lend me your yellow gown that you wear at home everyday?"

"What! Lend my clothes to such a dirty Cinderella! I should be a fool!"

Cinderella well enough expected such an answer, and she was glad for it.

Next day the two sisters again went off to the ball, and so did Cinderella — dressed even more magnificently than before.

The King's son stayed by her side, never ceasing to pay her compliments and kindness, to the point that she forgot to watch the clock. The hour of twelve was striking when she thought it still no more than eleven. At once she arose and fled, as nimble as a deer.

The Prince followed Cinderella, but could not overtake her. However, he was able to pick up one of her glass slippers which had fallen off and been left behind.

Cinderella reached home quite out of breath, wearing her shabby old clothes, and holding one of the little slippers she had dropped.

The guards at the palace gate, when asked, said that they had not seen a princess go out. They had, however, seen a poor country girl, in very ragged clothes.

When the two sisters returned from the ball Cinderella asked them if they had been well entertained, and if the beautiful princess had come again.

They answered that she had been there but that she had hurried away when the clock struck twelve, and with such haste that she dropped one of her little glass slippers, which the King's son had picked up. He had eyes for no one else at the ball and obviously was much in love with the princess who owned the glass slipper.

This was all true. A few days later, the King's son proclaimed by trumpet that he sought to marry the one whose foot the slipper would fit. He was employing a servant to try it upon the princesses, the duchesses, and the other court ladies — but in vain.

When the time came for each of her sisters to try the slipper, Cinderella stood by and watched. Knowing that it was her slipper, she finally said, "Let me see if it will fit me."

Her sisters burst out laughing. But the servant with the slipper looked at Cinderella and said that she should try. Furthermore, he had been ordered to let everybody put on the slipper.

He asked Cinderella to sit down and, sliding the slipper on to her foot, found it a perfect fit. The sisters were astonished, and even more so when Cinderella pulled out of her pocket the matching slipper and put it on her other foot.

Thereupon, in came the godmother who once more touched Cinderella's clothes with her wand and made them even richer than those she had worn before.

Now Cinderella's two sisters saw that she was the beautiful girl they had seen at the ball. They threw themselves at her feet to beg pardon for their ill treatment of her. As Cinderella embraced her sisters, she cried out that she forgave them entirely, and desired them always to love her. She herself was led to the young Prince who found her more charming than ever. And in a few days he married her.

Because Cinderella was no less good than she was beautiful, she gave her sisters rooms in the palace and even arranged marriages between them and two of the lords of the Court.

ACTIVITIES

VOCABULARY

haughty, adj.—overly proud
wretched, adj.—very poor in quality, miserable
pallet, n.—a straw filled mattress
garret, n.—a room just under the roof, an attic room
plait, v.—to pleat, fold
livery, n.—a uniform worn by servants of wealthy households
alight, v.—to get down, descend
nimble, adj.—quick and light in motion

CINDERELLA

by the Brothers Grimm from *The Complete Grimm's Fairy Tales*

T he wife of a rich man fell sick, and as she felt that her end was drawing near, she called her only daughter to her bedside and said: "Dear child, be good and pious, and then the good God will always protect you, and I will look down on you from heaven and be near you." Thereupon she closed her eyes and departed. Every day the maiden went out to her mother's grave and wept, and she remained pious and good. When winter came the snow spread a white sheet over the grave, and by the time the spring sun had drawn it off again, the man had taken another wife.

The woman had brought with her into the house two daughters who were beautiful and fair of face, but vile and black of heart. Now began a bad time for the poor step-child. "Is the stupid goose to sit in the parlor with us?" they said. "He who wants to eat bread must earn it; out with the kitchen-wench." They took her pretty clothes away from her, put an old grey bedgown on her, and gave her wooden shoes. "Just look at the proud princess, how decked out she is!" they cried, and laughed, and led her into the kitchen. There she had to do hard work from morning till night, get up before daybreak, carry water, light fires, cook and wash. Besides this, the sisters did her every imaginable injury — they mocked her and emptied her peas and lentils into the ashes, so that she was forced to sit and pick them out again. In the evening when she had worked till she was weary she had no bed to go to, but had to sleep by the hearth of cinders. And as on that account she always looked dusty and dirty, they called her Cinderella.

It happened that the father was once going to the fair, and he asked his two step-daughters what he should bring back for them. "Beautiful dresses," said one, "pearls and jewels," said the second. "And you, Cinderella," said he, "what will you have?" "Father, break off for me the first branch which knocks against your hat on your way home." So he bought beautiful dresses, pearls and jewels for his two step-daughters, and on his way home, as he was riding through a green thicket, a hazel twig brushed against him and knocked off his hat. Then he broke off the branch and took it with him. When he reached home he gave his stepdaughters the things which they had wished for, and to Cinderella he gave the branch from the hazel-bush. Cinderella thanked him, went to her mother's grave and planted the branch on it, and wept so much that the tears fell down on it and watered it. And it grew and became a handsome tree. Thrice a day Cinderella went and sat beneath it, and wept and prayed, and a little white bird always came on the tree, and if Cinderella expressed a wish, the bird threw down to her what she had wished for.

It happened, however, that the King gave orders for a festival which was to last three days, and to which all the beautiful young girls in the country were invited, in order that his son might choose himself a bride. When the two step-sisters heard that they too were to appear among the numbers, they were delighted, called Cinderella and said: "Comb our hair for us, brush our shoes and fasten our buckles, for we are going to the wedding at the King's palace." Cinderella obeyed, but wept, because she too would have liked to go with them to the dance, and begged her step-mother to allow her to do so. "You go, Cinderella!" said she; "Covered in dust and dirt as you are, and would go to the festival? You have no clothes and shoes, and yet would dance!" As, however, Cinderella went on asking, the step-mother said at last: "I have emptied a dish of lentils into the ashes for you, if you have picked them out again in two hours, you shall go with us." The maiden went through the back door into the garden, and called: "You tame pigeons, you turtledoves, and all you birds beneath the sky, come and help me to pick

> The good into the pot,
> the bad into the crop."

Then two white pigeons came in by the kitchen-window, and afterwards the turtle-doves, and at last all the birds beneath the sky, came whirring and crowding in, and alighted amongst the ashes. And the pigeons nodded with their heads and began pick, pick, pick, pick and the rest began also pick, pick, pick, pick and gathered all the good grains into the dish. Hardly had one hour passed before they had finished, and all flew out again. Then the girl took the dish to her step-mother, and was glad, and believed that now she would be allowed to go with them to the festival. But the step-mother said: "No, Cinderella, you have no clothes and you cannot dance; you would only be laughed at." And as Cinderella wept at this, the step-mother said: "If you can pick two dishes of lentils out of the ashes for me in one hour, you shall go with us." And she thought to herself: "That she most certainly cannot do again." When the step-mother had emptied the two dishes of lentils amongst the ashes, the maiden went through the back-door into the garden and cried: "You tame pigeons, you turtle-doves and all you birds beneath the sky, come and help me to pick

The good into the pot,
the bad into the crop."

Then two white pigeons came in by the kitchen-window, and afterwards the turtle-doves, and at length all the birds beneath the sky, came whirring and crowding in, and alighted amongst the ashes. And the doves nodded with their heads and began pick, pick, pick, pick and the others began also pick, pick, pick, pick, and gathered all the good seeds into the dishes, and before half an hour was over they had already finished, and all flew out again. Then the maiden carried the dishes to the step-mother and was delighted, and believed that she might now go with them to the wedding. But the step-mother said: "All this will not help; you cannot go with us, for you have no clothes and cannot dance; we should be ashamed of you!" On this she turned her back on Cinderella and hurried away with her two proud daughters.

As no one was now at home, Cinderella went to her mother's grave beneath the hazel-tree, and cried:

"Shiver and quiver, little tree,
Silver and gold throw down over me."

Then the bird threw a gold and silver dress down to her, and slippers embroidered with silk and silver. She put on the dress with all speed, and went to the wedding. Her step-sisters and the step-mother however did not know her, and thought she must be a foreign princess, for she looked so beautiful in the golden dress. They never once thought of Cinderella, and believed that she was sitting at home in the dirt, picking lentils out of the ashes. The prince approached her, took her by the hand and danced with her. He would dance with no other maiden, and never let loose of her hand, and if any one else came to invite her, he said: "This is my partner."

She danced till it was evening, and then she wanted to go home. But the King's son said: "I will go with you and bear you company," for he wished to see to whom the beautiful maiden belonged. She escaped from him, however, and sprang into the pigeon house. The King's son waited until her father came, and then he told him that the unknown maiden had leapt into the pigeon house. The old man thought: "Can it be Cinderella?" and they had to bring him an axe and a pickaxe that he might hew the pigeon-house to pieces, but no one was inside it. And when they got home Cinderella lay in her dirty clothes among the ashes, and a dim little oil-lamp was burning on the mantle-piece, for Cinderella had jumped quickly down from the back of the pigeon-house and had run to the little hazel-tree, and there she had taken off her beautiful clothes and laid them on the grave, and the bird had taken them away again, and then she had seated herself in the kitchen amongst the ashes in her grey gown.

Next day when the festival began afresh, and her parents and the step-sisters had gone once more, Cinderella went to the hazel-tree and said:

> *"Shiver and quiver, my little tree,*
> *Silver and gold throw down over me."*

Then the bird threw down a much more beautiful dress than on the preceding day. And when Cinderella appeared at the wedding in this dress, every one was astonished at her beauty. The King's son had waited until she came, and instantly took her by the hand and danced with no one but her. When others came and invited her, he said: "This is my partner." When evening came she wished to leave, and the King's son followed her and wanted to see into which house she went. But she sprang away from him, and into the garden behind the house. Therein stood a beautiful tall tree on which hung the most magnificent pears. She clambered so nimbly between the branches like a squirrel that the King's son did not know where she was gone. He waited until her father came, and said to him: "The unknown maiden has escaped from me, and I believe she has climbed the pear-tree." The father thought: "Can it be Cinderella?" and had an axe brought and cut the tree down but no one was in it. And when they got into the kitchen, Cinderella lay there among the ashes, as usual, for she had jumped down on the other side of the tree, had taken the beautiful dress to the bird on the little hazel-tree, and put on her grey gown.

On the third day, when the parents and sisters had gone away, Cinderella went once more to her mother's grave and said to the little tree:

> *"Shiver and quiver, my little tree,*
> *Silver and gold throw down over me."*

And now the bird threw down to her a dress which was more splendid and magnificent than any she had yet had, and the slippers were golden. And when she went to the festival in the dress, no one knew how to speak for astonishment. The King's son danced with her only, and if any one invited her to dance, he said: "This is my partner."

When evening came, Cinderella wished to leave, and the King's son was anxious to go with her, but she escaped from him so quickly that he could not follow her. The King's son, however, had employed a ruse, and had caused the whole staircase to be smeared with pitch, and there, when she ran down, the maiden's left slipper remained stuck. The King's son picked it up, and it was small and dainty, and all golden. Next morning, he went with it to the father, and said to him: "No one shall be my wife but she whose foot this golden slipper fits." Then were the two sisters glad, for they had pretty feet. The eldest went with the shoe into her room and wanted to try it on, and her mother stood by. But she could not get her big toe into it, and the shoe was too small for her. Then her mother gave her a knife and said: "Cut the toe off; when you are Queen you will have no more need to go on foot." The maiden cut the toe off, forced the foot into the shoe, swallowed the pain, and went out to the King's son. Then he took her on his horse as his bride and rode away with her. They were obliged, however, to pass the grave, and there, on the hazel-tree, sat the two pigeons and cried:

> *"Turn and peep, turn and peep,*
> *There's blood within the shoe,*
> *The shoe it is too small for her,*
> *The true bride waits for you."*

Then he looked at her foot and saw how the blood was trickling from it. He turned his horse round and took the false bride home again, and said she was not the true one, and that the other sister was to put the shoe on. Then this one went into her chamber and got her toes safely into the shoe, but her heel was too large. So her mother gave her a knife and said: "Cut a bit off your heel; when you are Queen you will have no more need to go on foot." The maiden cut a bit off her heel, forced her foot into the shoe, swallowed the pain, and went out to the King's son. He took her on his horse as his bride and rode away with her, but when they passed by the hazel-tree, the two little pigeons sat on it and cried:

> *"Turn and peep, turn and peep,*
> *There's blood within the shoe,*

The shoe it is too small for her,
The true bride waits for you."

He looked down at her foot and saw how the blood was running out of her shoe, and how it had stained her white stocking quite red. Then he turned on his horse and took the false bride home again. "This also is not the right one," said he, "have you no other daughter?" "No," said the man, "there is still a little stunted kitchen wench which my late wife left behind her, but she cannot possibly be the bride." The King's son said he was to send her up to him; but the mother answered: "Oh no, she is much too dirty, she cannot show herself!" But he absolutely insisted on it, and Cinderella had to be called. She first washed her hands and face clean, and then went and bowed down before the King's son, who gave her the golden shoe. Then she seated herself on a stool, drew her foot out of the heavy wooden shoe, and put it into the slipper, which fitted like a glove. And when she rose up and the King's son looked at her face he recognized the beautiful maiden who had danced with him and cried: "That is the true bride!" The stepmother and the two sisters were horrified and became pale with rage; he, however, took Cinderella on his horse and rode away with her. As they passed by the hazel-tree, the two white doves cried:

"Turn and peep, turn and peep,
No blood is in the shoe,
The shoe is not too small for her,
The true bride rides with you,"

and when they cried that, the two came flying down and placed themselves on Cinderella's shoulder, one on the right, the other on the left, and remained sitting there.

When the wedding with the King's son was to be celebrated, the two false sisters came and wanted to get into favor with Cinderella and share her good fortune. When the betrothed couple went to church, the elder was at the right side and the younger at the left, and the pigeons pecked out one eye from each of them. Afterwards as they came back, the elder was at the left, and the younger at the right, and then the pigeons pecked out the other eye from each. And thus, for their wickedness and falsehood, they were punished with blindness all their days.

ACTIVITIES

FOR DISCUSSION

A. Almost certainly, the most familiar version of the Cinderella story involves a fairy godmother who magically transforms a pumpkin into a beautiful coach. This version was made popular in the United States by Walt Disney, who adapted his Cinderella story from the version originally told by Charles Perrault. The Brothers Grimm, however, tell a significantly different tale. In as much detail as possible discuss the differences. As part of your discussion, think about the significance of the differences. Use the following list to begin:

- the importance of Cinderella's mother
- the role of Cinderella's father
- the description of the step-sisters
- Cinderella's chores
- the way Cinderella's wishes are fulfilled
- the reason behind Cinderella's departure from the ball
- the search for the real Cinderella
- the role of the prince
- the ending

Compare the character of Cinderella in the two versions. What kind of person was Cinderella in each story? In which story was she more her own person? Which Cinderella do you like better? Which ending do you prefer? Why?

B. Even children know that the story of Cinderella isn't "true." Yet it has been told for centuries. Stories last because they contain truths. Discuss the different meanings of the word "true." What ideas in the story have made it last? Explain which of the two versions is most "true."?

C. Remember that many stories contain symbols. These symbols can stand for inner states of the mind or the soul. Think of the image of the hazel-tree.

How does the tree and Cinderella's relationship with it change. How might changes in the tree reflect Cinderella's own development?

D. Most of us are startled by the scene where Cinderella's sisters cut off part of their feet in order to fit into the golden slipper. This mutilation is a symbol for the way people can sometimes act. What are some of the ways that people actually harm themselves in order to "fit" or to be accepted?

E. Some parts of the story, like the step-mother's treatment of Cinderella, express true feelings even though the actions seem exaggerated. Where else in the story do the feelings seem real to you even if the actions don't?

F. What kinds of love are found in "Cinderella?" What do you think about the prince's love for Cinderella? In what way does he get to know her better in the Grimms' version? Was it just her beautiful dress and face that attracted him? Do people really fall in love that fast? What about love at first sight? Can it last? Do you believe that somewhere a perfect "prince" or "princess" awaits you?

G. In "Cinderella" the true mother and the step-mother are two different people. People who study fairy tales suggest that the two are symbols for different parts of the same mother. Think of your own mother or father as two people. Which parts would you call the "real" parent and which parts would you call the "step-parent?" How might the "wicked stepmother" image be considered unfair?

THE CITY OF TREMBLING LEAVES

by Walter Van Tilburg Clark

fter supper, Billy led them all into the living room. "Let's play something," he said.

"What?"

"I know," one of the girls said. "Drop the handkerchief."

There was groaning. She was questioned about her age and mentality.

"Charades," another girl said, and there was more groaning.

There was some hope about musical chairs, but Billy said they couldn't play that because of the new floor, and anyway there was no piano and the new phonograph hadn't come yet.

There was more groaning about Teakettle.

"Oh, let's play something that's some fun," Billy said. "I'll tell you what. Let's play spin-the-bottle."

Tim didn't know what spin-the-bottle was, except that it was probably a boy-girl game and embarrassing, because several of the boys whooped and laughed, and the girl with the big mouth suddenly clutched him by the arm, as if to save herself from falling into a paroxysm of laughter, and when she got barely enough breath, squealed, "He would want to play that."

Tim saw that Rachel also either didn't know the game, or was afraid of it. She was standing like a soldier by herself at the other end of the couch, try-ing to smile and look as if she understood. There was a row of many, small, red-and-yellow plaid buttons down the front of her velvet jacket. They bound the jacket closely over her sharp, small breasts, and he could see how quickly she was breathing.

Some of the boys were pushing the couch out of the way against the

113

fireplace. Tim helped to roll the rug and put it against the wall. Billy stood out in the middle of the shining floor with an empty pop bottle in his hand.

"O.K., here we go," he yelled. "Everybody get in a big ring. First a boy, then a girl, all the way round like that."

He came over and dragged Rachel into the ring, and then went back out in the middle. "O.K.," he said again. "No moving. You gotta stay right where you are."

He laid the bottle down on its side, and spun it between his thumb and finger. The bottle twinkled rapidly, glittered as it slowed down, and finally lay still and gleaming, with its neck pointing at a boy. There was lamentation, as if this were a disappointment.

"Be a fish," Billy told him.

The boy lay down full length on the floor, and vaguely imitated some sort of a swimming creature. He was mildly applauded and heavily insulted.

"You spin now," Billy told him.

The game went on. The modest purpose of its first stage was to inflict upon the person chosen by the bottle a physical maneuver entailing some indignity. The transition period began when the dark boy called Sheik, who wore a college-cut suit and a red necktie, was told to go around the circle and bow to each girl and kiss her hand. There were fake protests from the girls and cheers from the boys. One boy yelled, "That ain't nothin' for you, is it, Sheik?" When Sheik went around the circle the girls giggled and posed haughtily, like movie countesses. Rachel became red and then white, and Sheik had to reach for her hand. When he kissed it, she had a spasm of laughter.

After that all the penalties were of the same sort, and everyone watched the spinning bottle intently, and sometimes a victim would try to change his place when he saw that the bottle might pick him. Timmy had to get down on his knees before each girl, and touch his forehead to her right hand, as in token fealty. When he finished this labor he was sweating, although it wasn't hot in the room, for the door and the windows were open, so that the night breathed in, and pale moths came and quivered upon the screens or drummed against them. He believed that the only hand he could still feel on his forehead was Rachel's, which was small and cold. He felt that probably there was a sacred mark left by her fingers, their imprint shining like a light.

It was Rachel who ended spin-the-bottle before its possibilities were fully explored. When the bottle picked her, the ringmaster ordered her to go around the circle and kiss each boy on both cheeks. Rachel stood like a soldier. The fields of her soul were given over to battle. Some of the boys offered loud advice. One of them cried that he would take two in the middle instead of one on each side, and everybody laughed explosively, and then stopped laughing suddenly, and only giggled. They all felt their personal futures involved in the battle Rachel was fighting.

Rachel was very red. She made quick little gasping laughs, and looked quickly at different girls, but when she wasn't laughing her lower lip trembled. Her hands were pulling at each other in front of her. She still didn't say anything. The circle broke up, and she was besieged. She began to shake her head. She was bombarded by arguments, ridicule and doubts of her innocence. She kept shaking her head and trying hard to laugh, but getting further and further from really laughing. Tim was a prisoner watching his own destroyed. Even Billy's powers were weakened by internal dissension. His desire to remain the champion of the liberals was checked by the threat to his personal privilege.

The siege was lifted by accident. One of the boys, intending only to add his bit to the popular pressure, yelled, "I know what's the trouble with her. She wants to play post-office, so we can't see her, don't you, Rachy?" But the suggestion turned a common desire, and at once pressure groups began to form to make it a real plan. A few extremists continued the personal fight though. They agreed to post-office, but worked up a chant, "Rachy has to go first, Rachy has to go first."

Rachel dumbly opposed this action also, and finally the chant died because she could hardly keep herself from crying. The debate shifted to method. One faction insisted that the choice should be personal, and the other that the names should be drawn. Feeling the swing of opinion, Billy voiced the majority preference.

"We'll draw," he yelled. "Then it won't be just one fellow getting all our mail or something." He was cheered, and also accused of fearing to risk himself in open contest. He began to give orders.

"Everybody write his name on a slip of paper," he yelled. He went into a side room and came back with several sheets of paper and a fistful of pencils. While he was folding the sheets together and tearing them into strips, he was assailed as having had the whole thing plotted out beforehand. Tim signed like an illiterate putting his name to a contract before a lawyer he mistrusted. He didn't know how post-office was played either, except that it must be an advance over spin-the-bottle because there was secrecy connected with it. Billy collected all the boys' names in one hat, and the girls' in another.

"First one I pick is post-master," he announced.

There was silence as he drew a slip from the girls' hat.

"Pauline Chester," he announced.

There was an uproar. The bosomy girl in whom Tim's elbow had been buried at supper stepped forth.

"Where do I go?" she asked, when it was quiet.

"The study is the post-office," Billy announced. "You go on in," he said to Pauline. "Then I'll hold the hat in for you."

"No lights," somebody cried.

"No lights," everybody shouted.

"No fakes, either," somebody else shouted. "You have to really kiss. Anybody that won't really kiss has to kiss everybody." This rule was adopted by acclaim, although there were a few skeptics who wanted to know how it was going to be enforced when they couldn't see what was going on. "If they're both a-scared, how do we know what they did?"

This simple game did not grow dull. There was an outburst as each name was read. There was an intense quiet during each interval in which Billy held the hat, and the hand from the dark room reached out and chose a name. There was a fleeting expression of dread or doubt, but also the room was electrical with particular hopes. On a few faces was the blanched agony of the card players in the Suicide Club. As each post-master emerged, he was hailed, belittled and cross-examined. The girls all attempted to appear unmoved by this public prominence. The boys, assuming the license of the double standard, came out in different ways. Some looked knowing and remained silent. Some expressed glee. One skinny youth, blond and freckled, whose pants were too short, came out with his hands clasped before him, his face raised in praise of the Lord who gave such bliss, and his knees sagging and wavering. This interpretation was popular, and was played frequently, with variations. The most successful imitator was particularly original. He came out on his hands and knees, rolled over, and expired in jerking agony.

Even though the game was turned over to Fortune, the spear of personal implication was felt often. There was loud booing when one girl chanced to pick the name of a boy who spent most of his time with her anyway. There was laughter and satire when a notoriously unilateral affair attained the secret climax. Loud suggestions for deliberate manipulation were made to Billy, and he pretended to act upon them. Billy himself was called, and somebody else took over the hat. If the door opened too soon, the deed was questioned. If it remained closed a long time, protest, scandalized accusation, and expressions of envy rose into a storm.

Tim kept looking back at Rachel. The davenport had been turned around, and she was sitting on one arm of it. She laughed every time everybody laughed, but never said anything. Tim understood that she was practicing the art of disappearing into the background. He was saying a good many things himself, but they all arose from that same desire to appear inconspicuous, and most of them were just poor imitations of previous successes. Each time it was a girl's hand working around the door, his breath and his pulse were suspended. He took as a sweet if brief reprieve each period during which a boy held office. It was in these moments that he made his few really witty comments which could be quoted. Only one hope, and that half dread, remained constant in him. The numerical chances of entering the study with Rachel were small. Still, he kept thinking how it would be, and each time the chance came up that it might be, suddenly the inside diplomatic preliminaries appeared insurmountable, and a desert without water would begin to expand between his chair and the door of the study.

There were several repeats, one boy being called so often that there were accusations of fixing, and still Rachel wasn't called, and neither was Tim. Tim allowed himself guardedly to begin to hope both ways. He began to look at Rachel even more often, hoping to establish a union by means of their isolation, but she would accept no ally.

The skinny boy who had first swooned was acting as panderer. The dark boy with the red necktie was in the study. The dark hand held up the slip, and the skinny boy took it. He read solemnly, "Rachel Wells."

When the skinny boy said "Rachel" Tim's breath stopped as if it had been his own name. He didn't even hear as far as Wells.

"About time," somebody shouted.

"Do a good job on her, Sheik."

"One ain't enough, Sheik. Take one for all of us."

"Two, you mean," somebody amended.

This became a chorus. "Two for each of us, Sheik."

Finally Rachel got up and walked across to the study door quickly, smiling hard and with her arms straight down. She was cheered and hooted. At the door she stood and waited. She was speaking. Everybody became quiet. She was making a last desperate appeal to Pander.

"I don't have to pick one too, do I?"

She received a great many replies, among which Pander's was lost. It required another moment to quell her own rebellion and then she entered. The skinny boy put his finger to his lip and his ear to the door. There was silence outside. There was also silence inside. The skinny boy straightened up, shrugging his shoulders and spreading his hands.

The boy called Sheik chose to be non-committal when he came out, and so far as the public was concerned Rachel remained a figure of mystery, as inviolate as upon her entrance. Her hand chose and the skinny boy intoned, "Tim Hazard."

This was also greeted as overdue, and Tim received a good many suggestions. The desert between his chair and the door swelled and sank under him. He entered the difficult portal, and it was closed behind him. He was standing in absolute darkness. He also felt that many-eared silence outside. He waited. Since she was already there, and had seen him come in, Rachel should make the overture. He didn't even know where she was in there. He couldn't even remember what shape the room was, or where the furniture was. He stood very still, except for the roaring in his brain, and listened. Rachel finally made the overture.

"Well," she whispered hard, "don't take all night. I don't want to be in here all night with any boy."

It was impossible to tell from the whisper how angry or tearful or merely matter-of-fact and in a hurry she was.

"Where are you?" he whispered.

This became at once, to him, a question of great significance. The dark study took on the dimensions of a dead planet in eternal night, and across its vast wastes, its tundras and glaciers and cold and whispering seas, he ran and swam and climbed frantically, in quest of a tiny, solitary, lost, perhaps dying, Rachel.

"Here," Rachel whispered.

"Right here," she whispered angrily, "behind the door."

It was shocking that she was so close. Even their whispering had not told him she was so close. He moved only one step, with his hand out, and touched her. He was shivering with expectation, dread and ignorance. It was the velvet jacket he had touched. He was terribly ashamed and bewildered. He didn't know what part of the velvet jacket he had touched. She didn't say anything, or move to help him.

"Is that you?" he asked. The word "you" in his mind began with a capital and from its letters arose tongues of oriflamme.

"It's my sleeve," she whispered.

He ventured to close her hand.

"Hurry up, will you?" she whispered sharply.

He felt that this was an accusation of timidity. He put his other arm around her waist. She was rigid and trembling. It was impossible to pass this barrier of fear. He was the hunter paralyzed by the eyes of the deer that has turned.

The tittering began outside. It had seemed to Tim that the laws of time were revoked. Now they returned in force, at once, and even retroactively. Probably he had been in this darkness with Rachel for a hundred years, and they would never dare to come out. The comments began in the living room.

"Hurry up, will you?" Rachel said again, almost out loud this time. He felt a paroxysm, as of a breath of wind through the aspen, pass down the little body in his arm.

He stammered when he whispered, "You don't really want me to kiss you really, do you?"

"I don't care what you do," she whispered, "only for goodness' sakes do something, will you?"

Tim was bewildered by a great tenderness. He was trembling more than she was. He had no pride and wanted only to do what she wished.

The comments outside had become a clamor.

Suddenly she was pushing him off and whispering, "Let go of me, will you? Let go of me."

She got him loose from her, and scurried past him, and he heard the door knob rattle as she found it, and then saw her in the beam of light as she opened the door quickly. She controlled herself enough to go out slowly, but her face must have given something away about which he wasn't sure himself, because she was met by a sudden outburst of laughter and cries.

Tim started to follow her out, and this brought on another burst of laughter.

"Oh, no you don't," the skinny boy said, and pushed him back in. Tim remembered that he was supposed to pick a name also.

"What's the matter, Tim? Want more?" somebody called.

Another answered him. "Go on. I bet they didn't even kiss. I bet it was a fake. They just stayed in there to make us think it was something."

Everybody began to ask Rachel if it had been just a fake.

Tim reached into the hat in the opening of the doorway, and then the slip was taken from him.

After a moment the skinny boy announced, "Pauline Chester."

The bosomy girl, the girl like cushions or a woman, came in. The door closed. There was nothing religious about this encounter, but there was no delay either. There was nothing said. Tim reached out to let her know where he was. She took his hand and worked up along his arm and closed on him. He tried to simulate cooperation, but that probably wouldn't have mattered anyway. It was a long and suffocating kiss. For one minute he forgot Rachel, but not because of any change of heart.

ACTIVITIES

VOCABULARY

paroxysm, n. — a sudden violent emotion or action

lamentation, n. — a wailing or other expression of sorrow

fealty, n. — loyalty

dissension, n. — disagreement, quarrelling

liberal, n. — one who is not bound by traditional beliefs

illiterate, adj. — having little or no education; unable to read or write

skeptic, n. — a person slow to believe; a doubter

blanch, v. — to become white or pale

unilateral, adj — affecting one side only

reprieve, n. — a temporary escape

diplomatic, adj. — tactful, skillful in handling negotiations

ally, n. — one united with another for a specific purpose

swoon, v. — to faint

panderer, n. — a go-between in schemes of love

quell, v. — to quiet or calm down

inviolate, adj. — pure

intone, v. — to chant, to speak in prolonged tones

oriflamme, n.—a red banner carried into battle by kings

retroactive, adj.—extending backward

FOR DISCUSSION

A. To cover their embarrassment the boys at the party exchange wisecracks and the girls sit and giggle self-consciously. Everyone goes along with the crowd. Tim's thoughts are the only ones shared with the reader. How typical do you think he is? Do the other kids at the party share his feelings?

B. Tim is constantly described as being in battle. What are the two warring sides? What is the conflict? How is his self-image at risk?

C. Tim is very much aware of his sexuality and his attraction to Rachel, but he doesn't know what to do about it. It is as if he is visiting a foreign country and doesn't speak the language. Anytime we learn something new whether it is how to read, how to swim, or how to express love, there is a period of fumbling and awkwardness. It takes practice and considerable effort to develop any skill. In what way do party games like "spin-the-bottle" and "post-office" relieve some of the pressure of experimentation? On the other hand, in what way is the situation made more difficult than if Tim were alone with Rachel?

HOMEWORK ACTIVITY: Moments to Remember . . . or Forget

There was a time in our country when young, unmarried men and women were not allowed to be alone, and a proper young lady was always accompanied by a chaperone. Her suitor might formally kiss her hand upon their engagement, but any greater physical passion was supposedly reserved for after the wedding.

Today expectations are not so clearly defined. Neither boys nor girls are given clear guidelines, and everybody is afraid of looking foolish. Experimentation makes us vulnerable. Do we dare express our true feelings? Can we trust anyone not to laugh at us? What are the best circumstances for learning about love and sexuality?

Most people remember their first kiss. Ask parents or other adults who are eager to share their memories about their experiences. How did their first kiss happen? When, where, with whom? Were the circumstances comfortable? What would they change if they could do it all over again? Was it embarrassing? Tender? Was the other person caring and sincere? Were there any regrets? If you have time and your teacher is willing, interview him or her for practice.

After everybody in the class finishes the assignment, see what lessons can be learned from other people's experiences. Are there other ways of learning without painful first hand experiences? Can we expand our experiences through literature? Given all the information collected, what would be the ideal circumstances for learning about the physical expression of love? Write a paragraph or two in which you describe the setting and characters involved in this ideal situation.

SIXTEEN

by Maureen Daly

ow don't get me wrong. I mean, I want you to understand from the beginning that I'm not really so dumb. I know what a girl should do and what she shouldn't. I get around. I read. I listen to the radio. And I have two older sisters. So you see, I know what the score is. I know it's smart to wear tweedish skirts and shaggy sweaters with the sleeves pushed up and pearls and ankle-socks and saddle shoes that look as if they've seen the world. And I know that your hair should be long, almost to your shoulders, and sleek as a wet seal, just a little fluffed on the ends, and you should wear a campus hat or a dink or else a peasant hankie if you've that sort of face. Properly, a peasant hankie should make you think of edelweiss, mist and sunny mountains, yodeling and Swiss cheese. You know, that kind of peasant. Now, me, I never wear a hankie. It makes my face seem wide and Slavic and I look like a picture always in one of those magazine articles that run "And Stalin says the future of Russia lies in its women. In its women who have tilled its soil, raised its children." Well, anyway. I'm not exactly too small-town either. I read Winchell's column. You get to know what New York boy is that way about some pineapple princess on the West Coast and what Paradise pretty is currently the prettiest, and why someone, eventually, will play Scarlett O'Hara. It gives you that cosmopolitan feeling. And I know that anyone who orders a strawberry sundae in a drugstore instead of a lemon coke would probably be dumb enough to wear colored anklesocks with high-heeled pumps or use Evening in Paris with a tweed suit. But I'm sort of drifting. This isn't what I wanted to tell you. I just wanted to give you the general idea of how I'm not so dumb. It's important that you understand that.

You see, it was funny how I met him. It was a winter night like any other winter night. And I didn't have my Latin done either. But the way the moon tinseled the twigs and silverplated the snow drifts, I just couldn't stay inside. The skating rink isn't far from our house — you can make it in five minutes if the sidewalks aren't so slippery, so I went skating. I remember it took me a long time to get ready that night because I had to darn my skating socks first. I don't know why they always wear out so fast — just in the toes, too. Maybe it's because I have metal protectors on the toes of my skates. That probably is why. And then I brushed my hair — hard, so it clung to my hand and stood up around my head in a hazy halo.

My skates were hanging by the back door all nice and shiny, for I'd just gotten them for Christmas and they smelled so queer — just like a fresh-smoked ham. My dog walked with me as far as the corner. She's a red chow, very polite and well mannered, and she kept pretending it was me she liked when all the time I knew it was the ham smell. She panted along beside me and her hot breath made a frosty little balloon balancing on the end of her nose. My skates thumped me good naturedly on the back as I walked and the night was breathlessly quiet and the stars winked down like a million flirting eyes. It was all so lovely.

It was all so lovely I ran most of the way and it was lucky the sidewalks had ashes on them or I'd have slipped surely. The ashes crunched like crackerjack and I could feel their cindery shape through the thinness of my shoes. I always wear old shoes when I go skating.

I had to cut across someone's back garden to get to the rink and last summer's grass stuck through the thin ice, brown and discouraged. Not many people came through this way and the crusted snow broke through the little hollows between corn stubbles frozen hard in the ground. I was out of breath when I got to the shanty — out of breath with running and with the loveliness of the night. Shanties are always such friendly places. The floor all hacked to wet splinters from skate runners and the wooden wall frescoed with symbols of dead romance. There was a smell of singed wool as someone got too near the glowing isinglass grid of the iron stove. Girls burst through the door laughing with snow on their hair and tripped over shoes scattered on the floor. A pimply-faced boy grabbed the hat from the frizzled head of an eighth grade blonde and stuffed it into an empty galosh to prove his love and then hastily bent to examine his skate strap with innocent unconcern.

It didn't take me long to get my own skates on and I stuck my shoes under the bench—far back where they wouldn't get knocked around and would be easy to find when I wanted to go home. I walked out on my toes and the shiny runners of my new skates dug deep into the sodden floor.

It was snowing a little outside—quick, eager little Lux-like flakes that melted as soon as they touched your hand. I don't know where the snow came from for there were stars out. Or maybe the stars were in my eyes and I just kept seeing them every time I looked up into the darkness. I waited a moment. You know, to start to skate at a crowded rink is like jumping on a moving merry-go-round. The skaters go skimming round in a colored blur like gaudy painted horses and the shrill musical jabber re-echoes in the night from a hundred human calliopes. Once in, I went all right. At least, after I found out exactly where that rough ice was. It was "round, round, jump the rut, round, round, jump the rut, round, round—"

And then he came. All of a sudden his arm was around my waist so warm and tight and he said very casually, "Mind if I skate with you?" and then he took my other hand. That's all there was to it. Just that and then we were skating. It wasn't that I'd never skated with a boy before. Don't be silly. I told you before I get around. But this was different. He was a smoothie! He was a big shot up at school and he went to all the big dances and he was the best dancer in town except Harold Wright who didn't count because he'd been to college in New York for two years! Don't you see? This was different.

At first I can't remember what we talked about, I can't even remember if we talked at all. We just skated and skated and laughed every time we came to that rough spot and pretty soon we were laughing all the time at nothing at all. It was all so lovely.

Then we sat on the big snow bank at the edge of the rink and just watched. It was cold at first even with my skating pants on, sitting on that hard heap of snow, but pretty soon I got warm all over. He threw a handful of snow at me and it fell in a little white shower on my hair and he leaned over to brush it off. I held my breath. The night stood still.

The moon hung just over the warming shanty like a big quarterslice of muskmelon and the smoke from the pipe chimney floated up in a sooty fog. One by one the houses around the rink twinkled out their lights and somebody's hound wailed a mournful apology to a star as he curled up for the night. It was all so lovely.

Then he sat up straight and said, "We'd better start home." Not "Shall I take you home?" or "Do you live far?" but "We'd better start home." See, that's how I know he wanted to take me home. Not because he had to but because he wanted to. He went to the shanty to get my shoes. "Black ones," I told him. "Same size as Garbo's." And laughed again. He was still smiling when he came back and took off my skates and tied the wet skate strings in a soggy knot and put them over his shoulder. Then he held out his hand and I slid off the snow bank and brushed off the seat of my pants and we were ready.

It was snowing harder now. Big, quiet flakes that clung to twiggy bushes and snuggled in little drifts against the tree trunks. The night was an etching in black and white. It was all so lovely I was sorry I lived only a few blocks away. He talked softly as we walked as if every little word were a secret. "Did I like Wayne King, and did I plan to go to college next year and did I have a cousin who lived in Appleton and knew his brother?" A very respectable Emily Post sort of conversation, and then finally—"how nice I looked with snow in my hair and had I ever seen the moon so—close?" For the moon was following us as we walked and ducking playfully behind a chimney every time I turned to look at it. And then we were home.

The porch light was on. My mother always puts the porch light on when I go away at night. And we stood there a moment by the front steps and the snow turned pinkish in the glow of the colored light and a few feathery flakes settled on his hair. Then he took my skates and put them over my shoulder and said, "Good night now. I'll call you," he said.

I went inside then and in a moment he was gone. I watched him from my window as he went down the street. He was whistling softly and I waited until the sound faded away so I couldn't tell if it was he or my heart whistling out there in the night. And then he was gone, completely gone.

I shivered. Somehow the darkness seemed changed. The stars were little hard chips of light far up in the sky and the moon stared down with a sullen yellow glare. The air was tense with sudden cold and a gust of wind swirled his footprints into white oblivion. Everything was quiet.

But he'd said, "I'll call you." That's what he said, "I'll call you." I couldn't sleep all night.

And that was last Thursday. Tonight is Tuesday. Tonight is Tuesday and my homework's done, and I darned some stockings that didn't really need it, and I worked a cross-word puzzle, and I listened to the radio and now I'm just sitting. I'm just sitting because I can't think of anything else to do. I can't think of anything, anything but snowflakes and ice skates and yellow moons and Thursday night. The telephone is sitting on the corner table with its old black face turned to the wall so I can't see its leer. I don't even jump when it rings any more. My heart still prays but my mind just laughs. Outside the night is still, so I think I'll go crazy and the white snow's all dirtied and smoked into grayness and the wind is blowing the arc light so it throws weird, waving shadows from the trees onto the lawn — like thin, starved arms begging for I don't know what. And so I'm just sitting here and I'm not feeling anything. . . . I'm not even sad because all of a sudden I know. I can't sit here now forever and laugh and laugh while the tears run salty in the corners of my mouth. For all of a sudden I know, I know what the stars knew all the time — he'll never, never call — never.

ACTIVITIES

VOCABULARY

edelweiss, n. — a flowering plant common to the Alps
cosmopolitan, adj. — at home anywhere in the world or in many areas of interest
shanty, n. — a roughly built cabin or shack
fresco, v. — to paint on fresh plaster
singe, v. — to burn lightly
sodden, adj. — thoroughly soaked
gaudy, adj. — excessively bright, tastelessly showy
sullen, adj. — gloomy, dismal; dull or heavy in color
oblivion, n. — the state of being completely forgotten
leer, n. — an evil or sly glance

FOR DISCUSSION

A. The narrator, the "I" of the story, takes a long time to introduce herself before she begins to tell what happened. Why is it so important to her to prove that she is *"not really so dumb?"* What kind of details does she list as proof? By the end of the story, however, it becomes clear that she does, in fact, think she has been dumb. In what way?

B. The word "romantic" has several shades of meaning. One definition is *"given to thoughts or feelings of idealized love."* Others include *"imaginative but impractical"* and *"not based on fact; imaginary."* More poetically stated, it is *"the triumph of hope over reality."* We do learn about the narrator from what she tells us about herself, but we also learn about her more indirectly. The way she describes events and the world around her reveal character traits she may not even recognize in herself. How might she be considered romantic? Find evidence to support your answer.

C. When she describes her skating partner, the narrator insists repeatedly that this time was special, unlike the other times she had skated with boys: *"Don't you see? This was different."* We can't know what "he" was thinking on Thursday night or whether he felt the same way. We can only guess. Based on the few details we do learn about him, what do you feel is the most likely explanation for his not calling? If he never actually intended to call, is he being unfair or unkind by building up her hopes? How else might he have handled the situation more kindly?

D. This story was written about fifty years ago; find five details that help date it. Although setting and characters may seem far away or long ago, there is a timelessness or universality to good literature. That is, ideas, conflicts, and insights into human nature often remain similar across many generations or even centuries. What similarities and what differences do you see between you and your classmates, on the one hand, and the teenagers of the story, on the other?

E. The title of a story often highlights its central theme or main idea. Why do you think Maureen Daly chose "Sixteen?"

WRITING ASSIGNMENT: In the Mood

Choose either 1 or 2:

1. Describe the same night and the same events of the story from the point of view of the boy. Let him become the "I" and use your imagination to fill in enough details to reveal his character more fully.

2. No two people experience the same event or see the same scene in exactly the same way. We all bring our own experiences and attitudes into play when we interpret happenings. In fact, we may react differently on different days depending on what else is going on in our lives at the time. Early Thursday evening, in the story, *"the moon tinseled the twigs and silverplated the snow drifts" and "the stars winked down like a million flirting eyes."* The mood changes dramatically, however, and later on *"the stars were little hard chips of light far up in the sky and the moon stared down with a sullen yellow glare."*

Pick one of your favorite spots, either indoors or out, and describe it under two different circumstances. Rather than stating it directly, let your choice of words indicate your mood.

CLASS ACTIVITY: Young Love

Whether the final outcome is one of joy or pain, falling in love is always an intensely emotional experience. At the time, our passions may interfere with reason. It is sometimes not until we look back upon a romantic experience that we get a clear picture of it.

Interview at least one parent or other adult who is willing to talk about an early romance, preferably one from his or her teenage years. When was it? Where? Who was involved? What happened? Was it overall a happy experience? What changes would you make? Your class may decide to include more questions, but start with these.

After the interviews have been completed, see if any patterns emerge. Do most of these first romances occur during the summer? Do they have happy endings? Do both sexes have similar memories? Are similar lessons learned? (You will probably find it easier to make comparisons if everybody interviews two adults, one man and one woman).

PREFACE TO WHAT MEANS SWITCH

The Latin phrase "E Pluribus Unum" is engraved on the back of every U.S. penny. It means "from many - one" and is a tribute to the many different native and immigrant groups that have joined forces in this land of opportunity. Few other countries can boast of having such diversity in the racial, national, and religious heritage of its citizens.

At times, however, this mixture of cultures can lead to conflict and confusion. Immigrant parents may struggle to preserve the traditions and values of their heritage while their children head straight for the torn jeans, junk food, and hard rock. Cultures of class, age, education, geography, or special interest may further complicate communication among groups in America. What's "in" in one school may be "out" in a neighboring town.

Mona Chang tells us her story in "What Means Switch." She has learned in social studies that *"All over the world people have their own cultures,"* and she has been around enough to know the difference between living in Yonkers and living in Scarsdale. She also knows the difference between a "cool" psychedelic notebook and an embarrassing one with white kitty cats and blue bows. Mona rarely hesitates to show off when she gets a chance, and she fills her tale with the language of many cultures. The more familiar you are with these words and events, the more you can appreciate the humor of her story.

Before you read the story, take the following culture quiz. Identify as many of the following words or terms as you can. Are they of a particular ethnic origin? What do they mean? The words are important not only for their literal meaning but for their cultural associations. Share your responses as a class. If there are some terms that not even your teacher knows, where can you go for more information?

CULTURE QUIZ

Scarsdale	deli	Dutch colonial
Bronx River Parkway	Killington	Sugarbush
Virgin Islands	Yonkers	ginseng
karate	tea ceremony	Crayola
bar mitzvah	seder	mortar
schmaltz	goy	tofu
stir-fry	Cool Hand Luke	delivered out of Egypt
Ji nu shee veh	kamikaze	judo
Alexander's	Sak's Fifth Avenue	Lender's bagels
UNICEF	Japanese bowing	John Wayne
World War II	Hitler	Nazi
Pearl Harbor	Nanking Massacre	ovens
Lord and Taylor	broker	reparation

WHAT MEANS SWITCH

by Gish Jen

H ere we are, nice Chinese family—father, mother, two born-here girls. Where should we live next? My parents slide the question back and forth like a cup of ginseng neither one wants to drink. Until finally it comes to them, what they really want is a milkshake (chocolate) and to go with it a house in Scarsdale. What else? The broker tries to hint: the neighborhood, she says. Moneyed. Many delis. Meaning rich and Jewish. But someone has sent my parents a list of the top ten schools nationwide (based on the opinion of selected educators "and others"), and so, *many-deli* or not, we nestle into a Dutch colonial on the Bronx River Parkway. The road is winding where we are, very charming; drivers miss their turns, plow up our flower beds, then want to use our telephone. "Of course," my mom tells them, like it's no big deal, we can replant. We're the type to adjust. You know—the lady drivers weep, my mom gets out the Kleenex for them. We're a bit down the hill from the private-plane set, in other words. Only in our dreams do our parka zippers jam, what with all the lift tickets we have stapled to them. Killington on top of Sugarbush on top of Stowe, and we don't even know where the Virgin Islands are—although certain of us do know that virgins are like priests and nuns, which there were a lot more of in Yonkers, where we just moved from, than there are here.

This is my first understanding of class. In our old neighborhood everybody knew everything about virgins and nonvirgins, not to say the technicalities of staying in between. Or almost everybody, I should say; in Yonkers I was the laugh-along type. Here I'm an expert.

"You mean the man . . . ?" Pigtailed Barbara Gugelstein spits a mouthful of Coke back into her can. "That is so gross!"

Pretty soon I'm getting popular for a new girl. The only problem is Danielle Meyers, who wears blue mascara and has gone steady with two boys. "How do *you* know," she starts to ask, and proceeds to edify us all with how she French-kissed one boyfriend and just regular-kissed another. ("Because, you know, he had braces.") We hear about his rubber bands, how once one popped right into her mouth. I realize I need to find somebody to kiss too. But how? I can't do mascara—my eyelashes stick together. Plus, as Danielle the Great Educator points out, I'm *Chinese.*

Luckily, I just about then happen to tell Barbara Gugelstein I know karate. I don't know why I tell her this. My sister, Callie, is the liar in the family; ask anybody. I'm the one who doesn't see why we should have to hold our heads up. But for some reason I tell Barbara Gugelstein I can make my hands like steel by thinking hard. "I'm not supposed to tell anyone," I say.

She backs away, blinking. I could be the burning bush.

"I can't do bricks," I say—a bit of expectation management. "But I can do your arm if you want." I set my hand in chop position. "Uhh, it's okay," she says. "I know you can. I saw it on TV last night." That's when I recall that I, too, saw it on TV last night—in fact, at her house. I rush on to tell her I know how to get pregnant with tea.

"With *tea?*"

"That's how they do it in China."

She agrees that China is an ancient and great civilization that ought to be known for more than spaghetti and gunpowder. I tell her I know Chinese. *"Be-yeh-fa-foon,"* I say. *"Shee-veh. Ji nu."* Meaning, "Stop acting crazy. Rice gruel. Soy sauce." She's impressed. At lunch the next day Danielle Meyers and Amy Weinstein and Barbara's crush, Andy Kaplan, are all impressed too. Scarsdale is a liberal town, not like Yonkers, where the Whitman Road gang used to throw crab-apple mash at Callie and me and tell us it would make our eyes stick shut. Here we're like permanent exchange students. In another ten years there'll be so many Orientals we'll turn into Asians; but for now, the mid-sixties, what with civil rights on TV, we're not so much accepted as embraced. Especially by the Jewish part of town—which, it turns out, is not all of town at all. That's just an idea people have, Callie says, and lots of them could take or leave us same as the Christians, who are nice too; I shouldn't generalize. So let me not generalize except to say that pretty soon I've been to so many bar and bas mitzvahs that I can almost say myself whether the kid chants like an angel or like a train conductor, maybe they could use him on the commuter line. At seder I know to get a good pile of that mortar. Also, I know what is schmaltz. I know that I am a goy. This is not why people like me, though. People like me because I do not need to use deodorant, as I demonstrate in the locker room before and after gym. Also, I can explain to them, for example, what is tofu (der-voo, we say at home). Their mothers invite me to taste-test their Chinese cooking.

"Very authentic." I try to be reassuring. After all, they're nice people. "De-lish." I have seconds. On the question of what we eat, though, I have to admit, "Well, no, it's different from that." I have thirds. "What my mom makes is home style, it's not in the cookbooks."

Not in the cookbooks! Everyone's jealous. Meanwhile, the big deal at home is when we have turkey pot pie. Callie's the one who introduced them — Mrs. Wilder's, they come in this green-and-brown box — and when we have them, we both suddenly get interested in helping out in the kitchen. You know, we stand in front of the oven and help them bake. Twenty-five minutes. She and I have a deal, though, to keep it secret from school, since everybody else thinks they're gross. We think they're a big improvement over authentic Chinese home cooking. Oxtail soup — now, that's gross. Stir-fried beef with tomatoes. One day I say, "You know, Ma, I have never seen a stir-fried tomato in any Chinese restaurant we have ever been in, ever."

"In China," she says, pontifical, "we consider tomatoes a delicacy."

"Ma," I say. "Tomatoes are *Italian.*"

"No respect for elders." She wags her finger at me, but I can tell it's just to try and shame me into believing her. "I'm tell you, tomatoes *invented* in China."

"Ma."

"Is true. Like noodles. Invented in China."

"That's not what they said in *school.*"

"In *China,*" my mother counters, "we also eat tomatoes uncooked, like apple. And in summertime we slice them, and put some sugar on top."

"Are you sure?"

My mom says of course she's sure, and in the end I give in, even though she once told me that China was such a long time ago, a lot of things she can hardly remember. She said sometimes she has trouble remembering her characters, that sometimes she'll be writing a letter, just writing along, and all of a sudden she won't be sure if she should put four dots or three.

"So what do you do then?"

"Oh, I just make a little sloppy."

"You mean you *fudge*?"

She laughed then, but another time, when she was showing me how to write my name, and I said, just kidding, "Are you sure that's the right number of dots, now?" She was hurt.

"I mean, of course you know," I said. "I mean, *oy.*"

Meanwhile, what I know is that in the eighth grade what people want to hear does not include the revelation that Chinese people eat sliced tomatoes with sugar on top. For a gross fact, it just isn't gross enough. On the other hand, the fact that somewhere in China somebody eats or has eaten or once ate living monkey brains — now that's conversation.

"They have these special tables," I say, "kind of like a giant collar. With a hole in the middle, for the monkey's neck. They put the monkey in the collar, and then they cut off the top of its head."

"Whadda they use for cutting?"

I think. "Scalpels."

"*Scalpels?*" Andy Kaplan says.

"Kaplan, don't be dense," Barbara Gugelstein says. "The Chinese *invented* scalpels."

Once a friend said to me, You know, everybody is valued for something. She explained how some people resented being valued for their looks; others resented being valued for their money. Wasn't it still better to be beautiful and rich than ugly and poor, though? You should just be glad, she said, that you have something people value. It's like having a special talent, like being good at ice-skating, or opera singing. She said. You could probably make a career out of it.

Here's the irony: I am.

Anyway, I am ad-libbing my way through eighth grade, as I've described. Until one bloomy spring day I come in late to homeroom, and to my chagrin discover there's a new kid in class.

Chinese.

So what should I do, pretend to have to go to the girls' room, like Barbara Gugelstein the day Andy Kaplan took his ID back? I sit down; I am so cool I remind myself of Paul Newman. First thing I realize, though, is that no one looking at me is thinking of Paul Newman. The notes fly:

"I think he's cute."

"Who?" I write back. (I am still at an age, understand, when I believe a person can be saved by aplomb.)

"I don't think he talks English too good. Writes it either."

"Who?"

"They might have to put him behind a grade, so don't worry."

"He has a crush on you already, you could tell as soon as you walked in, he turned kind of orangish."

I hope I'm not turning orangish as I deal with my mail. I could use a secretary. The second round starts:

"What do you mean who? Don't be weird. Didn't you *see* him??? Straight back over your right shoulder!!!!"

I have to look; what else can I do? I think of certain tips I learned in Girl Scouts about poise. I cross my ankles. I hold a pen in my hand. I sit up as though I have a crown on my head. I swivel my head slowly, repeating to myself. I could be Miss America.

"Miss Mona Chang."

Horror raises its hoary head.

"Notes, please."

Mrs. Mandeville's policy is to read all notes aloud.

I try to consider what Miss America would do and see myself: back straight, knees together, crying. Some inspiration. Cool Hand Luke, on the other hand, would, quick, eat the evidence. And why not? I should yawn as I stand up, and boom, the notes are gone. All that's left is to explain that it's an old Chinese reflex.

I shuffle up to the front of the room.

"One minute, please," Mrs. Mandeville says.

I wait, noticing how large and plastic her mouth is.

She unfolds a piece of paper.

And, I Miss Mona Chang, who got almost straight A's her whole life except in math and conduct, am about to start crying in front of everyone.

I am delivered out of hot Egypt by the bell. General pandemonium. Mrs. Mandeville still has her hand clamped on my shoulder, though; and the next thing I know, I'm holding the new boy's schedule. He's standing next to me like a big blank piece of paper. "This is Sherman," Mrs. Mandeville says.

"Hello," I say.

"*Non how a,*" I say.

I'm glad Barbara Gugelstein isn't there to see my Chinese in action.

"*Ji nu,*" I say. "*Shee-veh.*"

Later I find out that his mother asked if there were any other Orientals in our grade. She had him put in my class on purpose. For now, though, he looks at me as if I'm much stranger than anything else he's seen so far. Is this because he understands that I'm saying "soy sauce rice gruel" to him or because he doesn't?

"Sherman," he says finally.

I look at his schedule card. Sherman Matsumoto. What kind of name is that for a nice Chinese boy?

(Later on, people ask me how I can tell Chinese from Japanese. I shrug. It's the kind of thing you just kind of know, I say. *Oy!*)

Sherman's got the sort of looks I think of as pretty-boy. Monsignor-black hair (not monk-brown, like mine), kind of bouncy. Crayola eyebrows, one with a round bald spot in the middle of it, like a golf hole. I don't know how anybody can think of him as orangish; his skin looks white to me, with pink triangles hanging down the front of his cheeks like flags. Kind of delicate-looking, but the only truly uncool thing about him is that his spiral notebook has a picture of a kitty cat on it. A big white fluffy one, with a blue ribbon above each perky little ear. I get much opportunity to view this, because all the poor kid understands about life in junior high school is that he should follow me everywhere. It's embarrassing. But he's obviously even more miserable than I am, so I try not to say anything. I decide to give him a chance to adjust. We communicate by sign language, and by drawing pictures, which he's better at than I am; he puts in every last detail, even if it takes forever, I try to be patient.

A week of this. Finally I enlighten him. "You should get a new notebook."

His cheeks turn a shade of pink you see mostly only in hyacinths.

"Notebook." I point to his. I show him mine, which is psychedelic, with purple and yellow stick-on flowers. I try to explain that he should have one like this, only without the flowers. He nods enigmatically, and the next day brings me a notebook just like his, except that this cat sports pink bows instead of blue.

"Pret-ty," he says. "You."

He speaks English! I'm dumbfounded. Has he spoken it all this time? I consider: Pretty. You. What does that mean? Plus actually he's said "*plit-ty*," much as my parents would; I'm assuming he means pretty, but maybe he means pity. Pity. You.

"Jeez," I say finally.

"You are wel-come," he says.

I decorate the back of the notebook with stick-on flowers, and hold it so that they show when I walk through the halls. In class I keep my book open. After all, the kid's so new; I think I ought to have a heart. And for a livelong day nobody notices.

Then Barbara Gugelstein sidles up. "Matching notebooks, huh?"

I'm speechless.

"First comes love, then comes marriage, and then come chappies in a baby carriage."

"Barbara!"

"Get it?" she says. "Chinese Japs."

"Bar-*bra*," I say to get even.

"Just make sure he doesn't give you any *tea*," she says.

Are Sherman and I in love? Three days later I hazard that we are. My thinking proceeds this way: I think he's cute, and I think he thinks I'm cute. On the other hand, we don't kiss and we don't exactly have fantastic conversations. Our talks *are* getting better, though. We started out, "This is a book."

"Book."

"This is a chair."

"Chair."

Advancing to, "What is this?"

"This is a book."

Now, for fun, he tests me. "What is this?" he says.

"This is a book," I say, as if I'm the one who has to learn how to talk. He claps. "Good!"

Meanwhile, people ask me all about him. I could be his press agent.

"No, he doesn't eat raw fish."

"No, his father wasn't a kamikaze pilot."

"No, he can't do karate."

"Are you sure?" somebody asks.

Indeed he doesn't know karate, but judo he does. I am hurt that I'm not the one to find this out; the guys know from gym class. They line up to be flipped, he flips them all onto the floor, and after that he doesn't eat lunch at the girls' table with me anymore. I'm more or less glad. Meaning, when he was there, I never knew what to say. Now that he's gone, though, I seem to be stuck at the "This is a chair" level of conversation. Ancient Chinese eating habits have lost their cachet; all I get are more and more inquiries about me and Sherman. "I dunno," I'm saying all the time. *Are* we going out? We do stuff, it's true. For example, I take him to the department stores, explain to him who shops in Alexander's, who shops in Saks. I tell him my family's the type that shops in Alexander's. He says he's sorry. In Saks he gets lost, though maybe I'm the lost one. (It's true I find him calmly waiting at the front door, hands behind his back, like a guard.) I take him to the candy store. I take him to the bagel store. Sherman is crazy about bagels. I explain to him that Lender's is gross, he should get his bagels from the bagel store. He says thank you.

"Are you going steady?" people want to know.

How can we go steady when he doesn't have an ID bracelet? On the other hand, he brings me more presents than I think any girl's ever gotten before. Oranges. Flowers. A little bag of bagels. But what do they mean? Do they mean thank you, I enjoyed our trip; do they mean I like you; do they mean I decided I liked the Lender's better even if they are gross, and you can have these? Sometimes I think he's acting on his mother's instructions. Also I know that at least a couple of items were supposed to go to our teachers. He told me that and turned red. I figured it still might mean something that he didn't throw them out.

More and more now, we joke. Like, instead of *I'm thinking*, he always says, "I'm sinking," which we both think is so funny that all either one of us has to do is pretend to be drowning and the other one cracks up. And he tells me things — for example, that electric lights are everywhere in Tokyo now.

"You mean you didn't have them before?"

"Everywhere now!" He's amazed too. "Since Olympics!"

"Olympics?"

He hums for me the Olympic theme song. "You know?"

"Sure," I say, and hum with him happily. We could be a picture on a UNICEF poster. The only problem is that I don't really understand what the Olympics have to do with the modernization of Japan, any more than I get this other story he tells me, about that hole in his left eyebrow, which is from some time his father accidentally hit him with a lit cigarette. When Sherman was a baby. His father was drunk, having been out carousing, his mother was very mad but didn't say anything, just cleaned the whole house. Then his father was so ashamed he bowed to ask her forgiveness.

"Your mother cleaned the house?"

Sherman nods solemnly.

"And your father *bowed*?" I find this more astounding than anything I ever thought to make up. "That is so weird," I tell him.

"Weird," he agrees. "This I no forget, forever. *Father* bow to *mother!*"

We shake our heads.

As for the things he asks me, they're not topics I ever discussed before. Do I like it here? Of course I like it here, I was born here, I say. Am I Jewish? Jewish! I laugh. *Oy!* Am I American? "Sure I'm American," I say. "Everybody who's born here is American, and also some people who convert from what they were before. You could become American." But he says no, he could never. "Sure you could," I say. "You only have to learn some rules and speeches."

"But I Japanese," he says.

"You could become American anyway," I say. "Like I *could* become Jewish, if I wanted to. I'd just have to switch, that's all."

"But you Catholic," he says.

I think maybe he doesn't get what means switch.

I introduce him to Mrs. Wilder's turkey pot pies. "Gross?" he asks. I say they are, but we like them anyway. "Don't tell anybody." He promises. We bake them, eat them. While we're eating, he's drawing me pictures.

"This American," he says, and he draws something that looks like John Wayne. "This Jewish," he says, and draws something that looks like the Wicked Witch of the West, only male.

"I don't think so," I say.

He's undeterred. "This Japanese," he says, and draws a fair rendition of himself. "This Chinese," he says, and draws what looks to be another fair rendition of himself.

"How can you tell them apart?"

"This way," he says, and he puts the picture of the Chinese so that it faces the pictures of the American and the Jew. The Japanese faces the wall. Then he draws another picture, of a Japanese flag, so that the Japanese is looking at his flag. "Chinese lost in department store," he says. "Japanese know how go." For fun he draws another Japanese flag, a bigger one, which he attaches to the refrigerator with magnets. "In school, in ceremony, we this way," he explains, and bows to the picture.

When my mother comes in, her face is so red that with the white wall behind her she looks a bit like the Japanese flag herself. Yet I get the feeling I better not say so. First she doesn't move. Then she snatches the flag off the refrigerator, so fast the magnets go flying. Two of them land on the stove. She crumples the paper. She hisses at Sherman, *"This is the U. S. of A., do you hear me!"*

Sherman hears her.

"You call your mother right now, tell her come pick you up."

He understands perfectly. I, on the other hand, am buffaloed. How can two people who don't really speak English understand each other better than I can understand them? "But, Ma," I say.

"Don't *Ma* me," she says.

Later on she explains that the Second World War was in China, too. "Hitler," I say. "Nazis. Volkswagens." I know the Japanese were on the wrong side, because they bombed Pearl Harbor. My mother explains about before that. The Napkin Massacre. *"Nan-king,"* she corrects me.

"Are you sure?" I say. In school they said the war was about putting the Jews in ovens.

"Also about ovens."

"About both?"

"Both."

"That's not what they said in school."

"Just forget about school."

Forget about school? "I thought we moved here for the schools."

"We moved here," she says, "for your education."

Sometimes I have no idea what she's talking about.

"I like Sherman," I say after a while.

"He's a nice boy," she agrees.

Meaning what? I would ask, except that my dad's just come home, which means it's time to start talking about whether they should build a brick wall across the front of the lawn. Recently a car made it almost into our living room, which was so scary that the driver fainted and an ambulance had to come. "We should have discussion," my dad said after that. It's what he says every time. And so for about a week, every night we *have* them.

"Are you just friends or more than just friends?" Barbara Gugelstein is giving me the cross-ex.

"Maybe," I say.

"Come on," she says. "I told you everything about me and Andy."

I actually *am* trying to tell Barbara *everything* about Sherman, but everything turns out to be nothing. Meaning I can't locate the conversation in what I have to say: Sherman and I go places, we talk, my mother once threw him out of the house because of the Second World War.

"I think we're just friends," I say.

"You think or you're sure?"

Now that I do less of the talking at lunch, I notice more what other people talk about — cheerleading, who likes who, this place in White Plains to get earrings. On none of these topics am I an expert. Of course, I'm still friends with Barbara Gugelstein, but I notice that Danielle Meyers has spun away to other groups.

Barbara's analysis goes this way: To be popular you have to have big boobs, a note from your mother that lets you use her Lord & Taylor credit card, and a boyfriend. On the other hand, what's so wrong with being unpopular? "We'll get them in the end," she says. It's what her dad tells her. "Like they'll turn out too dumb to do their own investing," she says, "and then they'll get killed in broker's fees and then they'll have to move to towns where the schools stink. And my dad should know," she winds up. "He's a broker."

"I guess," I say.

But the next thing I know, I have a true crush on Sherman Matsumoto. *Mis*ter Judo, the guys call him now, with real respect; and the more they call him that, the more I don't care that he carries a notebook with a cat on it.

I sigh, "Sherman."

"I thought you were just friends," Barbara Gugelstein says.

"We were," I say mysteriously. This, I've noticed, is how Danielle Meyers talks; everything's secret, she only lets out so much, it's apparent she didn't grow up with everybody telling her she had to share.

And here's the funny thing: The more I intimate that Sherman and I are hot and heavy, the more it seems we actually are. It's the old imagination giving reality a nudge. When I start to blush, he starts to blush; we reach a point where we can hardly talk at all.

"Well, there's first base with tongue and first base without," I tell Barbara Gugelstein.

In fact, Sherman and I have brushed shoulders and what actually happened was at least equivalent to first base, I was sure, maybe even second. I felt as though I'd turned into one huge shoulder; that's all I was, one huge shoulder. We not only didn't talk, we didn't breathe. But how can I tell Barbara Gugelstein that? So instead I say, "Well, there's second base and second base."

Danielle Meyers is my friend again. She says, "I know exactly what you mean," just to make Barbara Gugelstein feel bad.

"Like *what* do I mean?" I say.

Danielle Meyers can't answer.

"You know what I think?" I tell Barbara the next day. "I think Danielle's giving us a line."

Barbara pulls thoughtfully on one of her pigtails.

If Sherman Matsumoto is never going to give me an ID to wear, he should at least get up the nerve to hold my hand. I don't think he sees this. I think of the story he told me about his parents, and in a synaptic firestorm realize we don't see the same things at all.

So one day when we happen to brush shoulders again, I don't move away. He doesn't move away either. There we are. Like a pair of bleachers, pushed together but not quite matched up. After a while I have to breathe. I can't help it. I breathe in such a way that our elbows start to touch too. We are in a crowd, waiting for a bus. I crane my neck to look at the sign that says where the bus is going; now our wrists are touching. Then it happens: he links his pinky around mine.

Is that holding hands? Later, in bed, I wonder all night. One finger, and not even the biggest one.

Sherman is leaving in a month. Already! I think, well, I suppose he will leave and we'll never even kiss. I guess that's all right. Just when I've resigned myself to it though, we hold hands all five fingers. Once when we are at the bagel shop, then again in my parent's kitchen. Then, when we are on the playground, he kisses the back of my hand.

He does it again not too long after that, in White Plains.

I invest in a bottle of mouthwash.

Instead of moving on, though, he kisses the back of my hand again. And again. I try raising my hand, hoping he'll make the jump from my hand to my cheek. It's like trying to wheedle an inchworm out the window. You know, *This way, this way.*

All over the world people have their own cultures. That's what we learned in social studies.

If we never kiss, I'm not going to take it personally.

It is the end of the school year. We've had parties. We've turned in our textbooks. Hooray! Outside, the asphalt already steams if you spit on it. Sherman isn't leaving for another couple of days, though, and he comes to visit every morning, staying until the afternoon, when Callie comes home from her big-deal job as bank teller. We drink Kool-Aid in the back yard and hold hands until they are sweaty and make smacking noises coming apart. He tells me how busy his parents are, getting ready for the move. His mother, particularly, is very tired. Mostly we are mournful.

The very last day we hold hands and do not let go. Our palms fill up with water like a blister. We do not care. We talk more than usual. How much will it cost to send an airmail letter to Japan, that kind of thing. Then suddenly he asks, will I marry him?

I'm only thirteen.

But when old? Sixteen?

If you come back to get me, I come.

Or you can come to Japan, be Japanese.

How can I be Japanese?

Like you become American. Switch.

He kisses me on the cheek, again and again and again.

His mother calls to say that she's coming to get him. I cry. I tell him how I've saved every present he's ever given me—the ruler, the pencils, the bags from the bagels, all the flower petals. I even have the orange peels from the oranges.

All?

I put them in a jar.

I'd show him, except we're not allowed to go upstairs to my room.

Anyway, something about the orange peels seems to choke him up too. *Mis*ter Judo, but I've gotten him in a soft spot. We are going together to the bathroom to get some toilet paper to wipe our eyes when poor tired Mrs. Matsumoto, driving her family's car, skids up onto our lawn.

"Very sorry!"

We race outside.

"Very sorry!"

Mrs. Matsumoto is so short that all we can see of her is a green cotton sun hat, with a big brim. It's tied on. The brim is trembling.

I hope my mom's not going to start yelling about the Second World War.

"It's all right, no trouble," she says, materializing on the steps, behind me and Sherman. She's propped the screen door wide open; when I turn, I see she's waving. "No trouble, no trouble!"

"No trouble, no trouble!" I echo, twirling a few times with relief.

Mrs. Matsumoto keeps apologizing; my mom keeps insisting she shouldn't feel bad, it was only some grass and a small tree. Crossing the lawn, she insists that Mrs. Matsumoto get out of the car, even though it means trampling some lilies-of-the-valley. She insists that Mrs. Matsumoto come in for a cup of tea. Then she will not talk about anything unless Mrs. Matsumoto sits down, and unless she lets my mom prepare her a small snack. The coming in and the tea and the sitting down are settled pretty quickly, but they negotiate ferociously over the small snack, which Mrs. Matsumoto will not eat unless she can call Mr. Matsumoto. She makes the mistake of linking Mr. Matsumoto with a reparation of some sort, which my mom will not hear of.

"Please!"

"No no no no."

Back and forth it goes.

"No no no no." "No no no no." "No no no no."

What kind of conversation is that? I look at Sherman, who shrugs. Finally Mr. Matsumoto calls on his own, wondering where his wife is. He comes over in a taxi. He's a heavy-browed businessman, friendly but brisk—not at all a type you could imagine bowing to a lady with a taste for tie-on sun hats. My mom invites him in as if it's an idea she just had this moment thought of. And would he maybe have some tea and a small snack? Sherman and I sneak back outside for another farewell by the side of the house, behind the forsythia bushes. We hold hands. He kisses me on the cheek again, and then — just when I think he's finally going to kiss me on the lips — he kisses me on the neck.

Is this first base?

He does it more. Up and down, up and down. First it tickles, and then it doesn't. He has his eyes closed. I close my eyes too. He's hugging me. Up and down. Then down.

He's at my collarbone.

Still at my collarbone. Now his hand's on my ribs. So much for first base. More ribs. The idea of second base would probably make me nervous if he weren't on his way back to Japan and if I really thought we were going to get there. As it is, though, I'm not in much danger of wrecking my life on the shoals of passion; his unmoving hand feels more like a growth than a boyfriend. He has his whole face pressed to my neck skin so I can't tell his mouth from his nose. I think he may be licking me.

From indoors, a burst of adult laughter. My eyelids flutter. I start to try and wiggle such that his hand will maybe budge upward.

Do I mean for my top blouse button to come accidentally undone?

He clenches his jaw, and when he opens his eyes, they're fixed on that button like it's a gnat that's been bothering him for far too long. He mutters in Japanese. If later in life he were to describe this as a pivotal moment in his youth, I would not be surprised. Holding the material as far from my body as possible, he buttons the button. Somehow we've landed up too close to the bushes.

What to tell Barbara Gugelstein? She says, "Tell me what were his last words. He must have said something last."

"I don't want to talk about it."

"Maybe he said, 'Good-bye?'" she suggests. "'*Sayonara?*'" She means well.

"I don't want to talk about it."

"Aw, come on, I told you everything about . . ."

I say, "Because it's private, excuse me."

She stops, squints at me as though I were a far-off face she's trying to make out. Then she nods and very lightly places her hand on my forearm.

The forsythia seemed to be stabbing us in the eyes. Sherman said, more or less, *You will need to study how to switch.*

And I said, *I think you should switch. The way you do everything is weird.*

And he said, *You just want to tell everything to your friends. You just want to have a boyfriend to become popular.*

Then he flipped me. Two swift moves, and I went sprawling through the air, a flailing confusion of soft human parts such as had no idea where the ground was, much less how hard it could be.

It is the fall and I am in high school, and still he hasn't written, so finally I write him.

I still have all your gifts, I write. *I don't talk as much as I used to. Although I am not exactly a mouse either. I don't care about being popular anymore. I swear. Are you happy to be back in Japan? I know I ruined everything. I was just trying to be entertaining. I miss you with all my heart, and hope I didn't ruin everything.*

He writes back, *You will never be Japanese.*

I throw all the orange peels out that day. Some of them, it turns out, were moldy anyway. I tell my mother I want to move to Chinatown.

"Chinatown!" she says.

I don't know why I suggested it.

"What's the matter?" she says. "Still boy-crazy? That Sherman?"

"No."

"Too much homework?"

I don't answer.

"Forget about school."

Later she tells that if I don't like school, I don't have to go every day. Some days I can stay home.

"Stay home?" In Yonkers, Callie and I used to stay home all the time, but that was because the schools there were *waste of time.*

"No good for a girl be too smart anyway."

For a long time I think about Sherman. But after a while I don't think about him so much as I just keep seeing myself flipped onto the ground, lying there shocked as the Matsumotos get ready to leave. My head has hit a rock; my brain aches as though it's been shoved to some new place in my skull. Otherwise I am okay. I see the forsythia, all those whippy branches, and I can't believe how many leaves there are on a bush — every one green and perky and durably itself. And past them real sky. I try to remember why the sky's blue, even though this one's gone the kind of indescribable gray you associate with the insides of old shoes. I smell grass. Probably I have grass stains all over my back. I hear my mother calling through the back door, "Mona! Everybody's leaving now," and "Not coming to say good-bye?" I hear Mr. and Mrs. Matsumoto bowing as they leave — or at least I hear the embarrassment in my mother's voice as they bow. I hear their car start. I hear Mrs. Matsumoto directing Mr. Matsumoto how to back off the lawn so as not to rip any more of it up. I feel the back of my head for blood — just a little. I hear their chug-chug grow fainter and fainter, until it has faded into the whuzz-whuzz of all the other cars. I hear my mom singing, "*Mon*-a! *Mon*-a!" until my dad comes home. Doors open and shut. I see myself standing up, brushing myself off so I'll have less explaining to do if she comes out to look for me. Grass stains — just like I thought.

I see myself walking around the house, going over to have a look at our churned-up yard. It looks pretty sad, two big brown tracks, right through the irises and the lilies of the valley, and that was a new dogwood we'd just planted. Lying there like that. I find myself thinking about my father, having to dig it up all over again. Adjusting. I think how we probably ought to put up that brick wall. And sure enough, when I go inside, no one's worrying about me, or that little bit of blood at the back of my head, or the grass stains — that's what they're talking about: that wall. Again. My mom doesn't think it'll do any good, but my dad thinks we should give it a try. Should we or shouldn't we? How high? How thick? What will the neighbors say? I plop myself down on a hard chair. And all I can think is, we are the complete only family that has to worry about this. If I could, I'd switch everything to be different. But since I can't, I might as well sit here at the table for a while, discussing what I know how to discuss. I nod and listen to the rest.

ACTIVITIES

VOCABULARY

chagrin, n. — annoyance caused by failure or disappointment
aplomb, n. — self-confidence, poise
hoary, adj. — very old, white with age
enigmatic, adv. — puzzling, hard to understand or explain
cachet, n. — appeal, prestige
carouse, v. — to celebrate wildly or drunkenly
shoal, n. — a shallow place

FOR DISCUSSION

A. The junior high and early high school years are often thought to be carefree times, at least in comparison to the responsibilities of earning a living and caring for a family. But during this stage of our lives we don't always feel that life is so easy. What are the pressures that Mona is feeling at the beginning of the story? Does she feel these pressures because she is Chinese or because she is a teenager? Are the same pressures common in your school?

B. What does Mona say it takes to be popular in her school? What does it take in yours? Do all cultures value the same qualities in friendships of the same sex? In friendships of the opposite sex?

C. Regardless of cultural differences, we've all felt awkward and self-conscious in unfamiliar situations. Often one of the most uncomfortable times is when we are beginning to socialize with the opposite sex. For example, Mona's flirtations with Sherman are painful and thrilling at the same time. Neither quite knows what to do when it comes to showing affection physically. Are your feelings similar to Mona's? What kind of worries or concerns do you have? Do you have thoughts you are willing to share with your classmates?

CLASS ACTIVITY: The Voices of Experience

Developing social skills takes practice just as it does when we first learn to walk or talk or drive a car, and it may seem that some people are naturally more expert than others. We learn from our own first hand experiences, but we can also learn from the experiences of others, whether fictional or real. We learn best from the experiences of others when we take the time to discuss carefully how we compare with them.

Invite five or six guests of both sexes, different ages, and varying cultural backgrounds to visit your classroom. Ask them to share their memories of first crushes and early romances. Do they recall particular moments of terror or joy? How old were they? Have intervening years given them any insights on those times? Do they offer any words of wisdom?

CLASS ACTIVITY: What Means Love?

Barbara's teasing about Sherman starts Mona wondering whether she and Sherman are really in love. Since she is obviously rather inexperienced in such matters, she isn't quite sure what it means to be in love. Mona also talks about being "just friends" and having "a true crush." What differences can you distinguish among these three kinds of feelings? Where does infatuation fit in? By the end of the story Mona has changed. The letter she writes to Sherman hints at the lessons she has learned. Although their cultural differences may be too big an obstacle to overcome, Mona has gained some valuable experience and should be far wiser the next time she becomes involved with a boy. In what ways has she matured? Study the Scale of Maturity on the next page and decide where you would place Mona between one and ten. Are there any signs that she is ready at the beginning of the story for intimacy based upon caring, respect, responsibility, and knowledge? At the end? Do we need different Scales of Maturity for different cultures?

THE SCALE OF MATURITY

| LOW | HIGH |

Immaturity	**Maturity**
Self-centered, concerned only about "me."	Caring and kind toward others, secure enough to give of oneself, not just take from others.
Focuses on immediate pleasure, the here and now; unconcerned about the future.	Aware of long-term consequences, accepts responsibility for decisions.
Insecure, needs to go along with the crowd.	Independent, knows one's mind and values; resists peer pressure.
Sees boys and girls in stereotyped roles, macho and dependent.	Understands complexity of sexuality, the interplay of gentleness and strength.
Confuses love with physical attraction.	Sees physical and emotional components of love as inseparable.

*Use the comparisons on the next two pages to add to this list.

CLASS ACTIVITY: Love or Infatuation?

1. Infatuation almost always leaps quickly into bloom. Love usually takes root more slowly and it always grows with time.

2. Infatuation is accompanied by a sense of uncertainty. You are stimulated, thrilled, and filled with a kind of feverish excitement. You are miserable when he or she is absent. You can't wait until you see him or her again. Love brings with it a feeling of security. You are warm with a sense of nearness, even when he/she is far away. Miles do not really separate you. You want him/her near, but you know you can wait. You belong to each other; others are on the outside.

3. When you're infatuated, you may lose your appetite. You may daydream a lot. You can't concentrate. You can't study. You can't keep your mind on your work. You may be short tempered and unpleasant with your family. When you're in love you're just the opposite. You can be sensible about your loved one. You feel more secure and trusting. Love gives you new energy and inspires you to do more than you ever dreamed possible.

4. Infatuation brings the feeling that you must get married right away. You can't wait. You musn't take the chance of losing him/her. When you're in love you know you can wait. You are sure of one another. You can plan your future with complete confidence.

5. Infatuation may stem from a desire for self-gratification. You wish to be identified with him/her. You want your friends to see that he/she has chosen you. When in love, there is always a deep concern for the welfare of the loved one. Outside criticism does not dull your attachment. It sharpens it. Misfortune which may take away your "hero" status is of no consequence to you.

6. Infatuation may be merely physical attraction. If you are honest, you may discover that it is often difficult to enjoy each other unless you are leading up to sexual activity. Sex is also a natural and spontaneous part of love, but only a part. If your love is real, you will enjoy a sweet comradeship with the loved one. You like each other. You are friends as well as lovers.

7. Infatuated couples may find it easy to disagree. When you're in love, although your personalities may be quite different, there is an eagerness to hear the other side; to give as well as take; to compromise.

8. Infatuation hardly ever thinks of the far future. What will she/he be like thirty years from now? What kind of parent will he/she make? What kind of home life will we have? Love is very much concerned with the future, not in a materialistic sense, but in the sense of wanting to grow and build a life together.

9. You may fall into infatuation, but you never "fall" in love. Infatuation may lead you to do things you feel are wrong, things which worry you. "'Why do I love you?' I love you not only for what you are, but for what I am when I am with you." (from the poem "Why do I Love You?" by Carolyn Davies)

10. ?????? Most agree that love results from being together and sharing, usually for a long time. Infatuation is built on a less solid foundation. The truth is that the emotions for both often seem the same. Keep this in mind and create your own comparison.

THE MAKEOVER OF MEREDITH KAPLAN

by Barbara Girion

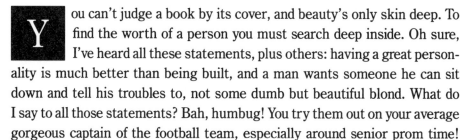ou can't judge a book by its cover, and beauty's only skin deep. To find the worth of a person you must search deep inside. Oh sure, I've heard all these statements, plus others: having a great personality is much better than being built, and a man wants someone he can sit down and tell his troubles to, not some dumb but beautiful blond. What do I say to all those statements? Bah, humbug! You try them out on your average gorgeous captain of the football team, especially around senior prom time!

I learned that early in life. When I was about eleven years old I heard my Aunt Doris say to my mother, "Meredith is such a kind child. I'm sure that after the braces come off and she has a good haircut she'll have her own special look."

I guess that's what you get for listening in on conversations you're not supposed to hear. Anyway, I'm seventeen and in my senior year at J.F.K. High, the braces have been off for four years. I've had dozens of haircuts, and believe me, I'd trade *special* to hear the word *pretty* any day of the week. Of course I'd never admit it, not even to my best friend Lisa, who is as different from me as a best-selling record. You know, she's the hit single and I'm the quiet, subdued tag-along they had to record on the flip side.

Anyway, I've really been too busy during my four years of high school to get myself crazy over a zit on my nose, or scraggly eyebrows, or even half-bitten fingernails. With two brothers and two sisters already in college and grad school, my parents told me from the very beginning that without a scholarship my immediate future would be narrowed down to the community college in our area or night school if I worked during the day. They didn't intend to be mean or discouraging; it's just the fact of my life, and they always wanted me to face it.

So in the hierarchy of high school I guess you would categorize me as a "grind," but an active grind because I've had to go out for all sorts of extracurricular activities to round out my college applications. When colleges say they want a "well-rounded" student before they hand out scholarships, they're not referring to your figure.

Lisa and I were filling out our activities sheets one night. Mine covered two pages. I'm editor of the yearbook, which I'm really proud of, but I've also served hot dogs during half-time at the football games, been chairperson of both the spring and fall class carwash, and worked as a candystriper in our local hospital.

Here I am in the second half of my senior year, with all my college applications sent out and most of my tough schoolwork finished. So I'm able to take a breath and enjoy putting the yearbook together. It's kind of like a puzzle. Lisa likes to interview people and write things up with razzle-dazzle and then throw stuff on my desk to lay out and organize. I guess it sounds as if I'm jealous of her. I don't like to think so, but maybe I am deep, deep down in the tiny bottom of my heart. After all, it's pretty hard not to be jealous of a Brooke Shields look-alike, dress-alike who is also nice. It's not really a nasty jealous, just a kind of jealousy like "Gee whiz, she has so much. Why couldn't I have been given her eyelashes?" Just the top pair would have been sufficient.

As of January first all my classmates seemed to be senior prom buggy, which is premature, since the prom is in June. Of course the girls who are going with someone don't have to worry, unless the romance breaks up. The boys never have to worry: they can always ask one of the underclass girls. There are always sophomore girls batting their eyes and giggling hysterically at everything that comes out of the mouth of a senior boy. I watched all these silly maneuverings with a very superior air. Catch me worrying over a prom date? *Never*!

Lisa plunked herself down at my desk one afternoon in early March.

"We have to talk about the prom, Meredith."

"We do? Please move, Lisa, you're crumpling up the English Department." I was editing that section of the yearbook.

She slapped my hands. "Forget the English Department and the year-book. We have to talk about the prom."

"Oh for heaven's sake, it's three months off." It isn't as though I didn't go out during my four years at J.F.K. High. I was always included in groups. You know, "the good old sport." I went to the games and picnics, but I guess I never had what you would call a real boyfriend. Lisa always said it was my fault. Not only did I not pay enough attention to my appearance, I was always too businesslike and sharp. Well, I don't have time to be soft and kittenish and sweet like Lisa. Besides, there was always Clay Wells. He was the editor of the literary magazine and the statistician of the basketball team, and he already had a scholarship to M.I.T., where he was going to major in comput-ers, if there was anything left about computers that M.I.T. could teach him. I guess Clay was really the stereotype of the class grind. But he was a good guy, and when people would couple off at picnics or parties we would wind up together. We would talk mostly about the future, and Clay would occasion-ally try to aim a few computer planned kisses somewhere near the vicinity of my mouth, but other than that we were strictly friends. I mean, he didn't make any bells ring or my knees turn to water, and I certainly didn't see rainbows when he kissed me good night.

We made a special pact. If either one of us was stuck in a situation where we needed an escort of the opposite sex, we would call on each other. Now, mostly just to get rid of Lisa, I said, "Look, stop worrying. Clay and I will go to the prom together just like we did to the junior dance and the sophomore drag."

"Aha, Miss Smarty . . ."

"Ms., if you please, and stop swinging your legs, Lisa. You're giving me a headache."

"Very well, Ms. Smarty. But please take a minute to surface through this stuff you've buried yourself under. And speaking of burying, your bangs need to be trimmed again. I told you your eyes are your best feature, and they're buried under all that hair. How long has it been this time?"

I blushed, couldn't help it. She had gotten me this time. My bangs were scraggling into my eyes. I had borrowed two clips from Barbara Ann during gym period and pinned them back. The trouble was that one clip was tortoise shell and the other bright blue, and the rubber band holding the rest of my scrags back in a ponytail was yellow striped.

"Now hear this. For the past three weeks, Clay Wells has been seeing," now get this, seeing, which means . . ." Lisa counted on her fingers, the tip of every one of which was polished with a pearly pink sheen, shaped into perfect little ovals without a hangnail in sight. I sat on my hands before she had a chance to notice that my fiftieth resolution not to bite, pick, or otherwise maim my nails was no longer in effect. ". . . two movies, cute little late night tete-a-tetes at King's Pizza, holding hands in front of her locker — her locker, mind you — Sara Woodruff."

I looked puzzled but my stomach felt a little sick.

"Sara Woodruff, junior class treasurer, blond, blue eyes, just loaded with Fair Isle sweaters that match those baby blues and with eight beads on her gold add-a-bead necklace."

I still couldn't see what she was leading up to. Of course I knew who Sara was.

"Well, accurate rumor has it that Clay has offered, and little Sara has accepted, his kind invitation to join him at the senior prom." There were two ways I could react, and Lisa was watching me closely. First I thought, what a fink! Clay could have gone with me and we could have spent the evening drinking punch and mocking the starlight that was bound to be shining out of the eyes of all the couples. Those kids were determined to press prom night firmly into their memories as the best night of their lives, just as the girls would press their flower corsages in the pages of some thick book. Why, I wouldn't even have cared if he didn't shave too closely, or if he did and patched himself up with a wide Band-Aid. And Clay would have laughed rather than lectured me if my fresh manicure was half peeled off before we got to the punch bowl. But then, I felt kind of relieved. Underneath my mocking exterior I think I am romantic. I would like to dance away prom night under the stars with someone who could make me quiver like Jell-O, whatever that means — someone who would think I was pretty or cute, not just a really good sport and "one of the guys." Of course how could you admit this to someone who looked like Lisa? It had always been so easy for her. Even when she was little, she was what everyone referred to as a beauty.

I'm just as nice a person. The trouble is that people look first before they decide to get to know you. And now apparently my friend Clay, who had always seemed to share my scorn for the dating practices of our peers, had himself fallen under the spell of two blue eyes and a shape that could fill an ad for jeans!

"Well, I shall just have to find someone else. Of course I could always go stag and stand behind the punch bowl and serve. Or visit my grandmother in Cleveland a little early."

"Oh, come on, Meredith, quit joking. It's probably the best thing that could have happened. Now you'll start thinking seriously about a date for the prom."

"Right now I'm afraid, Lisa, I shall have to copy a phrase from Scarlett O'Hara and 'think about it tomorrow,' because I've got to lay out the ad pages. The sponsors are coming in at a terrific rate."

And so with my usual good humor, I managed to change the subject around. The next couple of weeks passed quickly, but I began to notice that Clay was different. Oh, we still kibitzed and joked with each other when we passed in the halls, but the first thing I noticed was his chin. No more gucky-looking Band-Aids stuck all over.

One day he asked me to read his history notes. I looked around to see where that spicy smell was coming from. Then I realized that Clay had on aftershave lotion! And his favorite brown-and-tan lumber shirt was pressed and tucked into his jeans, which were belted with wide, dark tan leather and a large gold clasp. And for the first time in about four years, I actually saw his ears, because his hair had been clipped neatly around them.

"Clay, are your eyes blue-green?"

"What did you say, Meredith?"

"Your eyes. I don't think I ever noticed them before. Your glasses! What happened to your glasses? You can't see three inches in front of you without them."

"Contacts." He lowered his head and blushed. "It took me a few weeks to get used to them, but now they're great. My parents gave me an early graduation present. Do you like them?"

He actually had thick, curly lashes, almost as long as Lisa's.

"Well, it must be terrific to be in love. Did Sara cause all these changes?"

"No, not exactly. I thought I'd just kind of change my image, to get ready for college next year. Listen, about Sara. I know we always had this understanding about sticking together for special dances and things."

I held up my hands. "Say no more, Clay. I'm sure that Sara's very sweet and I suppose it's good for everyone's morale to have a real date."

"Thanks. And listen, my cousin Ned lives in Irvington. You remember him? I could always get him to take you to the prom."

Strangely enough, my eyes filled with tears and I had to blink quickly before they spilled over. "Hey, no sweat. If and when I decide to go to the prom, I'm sure I can arrange my own date."

"Hey, Meredith, don't get mad. I just don't want you left out."

"Don't worry about me, Clay Wells. I'm sure I can get a date, and without spraying myself to imitate a spice cabinet."

"Oh, my aftershave. Do you like it? Sara said it was her favorite scent."

"Later, Clay." And off I stalked down the hall, trying to decide why I felt so darn upset.

Lisa and I had to go to the shopping mall that Saturday. We were trying to collect more ads for the yearbook by visiting merchants in person.

There was a huge crowd standing under colored balloons and banners in the middle of the plaza on the first floor. Lisa and I edged our way through to see what was going on.

"Oh Meredith, look!"

A small stage had been set up with tables and chairs arranged around the edges. There were six young men and women fussing over girls who were seated in the chairs. The loudspeakers were blaring out music.

"It's a makeover," Lisa shouted above the din.

Then I noticed the posters. "Today's Teen magazine is in Millburn to make over twelve lucky young ladies."

"Oh, isn't this fun!" Lisa pushed me closer 'til we were right against the stage.

It was littered with blond, black, and all shades of red hair that had been clipped from the heads of the girls sitting in front of the tables. Some were having make-up applied, eyebrows tweezed, their hair set in hot rollers or blown free. It was as if a bunch of magicians were hovering over the stage. Their liquids and powders were magic potions, and hairbrushes and scissors were turned into magic wands.

The audience was full of oohs and aahs, and even I was fascinated at the transformation taking place.

"Miss, oh miss, could I speak to you for a minute?" Lisa was trying to get the attention of one of the cosmeticians. What would she ever want to be made over for? I thought. What more can you do with perfect? Then I realized.

"Oh, no, Lisa. I know what you're thinking. Absolutely not. Do you think I would make a public display of myself?"

I don't know what happened. I tried to get away but I was hemmed in by the crowd. Lisa spoke to someone important, one of the tables emptied as a newly transformed Cinderella left the stage to applause and cat calls and I found myself in the still warm wooden chair. A cape was tied under my chin and a hairdresser called over. There was a standing mirror in front of me. I tried to tell myself this wasn't happening. I felt like Alice when she'd just fallen down the rabbit hole.

After a quick look the hairdresser soaked my hair with water and began clipping away. The cosmetician dipped cotton and sponges into all kinds of liquids and oils and spread them on my face.

Lisa was yelling encouragement from the sidelines like a cheerleader. I tried to close my eyes, grit my teeth, and think of two hundred and seven ways I would personally maim, torture, and finally kill Lisa when I left the platform.

After what seemed like hours, I opened my eyes to hear the cosmetician's instructions. "We've written everything on this sheet of paper for you. You have beautiful eyes and absolutely gorgeous cheekbones. If you keep your eyebrows cleaned of all those extra hairs, your make-up will show. Come on, look in the mirror. Carlos just used a blower on your hair. You have a great natural wave."

Natural wave, beautiful eyes, gorgeous cheekbones, could he actually be talking about Meredith Kaplan? I looked in the mirror expecting to see one of those painted china dolls with ruby cheeks and thick goopy eyelids. But there was an absolutely dynamite-looking girl, and it was me! It was Meredith Kaplan. I know because I saw the tiny round birthmark under my left eye.

My bangs were trimmed and tapered and the rest of my hair had been layered. It fell back from my face in soft feathery waves. I have brown eyes, and they had been accented with a little bit of pale green shadow and brown mascara. My eyes were sparkling and shiny, out from under the thick eyebrows that used to run together across the bridge of my nose. There was just a little bit of blush high on my cheekbones, and with the faintest pink gloss my lips actually looked kissable.

"Shake your head back and forth," instructed Carlos. I did and watched my hair spin out gently and fall right back into place perfectly. "If you have a good cut, your hair will always look like this."

Before I knew it I was descending the steps, instruction sheets in hand, and this time the applause and whistles were for me.

Lisa raved and raved. I walked gingerly through the mall, stopping now and then to look at the sleek and pretty, that's right, pretty image that stared back at me from the store windows.

"I knew there was something under all that. Meredith, you look absolutely wild. Wait until the kids in school see you."

I was happy that she was raving but also felt that I must have been an absolutely number one slob in my "before" period, which was approximately 67 minutes ago. My chest puffed out as I began to float along. Why, with my looks and my "nice" personality, there probably was no male who would be immune to me for long.

"When I think of those wasted years, I could cry," said Lisa.

I didn't tell her, but I was thinking the same thing. Where had I gotten the idea that all attempts at self-improvement were strictly for the vain and frivolous? I had spent most of my high school days with only one of my oars in the water—when I, like everyone else, had two to paddle with!

I soon realized why the Fairy Godmother gave Cinderella a 12 o'clock curfew after her transformation. It's pretty hard to be a princess twenty-four hours a day. First I had to cope with my family's reaction. As an indication of their astonishment, my sister Sally gave me a small bottle of her favorite lily of the valley perfume. "It would have been wasted on the old you," she said.

The kids at school were equally astounded. I found myself running into the bathroom between periods to make sure I still had on lip gloss or that my mascara hadn't smeared. The first night I washed my hairdo I had been really frightened. How would I ever get it to look the same? I needn't have worried. It wasn't as perfect as Carlos had done it, but I managed to flip it back into place with my hairbrush. Being beautiful became a full time commitment, and I didn't have time to think of a wisecrack or something funny to keep me in the public eye.

When Clay and I met for our weekly study period, he was mesmerized. "You look fantastic, Meredith. And what do you have on? You smell like a flower garden."

Hmm. One for me, I thought. Let him tell good old Sara that. Quite a few boys who wouldn't have looked at me at all except to say, "How you doing, pal?" now stopped at my table in the lunchroom to talk.

I went out with Michael Brady about three times. He wasn't exactly the captain of the football team, but he was still part of the popular crowd and very good looking. Then on our fourth date, over pizza—which I didn't dare eat because it would have smeared on my lips — he asked me to the prom. "That is, if you don't have a date."

That was it, the high point of my life. I should have been in ecstasy, but I wasn't. Of course I accepted and, since it was now April, breathed a sigh of relief that I could finally relax and let June come.

Lisa was overjoyed and began badgering me over the gown I would have to buy for the big night.

"Oh, give me a chance to relax. I've got my sister Sally's gown. My mom said she'd fix it for me. You know we have a tight budget."

Lisa frowned. "Well, I wish you could have your very own dress, but I guess it'll be all right."

Michael and I were together every Friday and Saturday night. I wish that I could say he was my Prince Charming but I don't know, something was missing. All we ever talked about was the other kids, who was going with whom, what we would do at the prom, after the prom, and before the prom, and about the engine of his car. His kisses were nice, but I still didn't feel like Jell-O or rainbows or swinging garden gates. As a matter of fact, I yawned a lot.

At the end of April, Clay and I held our last study session. We were all alone in the classroom.

"Gee, I'm going to miss this next year when I'm at M.I.T."

"Miss what?" I looked around the room. "This smelly old school?"

"No, not the school building, but being with you these four years, studying. We've always had so much fun together."

Suddenly I realized that I would miss him, too. Good old Clay, we always had so much to talk about, laugh about. I reached for his hand to give it a gentle pat, somewhat like the way you would show kindness to a favorite pet. As my fingertips brushed his, I felt it, just for an instant. Then he grabbed my hand in his and reached over and kissed me right on my kissable lips. And then I knew he must have felt it, too: a tiny tingle that began in the tips of my fingers and ran up my shoulder and right down my spine to the tips of my toes. I tried to shuffle my feet and then I knew what it meant to have your legs turn to Jell-O. There was a soft, warm feeling all through me, and I gently pulled back to look at Clay.

"Your glasses are fogged up," I said. Then I looked again. "Hey, where are your contacts?"

"Oh, my eyes were a little irritated this week, so I've been giving them a rest."

He also had a Band-Aid on the right side of his chin where he had cut himself shaving, and his short sleeve shirt wasn't pressed. I nuzzled up to his cheek, sniffing. It didn't smell like spices anymore, but there was a nicer, better smell of soap and light sweat and Clay. Yes, he definitely smelled like the Clay I used to know.

I shook my hair out of my eyes and realized it had been six weeks since my makeover and that I hadn't gone back for a new haircut. I had also been in a rush this morning and left home without my blushed-on cheekbones, and my kissable lips must have been really kissable because I had lost the tube of gloss three days ago.

He kissed me again, and I tried to decide what tune the bells that were ringing through my head were playing and to enjoy all the colors of the rainbow that danced behind my closed eyes.

"You're terrific," he said.

"I know," I said.

"What was that?"

"Nothing, just keep kissing."

"Meredith, will you go to the prom with me?"

"Yes," I said. "Except I have a date already."

"I know," he said between kisses. "I have a date, too."

"We'll work it out," I said.

"You'd better believe it," he said. And then we didn't say anything at all.

ACTIVITIES

VOCABULARY

hierarchy, n. — a ranked order as from lower to higher

categorize, v. — to group or label

candy striper, n. — nickname for volunteer hospital workers who wear pink striped uniforms

stereotype, n. — a standardized, oversimplified mental picture of a kind of person, a group of people, or an idea; a fixed pattern

maim, v. — to cripple, to mutilate, to cut off parts of the body

morale, n. — mental and emotional attitude, sense of well-being

mesmerize, v. — to hypnotize

ecstasy, n. — a state of overwhelming emotion; overpowering joy

REVIEW QUESTIONS

1. What reason does Meredith give for being a "grind," that is, for being more concerned about her studies than her social life?

2. At the beginning of the story, Meredith lists two reasons why she has never had a real boyfriend. What are they?

3. What happens to make Meredith jealous of Sara Woodruff?

4. Why does Meredith compare the six young men and women in the mall to magicians?

5. How does Meredith's personality change when her appearance changes?

6. Meredith's dreams finally come true when she starts dating Michael Brady. How does she describe their relationship?

7. There are three references to the word "Jell-O" in the story. What feeling is "Jell-O" used to describe?

8. At the end of the story Meredith and Clay look about the same as they did at the beginning. But there has been a big change. What is different? In what way might you say there have been two makeovers of Meredith Kaplan?

FOR DISCUSSION

A "cliche" is a statement that is heard so frequently that it becomes stale from overuse. Perhaps these statements are quoted so frequently because they contain important truths about life and human nature. Meredith begins her story with two cliches, but others seem equally appropriate. Consider the meaning of the following cliches. Find one or more examples of each in "The Makeover of Meredith Kaplan." Can you think of other examples from your own experience?

A. "You can't judge a book by its cover."

B. "Beauty is only skin deep."

C. "The grass is always greener on the other side of the fence."

D. "Absence makes the heart grow fonder."

E. "Beauty is in the eye of the beholder."

F. "Handsome is as handsome does."

TOPICS FOR DEBATE OR WRITING ASSIGNMENT

By the end of the story Meredith has largely set aside her makeup, and her hair has become scraggly again. Clay similarly has relaxed his earlier attempts to improve his image. What does this change in attitude say about the characters? Pick either A or B and give evidence to support your position.

A. A sloppy appearance reflects a poor self-image. Meredith and Clay should take more pride in their appearance and should invest the time and money to look their best.

or

B. Meredith's and Clay's renewed disregard for appearances at the end of the story is a healthy sign. It reflects a mature understanding of who they are and what is most important to them.

SONNET 130

by William Shakespeare

M y mistress' eyes are nothing like the sun;
Coral is far more red than her lips' red;
If snow be white, why then her breasts are dun;
If hairs be wires, black wires grow on her head.
I have seen roses damasked, red and white,   5
But no such roses see I in her cheeks;
And in some perfumes is there more delight
Than in the breath that from my mistress reeks.
I love to hear her speak, yet well I know
That music hath a far more pleasing sound;   10
I grant I never saw a goddess go;
My mistress, when she walks, treads on the ground.
And yet, by heaven, I think my love as rare
As any she belied with false compare.

A NOTE ON READING POETRY:

Poets use language in a highly concentrated, intense way. They choose each word precisely and often link words in intricate ways. Reading poetry is a skill that takes practice, but a few simple tips may be helpful. First and most importantly, do not read line by line, pausing at the end of each one. It is not the division into lines that signals meaning; it is the punctuation. Read sentence by sentence, pausing briefly at commas and slightly longer at periods. If the sentence is confusing, look for the main subject and verb, then see where the other phrases and clauses fit in.

ACTIVITIES

A sonnet is a poem of fourteen lines and a standard rhyme scheme. In Shakespeare's time, the sixteenth century, a poet traditionally described the object of his passionate desire in extravagant verse. No mountain is too high to climb, no ocean is too deep to swim as proof of his undying love. The lady he worships is nothing short of a goddess. When she walks, she floats like an angel. Her voice is music to his ears, her breath the sweetest of perfumes. Her eyes sparkle like diamonds or are as bright as the sun, and each hair is a golden wire. Her cheeks are roses, her lips are tulips, and her teeth are pearls. Her skin is as pure and white as snow.

FOR DISCUSSION

In what way is Shakespeare's Sonnet 130 in agreement with the following statement from *Reason and Emotion* by John MacMurray?

> *"If you love a person you love him or her in their stark reality, and refuse to shut your eyes to their defects and errors. For to do that is to shut your eyes to their needs. Love cannot abide deceit, or pretense or unreality. It rests only in the reality of the loved one, demands that the loved one should be himself, so that it may love him for himself."*

How does "The Makeover of Meredith Kaplan" support this idea? Mac-Murray says *"love cannot abide deceit, pretense or unreality."* Can you build a loving relationship if there is deceit? If there is any degree of unreality?

LOVE POEM

by John Frederick Nims

My clumsiest dear, whose hands shipwreck vases,
At whose quick touch all glasses chip and ring,
Whose palms are bulls in china, burs in linen,
And have no cunning with any soft thing
Except all ill-at-ease fidgeting people;   5
The refugee uncertain at the door
You make at home; deftly, you steady
The drunk clambering on his undulant floor
Unpredictable dear, the taxi driver's terror,
Shrinking from far headlights pale as a dime   10
Yet leaping before red apoplectic streetcars —
Misfit in any space. And never on time.
A wrench in clocks and the solar system. Only
With words and people and love you move at ease.
In traffic of wit expertly maneuver   15
And keep us, all devotion, at your knees.
Forgetting your coffee spreading on our flannel,
Your lipstick grinning on our coat.
So gayly in love's unbreakable heaven,
Our souls on glory of spilt bourbon float.   20
Be with me darling, early and late.
I will study wry music for your sake,
for should your hands drop white and empty
All the toys of the world would break.

ACTIVITIES

VOCABULARY

deftly, adv. — skillfully
clamber, v. — climb
undulant, adj. — moving up and down, swinging
apoplectic, adj. — highly excited
wry, adj. — weird, cleverly humorous

FOR DISCUSSION

This poem was written nearly 400 years after Shakespeare's sonnet. How are the themes similar? What do you think is meant by the saying "Love is blind?" Is this a healthy or unhealthy characteristic of love? Why?

TOO EARLY SPRING

by Stephen Vincent Benét

I'm writing this down because I don't ever want to forget the way it was. It doesn't seem as if I could, now, but they all tell you things change. And I guess they're right. Older people must have forgotten or they couldn't be the way they are. And that goes for even the best ones, like Dad and Mr. Grant. They try to understand but they don't seem to know how. And the others make you feel dirty or else they make you feel like a goof. Till, pretty soon, you begin to forget yourself—you begin to think, "Well, maybe they're right and it was that way." And that's the end of everything. So I've got to write this down. Because they smashed it forever—but it wasn't the way they said.

Mr. Grant always says in comp. class: "Begin at the beginning." Only I don't know quite where the beginning was. We had a good summer at Big Lake but it was just the same summer. I worked pretty hard at the practice basket I rigged up in the barn, and I learned how to do the back jackknife. I'll never dive like Kerry but you want to be as all-around as you can. And, when I took my measurements, at the end of the summer, I was 5 ft. 9 3/4 and I'd gained 12 lbs. 6 oz. That isn't bad for going on sixteen and the old chest expansion was O.K. You don't want to get too heavy because basketball's a fast game, but the year before was the year when I got my height, and I was so skinny, I got tired. But this year Kerry helped me practice a couple of times, and he seemed to think I had a good chance for the team. So I felt pretty set up—they'd never had a Sophomore on it before. And Kerry's a natural athlete, so that means a lot from him. He's a pretty good brother too. Most Juniors at State wouldn't bother with a fellow in High.

It sounds as if I were trying to run away from what I have to write down, but I'm not. I want to remember that summer, too, because it's the last happy one I'll ever have. Oh, when I'm an old man—thirty or forty—things may be all right again. But that's a long time to wait and it won't be the same.

And yet, that summer was different, too, in a way. So it must have started then, though I didn't know it. I went around with the gang as usual and we had a good time. But, every now and then, it would strike me we were acting like awful kids. They thought I was getting the big head, but I wasn't. It just wasn't much fun—even going to the cave. It was like going on shooting marbles when you're in High.

I had sense enough not to try to tag after Kerry and his crowd. You can't do that. But when they all got out on the lake in canoes on warm evenings, and somebody brought a phonograph along, I used to go down to the Point, all by myself, and listen and listen. Maybe they'd be talking or maybe they'd be singing, but it all sounded mysterious across the water. I wasn't trying to hear what they said, you know. That's the kind of thing Tot Pickens does. I'd just listen, with my arms around my knees—and somehow it would hurt me to listen—and yet I'd rather do that than be with the gang.

I was sitting under the four pines, one night, right down by the edge of the water. There was a big moon and people were singing. It's funny how you can be unhappy and nobody knows it but yourself.

I was thinking about Sheila Coe. She's Kerry's girl. They fight but they get along. She's awfully pretty and she can swim like a fool. Once Kerry sent me over with her tennis racket and we had quite a conversation. She was fine. And she didn't pull any of this big sister stuff, either, the way some girls will with a fellow's kid brother.

And when the canoe came along, by the edge of the lake, I thought for a moment it was her. I thought maybe she was looking for Kerry and maybe she'd stop and maybe she'd feel like talking to me again. I don't know why I thought that—I didn't have any reason. Then I saw it was just the Sharon kid, with a new kind of bob that made her look grown-up, and I felt sore. She didn't have any business out on the lake at her age. She was just a Sophomore in High, same as me.

I chunked a stone in the water and it splashed right by the canoe, but she didn't squeal. She just said, "Fish," and chuckled. It struck me it was a kid's trick, trying to scare a kid.

"Hello, Helen," I said. "Where did you swipe the gunboat?"

"They don't know I've got it," she said. "Oh, hello, Chuck Peters. How's Big Lake?"

"All right," I said. "'How was camp?"

"It was peachy," she said. "We had a peachy counselor, Miss Morgan. She was on the Wellesley field-hockey team."

"Well," I said, "we missed your society." Of course we hadn't, because they're across the lake and don't swim at our raft. But you ought to be polite.

"Thanks," she said. "Did you do the special reading for English? I thought it was dumb."

"It's always dumb," I said. "What canoe is that?"

"It's the old one," she said. "I'm not supposed to have it out at night. But you won't tell anybody, will you?"

"Be your age," I said. I felt generous. "I'll paddle awhile, if you want," I said.

"All right," she said, so she brought it in and I got aboard. She went back in the bow and I took the paddle. I'm not strong on carting kids around, as a rule. But it was better than sitting there by myself.

"Where do you want to go?" I said.

"Oh, back towards the house," she said in a shy kind of voice. "I ought to, really. I just wanted to hear the singing."

"K.O.," I said. I didn't paddle fast, just let her slip. There was a lot of moon on the water. We kept around the edge so they wouldn't notice us. The singing sounded as if it came from a different country, a long way off.

She was a sensible kid, she didn't ask fool questions or giggle about nothing at all. Even when we went by Petters' Cove. That's where the lads from the bungalow colony go and it's pretty well populated on a warm night. You can hear them talking in low voices and now and then a laugh. Once Tot Pickens and a gang went over there with a flashlight, and a big Bohunk chased them for half a mile.

I felt funny, going by there with her. But I said, "Well, it's certainly Old Home Week" — in an offhand tone, because, after all, you've got to be sophisticated. And she said, "People are funny," in just the right sort of way. I took quite a shine to her after that and we talked. The Sharons have only been in town three years and somehow I'd never really noticed her before. Mrs. Sharon's awfully good-looking but she and Mr. Sharon fight. That's hard on a kid. And she was a quiet kid. She had a small kind of face and her eyes were sort of like a kitten's. You could see she got a great kick out of pretending to be grown-up—and yet it wasn't all pretending. A couple of times, I felt just as if I were talking to Sheila Coe. Only more comfortable, because, after all, we were the same age.

Do you know, after we put the canoe up, I walked all the way back home, around the lake? And most of the way, I ran. I felt swell too. I felt as if I could run forever and not stop. It was like finding something. I hadn't imagined anybody could ever feel the way I did about some things. And here was another person, even if it was a girl.

Kerry's door was open when I went by and he stuck his head out, and grinned.

"Well, kid," he said. "Stepping out?"

"Sure. With Greta Garbo," I said, and grinned back to show I didn't mean it. I felt sort of lightheaded, with the run and everything.

"Look here, kid—" he said, as if he was going to say something. Then he stopped. But there was a funny look on his face.

And yet I didn't see her again till we were both back in High. Mr. Sharon's uncle died, back East, and they closed the cottage suddenly. But all the rest of the time at Big Lake, I kept remembering that night and her little face. If I'd seen her in daylight, first, it might have been different. No, it wouldn't have been.

All the same, I wasn't even thinking of her when we bumped into each other, the first day of school. It was raining and she had on a green slicker and her hair was curly under her hat. We grinned and said hello and had to run. But something happened to us, I guess.

I'll say this now—it wasn't like Tot Pickens and Mabel Palmer. It wasn't like Junior David and Betty Page—though they've been going together ever since kindergarten. It wasn't like any of those things. We didn't get sticky and sloppy. It wasn't like going with a girl.

Gosh, there'd be days and days when we'd hardly see each other except in class. I had basketball practice almost every afternoon and sometimes evenings and she was taking music lessons four times a week. But you don't have to be always twos-ing with a person, if you feel that way about them. You seem to know the way they're thinking and feeling, the way you know yourself.

Now let me describe her. She had that little face and the eyes like a kitten's. When it rained, her hair curled all over the back of her neck. Her hair was yellow. She wasn't a tall girl but she wasn't chunky—just light and well made and quick. She was awfully alive without being nervous—she never bit her fingernails or chewed the end of her pencil, but she'd answer quicker than anyone in the class. Nearly everybody liked her, but she wasn't best friends with any particular girl, the mushy way they get. The teachers all thought a lot of her, even Miss Eagles. Well, I had to spoil that.

If we'd been like Tot and Mabel, we could have had a lot more time together, I guess. But Helen isn't a liar and I'm not a snake. It wasn't easy, going over to her house, because Mr. and Mrs. Sharon would be polite to each other in front of you and yet there'd be something wrong. And she'd have to be fair to both of them and they were always pulling at her. But we'd look at each other across the table and then it would be all right.

I don't know when it was that we knew we'd get married to each other, some time. We just started talking about it, one day, as if we always had. We were sensible, we knew it couldn't happen right off. We thought maybe when we were eighteen. That was two years but we knew we had to be educated. You don't get as good a job, if you aren't. Or that's what people say.

We weren't mushy either, like some people. We got to kissing each other good-by, sometimes, because that's what you do when you're in love. It was cool, the way she kissed you, it was like leaves. But lots of the time we wouldn't even talk about getting married, we'd just play checkers or go over the old Latin, or once in a while go to the movies with the gang. It was really a wonderful winter. I played every game after the first one and she'd sit in the gallery and watch and I'd know she was there. You could see her little green hat or yellow hair. Those are the class colors, green and gold.

And it's a queer thing, but everybody seemed to be pleased. That's what I can't get over. They liked to see us together. The grown people, I mean. Oh, of course, we got kidded too. And old Mrs. Withers would ask me about "my little sweetheart," in that awful damp voice of hers. But, mostly, they were all right. Even Mother was all right, though she didn't like Mrs. Sharon. I did hear her say to Father, once, "Really, George, how long is this going to last? Sometimes I feel as if I just couldn't stand it."

Then Father chuckled and said to her, "Now, Mary, last year you were worried about him because he didn't take any interest in girls at all."

"Well," she said, "he still doesn't. Oh, Helen's a nice child—no credit to Eva Sharon—and thank heaven she doesn't giggle. Well, Charles is mature for his age too. But he acts so solemn about her. It isn't natural."

"Oh, let Charlie alone," said Father. "The boy's all right. He's just got a one track mind."

But it wasn't so nice for us after the spring came. In our part of the state, it comes pretty late as a rule. But it was early this year. The little kids were out with scooters when usually they'd still be having snowfights and all of a sudden, the radiators in the classrooms smelt dry. You'd got used to that smell for months — and then, there was a day when you hated it again and everybody kept asking to open the windows. The monitors had a tough time, that first week — they always do when spring starts — but this year it was worse than ever because it came when you didn't expect it.

Usually, basketball's over by the time spring really breaks, but this year it hit us while we still had three games to play. And it certainly played hell with us as a team. After Bladesburg nearly licked us, Mr. Grant called off all practice till the day before the St. Matthew's game. He knew we were stale — and they've been state champions two years. They'd have walked all over us, the way we were going.

The first thing I did was telephone Helen. Because that meant there were six extra afternoons we could have, if she could get rid of her music lessons any way. Well, she said, wasn't it wonderful, her music teacher had a cold? And that seemed just like Fate.

Well, that was a great week and we were so happy. We went to the movies five times and once Mrs. Sharon let us take her little car. She knew I didn't have a driving license but of course I've driven ever since I was thirteen and she said it was all right. She was funny — sometimes she'd be awfully kind and friendly to you and sometimes she'd be like a piece of dry ice. She was that way with Mr. Sharon too. But it was a wonderful ride. We got stuff out of the kitchen — the cook's awfully sold on Helen — and drove way out into the country. And we found an old house, with the windows gone, on top of a hill, and parked the car and took the stuff up to the house and ate it there. There weren't any chairs or tables but we pretended there were.

We pretended it was our house, after we were married. I'll never forget that. She'd even brought paper napkins and paper plates and she set two places on the floor.

"Well, Charles," she said, sitting opposite me, with her feet tucked under, "I don't suppose you remember the days we were both in school."

"Sure," I said — she was always much quicker pretending things than I was — "I remember them all right. That was before Tot Pickens got to be President." And we both laughed.

"It seems very distant in the past to me—we've been married so long," she said, as if she really believed it. She looked at me.

"Would you mind turning off the radio, dear?" she said.

"This modern music always gets on my nerves."

"Have we got a radio?" I said.

"Of course, Chuck."

"With television?"

"Of course, Chuck."

"Gee, I'm glad," I said. I went and turned it off.

"Of course, if you want to listen to the late market reports—" she said just like Mrs. Sharon.

"Nope," I said. "The market—uh—closed firm today. Up twenty-six points."

"That's quite a long way up, isn't it?"

"Well, the country's perfectly sound at heart, in spite of this damn fool Congress," I said, like Father.

She lowered her eyes a minute, just like her mother, and pushed away her plate.

"I'm not very hungry tonight," she said. "You won't mind if I go upstairs?"

"Aw, don't be like that," I said. It was too much like her mother.

"I was just seeing if I could," she said. "But I never will, Chuck."

"I'll never tell you you're nervous, either," I said. "I—oh, gosh!"

She grinned and it was all right. "Mr. Ashland and I have never had a serious dispute in our wedded lives," she said, and everybody knows who runs that family. "We just talk things over calmly and reach a satisfactory conclusion, usually mine."

"Say, what kind of house have we got?"

"It's a lovely house," she said. "We've got radios in every room and lots of servants. We've got a regular movie projector and a library full of good classics and there's always something in the icebox. I've got a shoe closet."

"A shoe closet. All my shoes are on tipped shelves, like Mother's. And all my dresses are on those padded hangers. And I say to the maid, 'Elsie, Madam will wear the new French model today.'"

"What are my clothes on?" I said. "Christmas trees?"

"Well," she said. "You've got lots of clothes and dogs. You smell of pipes and the open and something called Harrisburg tweed."

"I do not," I said. "I wish I had a dog. It's a long time since Jack."

"Oh, Chuck, I'm sorry," she said.

"Oh, that's all right," I said. "He was getting old and his ear was always bothering him. But he was a good pooch. Go ahead."

"Well," she said, "of course we give parties-"

"Cut the parties," I said.

"Chuck! They're grand ones!"

"I'm a homebody," I said. "Give me — er — my wife and my little family and — say, how many kids have we got, anyway?"

She counted on her fingers. "Seven."

"Good Lord," I said.

"Well, I always wanted seven. You can make it three, if you like."

"Oh, seven's all right I suppose," I said. "But don't they get awfully in the way?"

"No," she said. "We have governesses and tutors and send them to boarding school."

"O.K.," I said. "But it's a strain on the old man's pocketbook, just the same."

"Chuck, will you ever talk like that? Chuck, when we're rich?" Then suddenly, she looked sad. "Oh, Chuck, do you suppose we ever will?" she said.

"Why, sure," I said.

"I wouldn't mind if it was only a dump," she said. "I could cook for you. I keep asking Hilda how she makes things."

I felt awfully funny. I felt as if I were going to cry.

"We'll do it," I said. "Don't you worry."

"Oh, Chuck, you're a comfort," she said.

I held her for a while. It was like holding something awfully precious. It wasn't mushy or that way. I know what that's like too.

"It takes so long to get old," she said. "I wish I could grow up tomorrow. I wish we both could."

"Don't you worry," I said. "It's going to be all right."

We didn't say much, going back in the car, but we were happy enough. I thought we passed Miss Eagles at the turn. That worried me a little because of the driving license. But, after all, Mrs. Sharon had said we could take the car.

We wanted to go back again, after that, but it was too far to walk and that was the only time we had the car. Mrs. Sharon was awfully nice about it but she said, thinking it over, maybe we'd better wait till I got a license. Well, Father didn't want me to get one till I was seventeen but I thought he might come around. I didn't want to do anything that would get Helen in a jam with her family. That shows how careful I was of her. Or thought I was.

All the same, we decided we'd do something to celebrate if the team won the St. Matthew's game. We thought it would be fun if we got a steak and cooked supper out somewhere — something like that. Of course we could have done it easily enough with a gang, but we didn't want a gang. We wanted to be alone together, the way we'd been at the house. That was all we wanted. I don't see what's wrong about that. We even took home the paper plates, so as not to litter things up.

Boy, that was a game! We beat them 36–34 and it took an extra period and I thought it would never end. That two-goal lead they had looked as big as the Rocky Mountains all the first half. And they gave me the full school cheer with nine Peters when we tied them up. You don't forget things like that.

Afterwards, Mr. Grant had a kind of spread for the team at his house and a lot of people came in. Kerry had driven down from State to see the game and that made me feel pretty swell. And what made me feel better yet was his taking me aside and saying, "Listen, kid, I don't want you to get the swelled head, but you did a good job. Well, just remember this. Don't let anybody kid you out of going to State. You'll like it up there." And Mr. Grant heard him and laughed and said, "Well, Peters, I'm not proselytizing. But your brother might think about some of the Eastern colleges." It was all like the kind of dream you have when you can do anything. It was wonderful.

Only Helen wasn't there because the only girls were older girls. I'd seen her for a minute, right after the game, and she was fine, but it was only a minute. I wanted to tell her about that big St. Matthew's forward and — oh, everything. Well, you like to talk things over with your girl.

Father and Mother were swell but they had to go on to some big shindy at the country club. And Kerry was going to the house in his car and he did. He's a great guy. He made jokes about my being the infant phenomenon of basketball, and they were good jokes too. I didn't mind them. But, all the same, when I'd said good night to him and gone into the house, I felt sort of let down.

I knew I'd be tired the next day but I didn't feel sleepy yet. I was too excited. I wanted to talk to somebody. I wandered around downstairs and wondered if Ida was still up. Well, she wasn't, but she'd left half a chocolate cake, covered over, on the kitchen table, and a note on top of it, "Congratulations to Mister Charles Peters." Well, that was awfully nice of her and I ate some. Then I turned the radio on and got the time signal — eleven — and some snappy music. But still I didn't feel like hitting the hay.

So I thought I'd call up Helen and then I thought — probably she's asleep and Hilda or Mrs. Sharon will answer the phone and be sore. And then I thought — well, anyhow, I could go over and walk around the block and look at her house. I'd get some fresh air out of it, anyway, and it would be a little like seeing her.

So I did — and it was a swell night — cool and a lot of stars — and I felt like a king, walking over. All the lower part of the Sharon house was dark but a window upstairs was lit. I knew it was her window. I went around back of the driveway and whistled once — the whistle we made up. I never expected her to hear.

But she did, and there she was at the window, smiling. She made motions that she'd come down to the side door.

Honestly, it took my breath away when I saw her. She had on a kind of yellow thing over her night clothes and looked so pretty. Her feet were so pretty in those slippers. You almost expected her to be carrying one of those animals that kids like — she looked young enough. I know I oughtn't to have gone into the house. But we didn't think anything about it — we were just glad to see each other. We hadn't had any sort of chance to talk over the game.

We sat in front of the fire in the living room and she went out to the kitchen and got us cookies and milk. I wasn't really hungry, but it was like that time at the house, eating with her. Mr. and Mrs. Sharon were at the country club, too, so we weren't disturbing them or anything. We turned off the lights because there was plenty of light from the fire and Mr. Sharon's one of those people who can't stand having extra lights burning. Dad's that way about saving string.

It was quiet and lovely and the firelight made shadows on the ceiling. We talked a lot and then we just sat, each of us knowing the other was there. And the room got quieter and quieter and I'd told her about the game and I didn't feel excited or jumpy any more — just rested and happy. And then I knew by her breathing that she was asleep and I put my arms around her for just a minute. Because it was wonderful to hear that quiet breathing and know it was hers. I was going to wake her in a minute. I didn't realize how tired I was myself.

And then we were back in that house in the country and it was our home and we ought to have been happy. But something was wrong because there still wasn't any glass in the windows and a wind kept blowing through them and we tried to shut the doors but they wouldn't shut. It drove Helen to distraction and we were both running through the house, trying to shut the doors, and we were cold and afraid. Then the sun rose outside the windows, burning and yellow and so big it covered the sky. And with the sun was a horrible, weeping voice. It was Mrs. Sharon's saying, "Oh, my God, oh my God."

I didn't know what had happened, for a minute, when I woke. And then I did and it was awful. Mrs. Sharon was saying "Oh Helen — I trusted you . . ." and looking as if she were going to faint. And Mr. Sharon looked at her for a minute and his face was horrible and he said, "Bred in the bone," and she looked as if he'd hit her. Then he said to Helen —

I don't want to think of what they said. I don't want to think of any of the things they said. Mr. Sharon is a bad man. And she is a bad woman, even if she is Helen's mother. All the same, I could stand the things he said better than hers.

I don't want to think of any of it. And it is all spoiled now. Everything is spoiled. Miss Eagles saw us going to that house in the country and she said horrible things. They made Helen sick and she hasn't been back at school. There isn't any way I can see her. And if I could, it would be spoiled. We'd be thinking about the things they said.

I don't know how many of the people know, at school. But Tot Pickens passed me a note. And, that afternoon, I caught him behind his house. I'd have broken his nose if they hadn't pulled me off. I meant to. Mother cried when she heard about it and Dad took me into his room and talked to me. He said you can't lick the whole town. But I will anybody like Tot Pickens. Dad and Mother have been all right. But they say things about Helen and that's almost worse. They're for me because I'm their son. But they don't understand.

I thought I could talk to Kerry but I can't. He was nice but he looked at me such a funny way. I don't know — sort of impressed. It wasn't the way I wanted him to look. But he's been decent. He comes down almost every weekend and we play catch in the yard.

You see, I just go to school and back now. They want me to go with the gang, the way I did, but I can't do that. Not after Tot. Of course my marks are a lot better because I've got more time to study now. But it's lucky I haven't got Miss Eagles though Dad made her apologize. I couldn't recite to her.

I think Mr. Grant knows because he asked me to his house once and we had a conversation. Not about that, though I was terribly afraid he would. He showed me a lot of his old college things and the gold football he wears on his watch chain. He's got a lot of interesting things.

Then we got talking, somehow, about history and things like that and how times had changed. Why, there were kings and queens who got married younger than Helen and me. Only now we lived longer and had a lot more to learn. So it couldn't happen now. "It's civilization," he said. "And all civilization's against nature. But I suppose we've got to have it. Only sometimes it isn't easy." Well somehow or other, that made me feel less lonely. Before that I'd been feeling that I was the only person on earth who'd ever felt that way.

I'm going to Colorado, this summer, to a ranch, and next year I'll go East to school. Mr. Grant says he thinks I can make the basketball team, if I work hard enough, though it isn't as big a game in the East as it is with us. Well, I'd like to show them something. It would be some satisfaction. He says not to be too fresh at first, but I won't be that.

It's a boys' school and there aren't even women teachers. And, maybe, afterwards, I could be a professional basketball player or something, where you don't have to see women at all. Kerry says I'll get over that; but I won't. They all sound like Mrs. Sharon to me now, when they laugh.

They're going to send Helen to a convent — I found out that. Maybe they'll let me see her before she goes. But, if we do, it will be all wrong and in front of people and everybody pretending. I sort of wish they don't — though I want to, terribly. When her mother took her upstairs that night — she wasn't the same Helen. She looked at me as if she was afraid of me. And no matter what they do for us now, they can't fix that.

ACTIVITIES

"Do as I say, not as I do!" is hardly a persuasive argument. Ideally parents and teachers should be strong role models. It is through them that values and morality are passed from one generation to the next. In this story, however, it is the adults who could learn from the teenagers.

FOR DISCUSSION

A. Chuck's and Helen's love for each other is much more than a hot romance, more than a physical attraction. Their relationship promises to endure and grow—until it is spoiled by false suspicions and rumors. In what ways do Chuck and Helen want their relationship to be different from the relationship of Mr. and Mrs. Sharon?

B. Why do Chuck and Helen care so much what others think of them? How is their self-respect and respect for each other tied to their reputations?

C. Chuck and Helen often seem more mature than many of their elders. For each of the traits listed below, find at least one instance where the young couple demonstrates the trait, and find another instance where adults lack it.
1. sense of responsibility
2. self-control
3. concern for others
4. fairness
5. sense of honor/concern for reputation

CLASS ACTIVITY: What Would You Do?

Parents are people, too, and all human beings make mistakes. Helen's parents think the worst when they find her in her nightgown asleep in Chuck's arms. Their outrage is so great that Chuck cannot bring himself to report most of what they say. *"I don't want to think of what they said. I don't want to think of any of the things they said. Mr. Sharon is a bad man. And she is a bad woman, even if she is Helen's mother. All the same, I could stand the things he said better than hers."*

Our sympathy is clearly with the innocent couple. Yet for a moment put yourself in the place of the parents. They supposedly love their daughter and want the best for her. They have had difficulties in their marriage but hope she can avoid similar problems. They have set high standards for her, and they have trusted her. Then suddenly all their efforts seem to be wasted. They are quick to jump to the wrong conclusion, but considering the circumstances perhaps their reaction is understandable.

You be the parent. How would you handle the situation if you found your own teenager in such a compromising situation? Pick someone in the class to be your son or daughter, and act out the confrontation. What do you say? (You may then reverse the roles if you wish).

from
THE HEART IS A LONELY HUNTER
by Carson McCullers

T*he next selection is taken from a novel about 300 pages long. The setting is a small town in the deep South, and the main character is a young girl named Mick Kelly. In this section Mick and her friend Harry bike 15 miles out of town to picnic and swim. You may wish eventually to read the entire book to learn more about these characters and their families. Meanwhile, this incident can stand by itself.*

It has often been said that experience is the best teacher. As you read about this important day in the lives of both Mick and Harry, consider whether or not you agree. Almost without knowing what is happening, Mick and Harry get carried away and have their first sexual experience. It is over very quickly, but the effects will be long lasting. How could they have been spared the pain of this experience?

Mick split open the biscuits and put slices of fried white meat inside them. She sat down on the back steps to eat her breakfast. The morning was warm and bright. Spareribs and Sucker were playing with George in the back yard. Sucker wore his sun suit and the other two kids had taken off all their clothes except their shorts. They were scooting each other with the hose. The stream of water sparkled bright in the sun. The wind blew out sprays of it like mist and in this mist there were the colors of the rainbow. A line of clothes flapped in the wind — white sheets, Ralph's blue dress, a red blouse and nightgowns — wet and fresh and blowing out in different shapes. The day was almost like summer-time. Fuzzy little yellowjackets buzzed around the honeysuckle on the alley fence.

"Watch me hold it up over my head!" George hollered. "Watch how the water runs down."

She was too full of energy to sit still. George had filled a meal sack with dirt and hung it to a limb of the tree for a punching bag. She began to hit this. Puck! Pock! She hit it in time to the song that had been in her mind when she woke up. George had mixed a sharp rock in the dirt and it bruised her knuckles.

"Aoow! You skeeted the water right in my ear. It's busted my eardrum. I can't even hear."

"Gimme here. Let me skeet some."

Sprays of the water blew into her face, and once the kids turned the hose on her legs. She was afraid her box would get wet, so she carried it with her through the alley to the front porch. Harry was sitting on his steps reading the newspaper. She opened her box and got out the notebook. But it was hard to settle her mind on the song she wanted to write down. Harry was looking over in her direction and she could not think.

She and Harry had talked about so many things lately. Nearly every day they walked home from school together. They talked about God. Sometimes she would wake up in the night and shiver over what they had said. Harry was a Pantheist. That was a religion, the same as Baptist or Catholic or Jew. Harry believed that after you were dead and buried you changed to plants and fire and dirt and clouds and water. It took thousands of years and then finally you were a part of all the world. He said he thought that was better than being one single angel. Anyhow it was better than nothing.

Harry threw the newspaper into his hall and then came over. "It's hot like summer," he said. "And only March."

"Yeah. I wish we could go swimming."

"We would if there was any place."

"There's not any place. Except that country club pool."

"I sure would like to do something—to get out and go somewhere."

"Me too," she said, "Wait! I know one place. It's out in the country about 15 miles. It's a deep, wide creek in the woods. The Girl Scouts have a camp there in the summer-time. Mrs. Wells took me and George and Pete and Sucker swimming there one time last year."

"If you want to I can get bicycles and we can go tomorrow. I have a holiday one Sunday a month."

"We'll ride out and take a picnic dinner," Mick said.

"O.K. I'll borrow the bikes."

It was time for him to go to work. She watched him walk down the street. He swung his arms. Halfway down the block there was a bay tree with low branches. Harry took a running jump, caught a limb, and chinned himself. A happy feeling came in her because it was true they were real good friends. Also he was handsome. Tomorrow she would borrow Hazel's blue necklace and wear the silk dress. And for dinner they would take jelly sandwiches and Nehi. Maybe Harry would bring something queer, because they are orthodox Jews. She watched him until he turned the corner. It was true that he had grown to be a very good-looking fellow.

Harry in the country was different from Harry sitting on the back steps reading the newspapers and thinking about Hitler. They left early in the morning. The wheels he borrowed were the kind for boys—with a bar between the legs. They strapped the lunches and bathing-suits to the fenders and were gone before nine o'clock. The morning was hot and sunny. Within an hour they were far out of town on a red clay road. The fields were bright and green and the sharp smell of pine trees was in the air. Harry talked in a very excited way. The warm wind blew into their faces. Her mouth was very dry and she was hungry.

"See that house up on the hill there? Let's stop and get some water."

"No, we better wait. Well water gives you typhoid."

"I already had typhoid. I had pneumonia and a broken leg and an infected foot."

"I remember."

"Yeah," Mick said. "Me and Bill stayed in the front room when we had typhoid fever and Pete Wells would run past on the sidewalk holding his nose and looking up at the window. Bill was very embarrassed. All my hair came out so I was bald-headed."

"I bet we're at least ten miles from town. We've been riding an hour and a half—fast riding, too."

"I sure am thirsty," Mick said. "And hungry. What you got in that sack for lunch?"

"Cold liver pudding and chicken salad sandwiches and pie."

"That's a good picnic dinner." She was ashamed of what she had brought. "I got two hard-boiled eggs—already stuffed—with separate little packages of salt and pepper. And sandwiches — blackberry jelly with butter. Everything wrapped in oil paper. And paper napkins."

"I didn't intend for you to bring anything." Harry said. "My mother fixed lunch for both of us. I asked you out here and all. We'll come to a store soon and get cold drinks."

They rode half an hour longer before they finally came to the filling-station store. Harry propped up the bicycles and she went in ahead of him. After the bright glare the store seemed dark. The shelves were stacked with slabs of white meat, cans of oil, and sacks of meal. Flies buzzed over a big, sticky jar of loose candy on the counter.

"What kind of drinks you got?" Harry asked.

The storeman started to name them over. Mick opened the ice box and looked inside. Her hands felt good in the cold water. "I want a chocolate Nehi. You got any of them?"

"Ditto," Harry said. "Make it two."

"No, wait a minute. Here's some ice-cold beer. I want a bottle of beer if you can treat as high as that."

Harry ordered one for himself, also. He thought it was a sin for anybody under 20 to drink beer — but maybe he just suddenly wanted to be a sport. After the first swallow he made a bitter face. They sat on the steps in front of the store. Mick's legs were so tired that the muscles in them jumped. She wiped the neck of the bottle with her hand and took a long, cold pull. Across the road there was a big empty field of grass, and beyond that a fringe of pine woods. The trees were every color of green — from a bright yellow-green to a dark color that was almost black. The sky was hot blue.

"I like beer," she said. "I used to sop bread down in the drops our Dad left. I like to lick salt out of my hand while I drink. This is the second bottle to myself I've ever had."

"The first swallow was sour. But the rest tastes good."

The storeman said it was twelve miles from town. They had four more miles to go. Harry paid him and they were out in the hot sun again. Harry was talking loud and he kept laughing without any reason.

"Gosh, the beer along with this hot sun makes me dizzy. But I sure do feel good," he said.

"I can't wait to get in swimming."

There was sand in the road and they had to throw all their weight on the pedals to keep from bogging. Harry's shirt was stuck to his back with sweat.

He still kept talking. The road changed to red clay and the sand was behind them. There was a slow colored song in her mind — one Portia's brother used to play on his harp. She pedaled in time to it.

Then finally they reached the place she had been looking for. "This is it! See that sign that says PRIVATE? We got to climb the bob-wire fence and then take that path there — see!"

The woods were very quiet. Slick pine needles covered the ground. Within a few minutes they had reached the creek. The water was brown and swift. Cool. There was no sound except from the water and a breeze singing high up in the pine trees. It was like the deep, quiet woods made them timid, and they walked softly along the bank beside the creek.

"Don't it look pretty."

Harry laughed. "What makes you whisper? Listen here!" He clapped his hand over his mouth and gave a long Indian whoop that echoed back at them. "Come on. Let's jump in the water and cool off."

"Aren't you hungry?"

"O.K. Then we'll eat first. We'll eat half the lunch now and half later on when we come out."

She unwrapped the jelly sandwiches. When they were finished Harry balled the papers neatly and stuffed them into a hollow tree stump. Then he took his shorts and went down the path. She shucked off her clothes behind a bush and struggled into Hazel's bathing-suit. The suit was too small and cut her between the legs.

"You ready?" Harry hollered.

She heard a splash in the water and when she reached the bank Harry was already swimming. "Don't dive yet until I find out if there are any stumps or shallow places," he said. She just looked at his head bobbing in the water. She had never intended to dive, anyway. She couldn't even swim. She had been in swimming only a few times in her life — and then she always wore water-wings or stayed out of parts that were over her head. But it would be sissy to tell Harry. She was embarrassed. All of a sudden she told a tale:

"I don't dive anymore. I used to dive, high dive, all the time. But once I busted my head open, so I can't dive any more." She thought for a minute. "It was a double jack-knife dive I was doing. And when I came up there was blood all in the water. But I didn't think anything about it and just began to do swimming tricks. These people were hollering at me. Then I found out where all this blood in the water was coming from. And I never have swam good since."

Harry scrambled up the bank. "Gosh! I never heard about that."

She meant to add on to the tale to make it sound more reasonable, but instead she just looked at Harry. His skin was light brown and the water made it shining. There were hairs on his chest and legs. In the tight trunks he seemed very naked. Without his glasses his face was wider and more handsome. His eyes were wet and blue. He was looking at her and it was like suddenly they got embarrassed.

"The water's about ten feet deep except over on the other bank, and there it's shallow."

"Let's get going. I bet that cold water feels good."

She wasn't scared. She felt the same as if she had got caught at the top of a very high tree and there was nothing to do but just climb down the best way she could—a dead-calm feeling. She edged off the bank and was in ice-cold water. She held to a root until it broke in her hands and then she began to swim. Once she choked and went under, but she kept going and didn't lose any face. She swam and reached the other side of the bank where she could touch bottom. Then she felt good. She smacked the water with her fists and called out crazy words to make echoes.

"Watch here!"

Harry shimmied up a tall, thin little tree. The trunk was limber and when he reached the top it swayed down with him. He dropped into the water.

"Me too! Watch me do it!"

"That's a sapling."

She was as good a climber as anybody on the block. She copied exactly what he had done and hit the water with a hard smack. She could swim, too. Now she could swim O.K.

They played follow the leader and ran up and down the bank and jumped in the cold brown water. They hollered and jumped and climbed. They played around for maybe two hours. Then they were standing on the bank and they both looked at each other and there didn't seem to be anything new to do. Suddenly she said:

"Have you ever swam naked?"

The woods was very quiet and for a minute he did not answer. He was cold. His titties had turned hard and purple. His lips were purple and his teeth chattered. "I—I don't think so."

This excitement was in her, and she said something she didn't mean to say. "I would if you would. I dare you to."

Harry slicked back the dark, wet bangs of his hair. "O.K."

They both took off their bathing-suits. Harry had his back to her. He stumbled and his ears were red. Then they turned toward each other. Maybe it was half an hour they stood there — maybe not more than a minute.

Harry pulled a leaf from a tree and tore it to pieces. "We better get dressed."

All through the picnic dinner neither of them spoke. They spread the dinner on the ground. Harry divided everything in half. There was the hot, sleepy feeling of a summer afternoon. In the deep woods they could hear no sound except the slow flowing of the water and the song-birds. Harry held his stuffed egg and mashed the yellow with his thumb. What did that make her remember? She heard herself breathe.

Then he looked up over her shoulder. "Listen here. I think you're so pretty, Mick. I never did think so before. I don't mean I thought you were very ugly — I just mean that — "

She threw a pine cone in the water. "Maybe we better start back if we want to be home before dark."

"No," he said. "Let's lie down. Just for a minute."

He brought handfuls of pine needles and leaves and gray moss. She sucked her knee and watched him. Her fists were tight and it was like she was tense all over.

"Now we can sleep and be fresh for the trip home."

They lay on the soft bed and looked up at the dark-green pine clumps against the sky. A bird sang a sad, clear song she had never heard before. One high note like an oboe — and then it sank down five tones and called again. The song was sad as a question without words.

"I love that bird," Harry said. "I think it's a vireo."

"I wish we was at the ocean. On the beach and watching the ships far out on the water. You went to the beach one summer — exactly what is it like?"

His voice was rough and low. "Well — there are the waves. Sometimes blue and sometimes green, and in the bright sun they look glassy. And on the sand you can pick up these little shells. Like the kind we brought back in a cigar box. And over the water are these white gulls. We were at the Gulf of Mexico — these cool bay breezes blew all the time and there it's never bakin' hot like it is here. Always — "

"Snow," Mick said. "That's what I want to see. Cold, white drifts of snow like in pictures. Blizzards. White, cold snow that keeps falling soft and falls on and on and on through all the winter. Snow like in Alaska."

They both turned at the same time. They were close against each other. She felt him trembling and her fists were tight enough to crack. "Oh God," he kept saying over and over. It was like her head was broke off from her body and thrown away. And her eyes looked up straight into the blinding sun while she counted something in her mind. And then this was the way.

This was how it was.

They pushed the wheels slowly along the road. Harry's head hung down and his shoulders were bent. Their shadows were long and black on the dusty road, for it was late afternoon.

"Listen here," he said.

"Yeah"

"We got to understand this. We got to. Do you—any?"

"I don't know. I reckon not."

"Listen here. We got to do something. Let's sit down."

They dropped the bicycles and sat by a ditch beside the road. They sat far apart from each other. The late sun burned down on their heads and there were brown, crumbly ant beds all around them.

"We got to understand this," Harry said.

He cried. He sat very still and the tears rolled down his white face. She could not think about the thing that made him cry. An ant stung her on the ankle and she picked it up in her fingers and looked at it very close.

"It's this way," he said. "I never had even kissed a girl before."

"Me neither. I never kissed any boy. Out of the family."

"That's all I used to think about—was to kiss this certain girl. I used to plan about it during school and dream about it at night. And then once she gave me a date. And I could tell she meant for me to kiss her. And I just looked at her in the dark and I couldn't. That was all I had thought about— to kiss her—and when the time came I couldn't."

She dug a hole in the ground with her finger and buried the dead ant. "It was all my fault. Adultery is a terrible sin any way you look at it. And you were two years younger than me and just a kid."

"No, I wasn't. I wasn't any kid. But now I wish I was, though."

"Listen here. If you think we ought to we can get married—secretly or any other way."

Mick shook her head. "I didn't like that. I never will marry with any boy."

"I never will marry either. I know that. And I'm not just saying so — it's true."

His face scared her. His nose quivered and his bottom lip was mottled and bloody where he had bitten it. His eyes were bright and wet and scowling. His face was whiter than any face she could remember. She turned her head from him. Things would be better if only he would just quit talking. Her eyes looked slowly around her — at the streaked red-and-white clay of the ditch, at a broken whiskey bottle, at a pine tree across from them with a sign advertising for a man for county sheriff. She wanted to sit quiet for a long time and not think and not say a word.

"I'm leaving town. I'm a good mechanic and I can get a job some other place. If I stayed home Mother could read this in my eyes."

"Tell me. Can you look at me and see the difference?"

Harry watched her face a long time and nodded that he could. Then he said:

"There's just one more thing. In a month or two I'll send you my address and you write and tell me for sure whether you're all right."

"How you mean?" she asked slowly.

He explained to her. "All you need to write is 'O.K.' and then I'll know."

They were walking home again, pushing the wheels. Their shadows stretched out giant-sized on the road. Harry was bent over like an old beggar and kept wiping his nose on his sleeve. For a minute there was a bright, golden glow over everything before the sun sank down behind the trees and their shadows were gone on the road before them. She felt very old, and it was like something was heavy inside her. She was a grown person now, whether she wanted to be or not.

They had walked the sixteen miles and were in the dark alley at home. She could see the yellow light from their kitchen. Harry's house was dark — his mother had not come home. She worked for a tailor in a shop on a side street. Sometimes even on Sunday. When you looked through the window you could see her bending over the machine in the back or pushing a long needle through the heavy pieces of goods. She never looked up while you watched her. And at night she cooked these orthodox dishes for Harry and her.

"Listen here —" he said.

She waited in the dark, but he did not finish. They shook hands with each other and Harry walked up the dark alley between the houses. When he reached the sidewalk he turned and looked back over his shoulder. A light shone on his face and it was white and hard. Then he was gone.

"This here is a riddle," George said.

"I'm listening."

"Two Indians was walking on a trail. The one in front was the son of the one behind but the one behind was not his father. What kin was they?"

"Let's see. His Stepfather."

George grinned at Portia with his little square, blue teeth.

"His uncle, then."

"You can't guess. It was his mother. The trick is that you don't think about a Indian being a lady."

She stood outside the room and watched them. The doorway framed the kitchen like a picture. Inside it was homey and clean. Only the light by the sink was turned on and there were shadows in the room. Bill and Hazel played black-jack at the table with matches for money. Hazel felt the braids of her hair with her plump, pink fingers while Bill sucked in his cheeks and dealt the cards in a very serious way. At the sink Portia was drying the dishes with a clean checked towel. She looked thin and her skin was golden yellow, her greased black hair slicked neat. Ralph sat quietly on the floor and George was tying a little harness on him made out of old Christmas tinsel.

"This here is another riddle, Portia. If the hand of a clock points to half-past two—"

She went into the room. It was like she had expected them to move back when they saw her and stand around in a circle and look. But they just glanced at her. She sat down at the table and waited.

"Here you come traipsing in after everybody done finished supper. Seem to me like I never will get off from work."

Nobody noticed her. She ate a big plateful of cabbage and salmon and finished off with a junket. It was her Mama she was thinking about. The door opened and her Mama came in and told Portia that Miss Brown had said she found a bedbug in her room. To get out the gasoline.

"Quit frowning like that, Mick. You're coming to the age where you ought to fix up and try to look the best you can. And hold on—don't barge out like that when I speak with you—I mean you to give Ralph a good sponge bath before he goes to bed. Clean his nose and ears good."

Ralph's soft hair was sticky with oatmeal. She wiped it with a dishrag and rinsed his face and hands at the sink. Bill and Hazel finished their game. Bill's long fingernails scraped on the table as he took up the matches. George carried Ralph off to bed. She and Portia were alone in the kitchen.

"Listen! Look at me. Do you notice anything different?"

"Sure I notice, Hon."

Portia put on her red hat and changed her shoes.

"Well—?"

"Just you take a little grease and rub it on your face. Your nose already done peeled very bad. They say grease is the best thing for bad sunburn."

She stood by herself in the dark back yard, breaking off pieces of bark from the oak tree with her fingernails. It was almost worse this way. Maybe she would feel better if they could look at her and tell. If they knew.

Her Dad called her from the back steps. "Mick! Oh, Mick!"

"Yes, sir."

"The telephone."

George crowded up close and tried to listen in, but she pushed him away. Mrs. Minowitz talked very loud and excited.

"My Harry should be home by now. You know where he is?"

"No, ma'am."

"He said you two would ride out on bicycles. Where could he be now? You know where he is?"

"No, ma'am," Mick said again.

ACTIVITIES

FOR DISCUSSION

Their sexual encounter has a dramatic effect on both Mick and Harry. It happens suddenly, unexpectedly, and almost innocently. But clearly they are not ready for such an experience, and they pay a heavy price. This first sexual experience is hardly what one dreams it should be.

Compare the feelings of Mick and Harry as they set out on their trip in the morning with the feelings they have later that same afternoon. Can you add to the following list of emotions?

MORNING (INNOCENCE):

A. ENERGY - It is a glorious day, and the young friends are alert to all its beauty, to the sights, sounds, and smells of spring. They are so full of life that both Mick and Harry have a hard time sitting still.

B. JOY - Their close friendship is a source of real happiness. They trust each other and enjoy sharing ideas and experiences.

C. CURIOSITY- Their world is a wondrous place, and they want to know all about life and death. They want to experience mysterious, adult things. There are new feelings in their changing bodies, and they want to investigate.

AFTERNOON (EXPERIENCE):

A. PAIN - Tears roll down Harry's cheeks, and Mick cannot bring herself to think about what has happened.

B. REGRET - Neither Mick nor Harry had even kissed a member of the opposite sex before. Now they both know they have made a mistake, but there is no way they can take it back.

C. FEAR -They worry about the possibility of pregnancy, and they also worry that people will be able to see the change in them.

D. CONFUSION - The sexual attraction Mick and Harry felt earlier has switched to a feeling of revulsion. They have experienced very conflicting feelings. At this point there is no way they can think of sex as something beautiful between people who love each other in a mature and responsible way. Both Mick and Harry vow never to marry.

E. DEPRESSION - Their carefree playfulness is gone as is their enthusiasm for life. The world weighs heavily on their shoulders, and they feel tired and old.

Identify the following quotations. Tell where each occurs in the story and what it shows about Mick and Harry. Where does it fit into the range of emotions listed above?

1. *"I think you're so pretty, Mick. I never did think so before. I don't mean I thought you were very ugly—I just mean that—"*

2. *"She was a grown person now, whether she wanted to be or not."*

3. *"Harry took a running jump, caught a limb, and chinned himself."*

4. *"Listen! Look at me. Do you notice anything different?"*

5. *"Nearly every day they walked home from school together. They talked about God. Sometimes she would wake up in the night and shiver over what they had said."*

6. *"Then they turned toward each other. Maybe it was half an hour they stood there—maybe not more than a minute."*

7. *"His nose quivered and his bottom lip was mottled and bloody where he had bitten it."*

8. *"It was like her head was broke off from her body and thrown away."*

9. *"Harry was talking loud and he kept laughing without any reason."*

10. *This excitement was in her, and she said something she didn't mean to say, "I would if you would. I dare you to."*

CLASS ACTIVITY: Stop, Look, and . . . Think!

If Mick and Harry had stopped to think and talk about their actions, they probably would have avoided later regrets. But circumstances work against them. The beauty of the day heightens their awareness of sensual pleasures. They are far from town and alone. The beer makes them feel good and weakens their self-control. Their changing bodies give them strong new messages.

Make a list of questions they could have asked themselves to judge their readiness for such intimate involvement. How might they have avoided such a painful lesson? What circumstances would have to change to make the experience a happy one?

READING CHALLENGE

The ideas in the following paragraph are complex. With the help of your teacher, study the paragraph sentence by sentence. What does Walter Lippmann say is the difference between sexual intimacy as an expression of mature love and sexual intimacy as simply an outlet for physical desire?

"When a man and woman are successfully in love, their whole activity is energized and victorious. They walk better, their digestion improves, they think more clearly, their secret worries drop away, the world is fresh

and interesting, and they can do more than they dreamed that they could do. In love of this kind, sexual intimacy is not the dead end of desire as it is in romantic or promiscuous love, but periodic affirmation of the inward delight of desire pervading an active life. Love of this sort can grow: it is not, like youth itself, a moment that comes and is gone and remains only a memory of something which cannot be recovered. It can grow because it has something to grow upon and to grow with; it is not contracted and stale because it has for its object, not the mere relief of physical tension, but all the object with which the two lovers are concerned. They desire their worlds in each other, and therefore their love is as interesting as their worlds and their worlds are as interesting as their love." (From *Preface to Morals* by Walter Lippmann)

For homework, double check your understanding by seeing how well you can explain the paragraph to an adult. Then have each adult select a phrase he or she finds most meaningful. When you come back together as a class compare the adults' selections.

UP ON FONG MOUNTAIN

by Norma Fox Mazer

TO: All Students Taking English 10
MEMO FROM: Carol Durmacher
DATE: February 3

"That favorite subject, Myself." —James Boswell

Your term project will be to keep a weekly Journal. Purchase a 7 3/4 x 5-inch ruled, wire-bound notebook. (Woolworth's at the Mall stocks them, so does Ready's Stationers on East Avenue.) Date each entry. Note the day, also. Make a minimum of two entries a week. The Journal must be kept to the end of the school year. It is to be handed in June 24.

I will not read these Journals—only note that they have been kept faithfully. There will be two marks for this project—Pass and Fail. Only those students not handing in a Journal or blatantly disregarding the few rules I have set down will receive a Fail.

In writing in your Journal, try to be as free as possible. This is your Journal: express yourself. Use the language that comes naturally to you. Express your true feelings without reservation. Remember, I will not read what you have written (unless you ask me to). Once I record your mark I will hand the Journal back to you. (You may be present while I check to see that the Journal has been kept in the required manner.)

These Journals are for YOU. To introduce you to the joy of record-keeping. To help you think about your lives, the small events, the little graces, the funny, sad, or joyful moments. Record these as simply and directly as possible.

A moment recorded is a moment forever saved.

February 6, Thursday

I don't know what to write really. I have never kept a journal before. Well, I better write something. I have to do this two times in the next three days. Miss Durmacher, you said, write your true feelings. My true feelings are that I actually have nothing to write. Well, I'll describe myself. My name is Jessie Granatstein. I'm fifteen years old. My coloring is sandy (I think you would call it that). I ought to lose ten pounds. My eyes are brown. I have thick eyebrows that my sister Anita says I ought to pluck. My father says I'm stubborn as a bulldog. He said that last week when we fought over the Sunday paper. I was up first and started to read it, then he got up and took it away from me. He says he ought to get it first, the whole paper, every section, because he's the father, the head of the household, and that I should learn to wait patiently. We argued for an hour. He didn't change my mind and I didn't change his. He got the paper first.

February 8, Saturday

Anita and I made a huge bowl of popcorn tonight, then ate it watching TV. Then we were still hungry, so we made a pot of spaghetti, slathered it with butter, and ate it straight from the pot. We had a good time till Mark came over, then Anita acted like I didn't exist.

February 12, Wednesday

Lincoln's birthday, also my parent's anniversary. Mom made a rib roast, baked Idaho potatoes with sour cream and chives, frozen corn on the cob, and strawberry shortcake with real whipped cream for topping. I stuffed myself like a pig. It half rained, half snowed all day. Why would anyone want to get married on Feb. 12, in the middle of winter? Mom just laughs when I ask her, and looks at Dad. "Sex rears its ugly head," I whispered to Anita. "Don't be vulgar," she said.

February 14, Friday

I don't have anything to write. I'm sorry, Miss Durmacher, but all I seem to be writing about is food. I had tuna fish with celery and mayo for lunch, plus two ice cream sandwiches which I should have resisted. Mom says not to worry about my weight, that I'm "appealing." She's nice.

February 18, Tuesday

Yesterday I was talking to Anita and we got called to supper right in the middle of a sentence. "Girls!" That's my father, he won't eat till we're all at the table, and he's hungry when he sits down, so he doesn't want to wait very long for us. Like, not one extra second.

But, anyway, that wasn't what I was going to write about today. I was going to write about Brian Marchant — Brian Douglas Marchant III. Kids call him BD. I'm pretty sure he was watching me in geometry class today. Fairly sure, although not positive. What I am positive of is that I was watching him. In fact — well, I'm not going to write any more about it. I thought I wanted to, but I take it back. And that's all I have to say today.

Feb. 21, Fri.

Well, Miss D., it's a Friday, it's winter, I feel sort of depressed. I wish I had someone I could really talk to. It snowed again today. I've always loved snow, loved to see it caked in big thick white clumps on all the trees when it first falls, loved to jump around in it. Today, for the first time ever I didn't like it. I hated it. And that depressed me even more.

And to tell you the truth, Miss D., while we're on depressing subjects, I just can't believe this journal. Almost three more months of my real thoughts and feelings — that's depressing!

Monday, February 24

Brian Marchant borrowed paper from me, and winked at me. I have always hated winking boys.

Feb 28, last day of the month, Friday

BD winked at me again.

I said, "Why are you winking at me?"

"What do you mean? I'm winking at you because I feel like winking at you."

"Don't," I said.

"Don't?" He looked at me in astonishment and amazement. I mean it, Miss Durmacher, like nobody ever said don't to him before.

"I think winking is dumb," I said.

He stared at me some more. Then he gave me a double wink.

March 3, Monday

I saw BD in the cafeteria today. I said, "Hi." He said, "Hi." I said, "Have you given up winking?" He said, "What?" Then he laughed. He has a nice big laugh.

Tues. Mar. 4

BD and I ate lunch together today. No winking.

Thursday, March 6

Lunch again with BD. I forgot to bring mine and didn't have any money with me, either. BD brings enormous lunches. Two peanut butter and jelly sandwiches, one tuna fish with pickle relish, one salami with cheese, three Hostess Twinkies, one bag of chips, an apple, an orange, a banana, plus he bought three cartons of milk and two ice cream sandwiches. And parted reluctantly with one of the pbj's for me. Also, he bigheartedly gave me half his apple.

And that makes three entries for this week, Miss Durmacher. Not bad, huh?

Tuesday, March 11

BD walked home with me and came in for cocoa. Then we went outside and he looked up at the fignut tree in the backyard which is almost the tallest tree around. "I think I could climb that, Jess," he said.

"Don't BD," I said.

"Why not? I like to climb trees."

"I don't like heights, and it might be slippery."

"You don't have to climb it," he said. And up he went. I could hardly bear to look. All I could think of was, he's going to fall. He's going to fall and crack his head.

When he got nearly to the top he yelled, "Jess-eee! Jess-eee!" I yelled back, "I hear you, Beee-Deee!" Then he came down, laughing all the way.

Wednesday, March 12

Anita said she thought BD was funny-looking. I said I didn't think he was funnier-looking than most human beings. She said, "You have to admit he's, one, shorter than you, and two, has got big pop eyes. Green pop eyes, like a frog. Also, a big mouth which looks like he could swallow your whole face when he kisses you."

"How do you know he kisses me, Anita?"

"Well, sister, I hope he kisses you! At your age, you're not going to tell me you're sweet fifteen and never been kissed! I had boys running after me and kissing me since I was nine years old!" She laughed merrily.

Are you reading this, Miss Durmacher? Don't, please. The truth is, I have only been kissed a few times — well, not even a few, three to be exact — at parties. But I'm not going to tell Anita that.

March 21, Friday

Anita doesn't stop making cracks about BD's looks. I just don't understand it. Her boyfriend, Mark Maloff, is supposed to be super-good-looking, but I really can't stand him. He wears pink ties and has a little green ring on his left hand. It's true BD looks as if he never thinks about what he's wearing. Nothing ever matches. But something about him really pleases me. Maybe it's the way he walks around with his hands stuck in his back pockets, sort of jaunty and jolly and swaggering. (The other day he was wearing one green sock and one dark blue. When I pointed it out to him, he said, "Really?" and looked down at his feet very interested. Then he said that his eyes were never really open in the morning, not til about ten o'clock, and by then, for better or worse, he was dressed.)

Saturday night, March 22

Miss Durmacher, don't read this — you said you wouldn't. I love kissing BD. I love it!

Wednesday, March 26

Mom thinks she and I are alike. She's always saying it. (She thinks Dad and Anita are alike, and she says they are both very good-looking. True. While she and I are both chunky and sandy-haired.) But Mom doesn't say boo to Dad, she's always very sweet to him. (Actually she's sort of sweet to everybody.) I'm not like her in that way AT ALL. I'M NOT SWEET. In that regard, I'm more like my father than Anita is. I became aware of this because of BD. I have been noticing that he likes things his own way. Most of the time he gets it. I have noticed, too, that I don't feel sweet about this at all!

March 29, Sat. afternoon

BD came over last night and said we were going bowling. I said why didn't we do something else, as we went bowling last week. He said he liked bowling and what else was there to do, anyway? I said we could go roller skating. BD laughed a lot. I said what's the problem with roller skating. I like roller skating. (Which I do.) BD said, "Jessie, why are you being so picky? Why are you being hard to get along with?" I thought, Right! Why am I?

And we went bowling. And then, later, I realized, just like that, he had talked me out of what I wanted to do and into what he wanted to do.

Monday, March 31, last day of the month

I don't even mind writing in here anymore, Miss Durmacher. I have plenty to write all the time. Now, lately, I've been thinking about what you wrote at the top of our assignment sheet. That favorite subject, Myself. Everyone got a laugh out of that when we first read it. Who wants to admit they are their own best, most favorite topic of conversation?

But I think it's the truth. Last night, at supper, Dad was talking, and I noticed how I was pretty much waiting to get my own two cents in. It seems Anita was, too, because she actually beat me to the punch. The only one who didn't rush to talk about herself was Mom, and sometimes I think that's just from long years of practice listening to Dad.

Also, today, I noticed when BD and I were hanging around school that he is another one whose most favorite subject is — myself. That is — HIMself. The thing is, I really like to listen to him go on because, mainly, I like him. But if he never wants to listen to me, after a while, I get this horrible lonely feeling. I think that's it. A lonely feeling. Sad.

April 2, Tuesday, no I mean, Wednesday

A dumb fight with BD today. He came home from school with me and not for the first time got going on his ancestors who came over here about 200 years ago. Pioneers, he said with a big happy delighted smile. As if because they got on a boat about 150 years earlier than my family this made them really special. So I said, "Well, BD, I think there's another word for your ancestors. Thieves."

"Thieves!" His cheeks puffed up.

"They stole Indian land, didn't they?" (I have just become aware of this lately from Mr. Happy's American History class.)

BD whipped out his map of the Northeast from his pocket and stabbed his finger about a dozen places all over Maine and Vermont. "Here's Marchantville, Jessie. Marchant River. Marchant's Corners. East Marchant, West Marchant, and Marchant's Falls!" He looked at me very triumphantly.

"BD," I said, "I've seen all that before." Which indeed, I have. In fact, the first time I realized BD actually carried the map around with him, I burst out laughing. And at the time he didn't take too kindly to that. But this time, I made him truly furious.

"You think thieves were the founders of all these places, Jessie? You think that's why all these rivers and towns were named after the Marchants? They were pioneers, Jess—" And he got that fanatical happy look on his face again at the mere sound of the word. "Pioneers, people who had the intelligence and foresight to go to the new country, the unexplored territory, the virgin lands—"

"Now listen, BD," I said, and I had to talk loud to slow him down. "Suppose a boatload of people came over here tomorrow from China and landed smack in the middle of our town, and pushed us all out—"

"The boat's in the middle of our town?" BD said.

"You know what I mean! The people, BD. The people from across the ocean. And they say to us, 'From now on, we're going to call this Fong City after our leader, Mao Tze Fong, and this river here, this is going to be Fong River, and over here we've got Fong Mountain—'"

"Jessie, that's dumb," BD yelled. "That's inaccurate, the comparison just won't work—"

Well I can yell, too. "Like I was saying, BD, although we don't know it, the Chinese have developed this ray gun. Instant death. Superior to anything we have. Okay? Now—"

"No, it's not okay. We've got atomic weapons, we've got sophisticated weapons, an army, police—"

"So here comes Mao Tze Fong," I went on, "and all the others with him and they've got these ray guns which we can't do anything against. They kill off a bunch of us, take over our houses and land, and the rest of us run to hide in the mountains—"

"Fong Mountain, I presume?" BD said.

"Right! We're up on Fong Mountain. From there we survivors would try to get our homes back, but after quite a few years of battling, the invaders would beat us enough so we'd have to agree to anything they said. Because, remember, we have just a few old hunting rifles against their ray guns. Then, after a while, they would let us have some land they didn't care about, some swamps and stuff, and they'd stick us all on it and call it a reservation. And meanwhile, meanwhile — BD, are you listening? — they'd have been wiping out all the old maps and making new ones. With Fong Mountain, East Fong, West Fong, Fong's Corners, and fongoo, BD, if you don't want to understand the point of what I'm saying!"

April 3, Thursday

In geometry class today: "How's your revered ancestors, BD?"

"How're things up on Fong Mountain, Jessie?"

April 6, Sunday

I talked to BD on the phone. We were peaceful. That's good. Because we have been fighting a good bit lately.

April 12, Saturday

Mom came into my room with a sweater she'd washed for me. "Oh, by the way, honey," she said (which is always the signal that she's going to be serious), "aren't you and Brian seeing an awful lot of each other?"

"Me and BD?" I said, sort of stalling for time.

"Yes. You saw him every single night this week. Do you think that's wise?"

"Wise?"

"I don't want you to be in a terrible hurry like I was."

"Terrible hurry?"

"To grow up," she said.

"Grow up?"

"Jessie! Do you have to repeat everything I say?" She flashed me a funny little smile. "When two people see a lot of each other, it's not always so wise. They might get too — they might get carried away."

"Oh," I said. "You don't have to worry, Mom. No one is going to carry me away."

Tuesday, April 15

Thinking about me and BD. At this point in my life, the way I feel is — my body is my body. And I don't care to share it with anyone. I don't know totally why I feel that way, and I don't think I have to know why. It's just the way I feel. Sometimes in the morning I look at myself in the mirror and I feel proud. I look myself over and I think, Hey, yeah, Jessie, that's your body. Terrific!

Sunday, April 20

A fight with BD last night. Please don't read this Miss Durmacher! It's private and personal. We were parked in the cemetery. BD said I was being mean. He said I was being selfish, and also unfair. I didn't know what to say in return, so I just got mad. I said, I'm going home! I wanted to get out of the car and walk but he wouldn't let me. He started the car and drove me home. I was furious. He won't even let me get mad in my own way.

Monday, April 21

Miss Durmacher, you didn't say how long or short the entries had to be. I'll describe the weather today. Sleaty gray air and the smell of garbage everywhere.

Tuesday, April 22

Today, in school, I saw BD in the halls, and I saw him in geometry class, and I saw him in the cafeteria. We looked at each other. He didn't say anything, and I didn't say anything.

After school I started home. After a few blocks I felt someone was following me. I turned around. There was BD behind me. I started walking again. Then I turned around. He was right behind me. He grabbed me in a big hug, knocking my books every which way and said, "Kiss! Kiss!" I was sort of shocked, but I couldn't help kissing him back. And then he laughed and laughed.

Wednesday, April 30

Today I tried to talk to BD. He says it's my fault we fight so much. He says I pick the fights, that I'm aggressive, he's peaceful. This might be true. He is peaceful when he gets his way. He said I didn't know how to give in gracefully. He might be right about this, too. I hate to lose a game or an argument. He says I'm a prickly character. He's started calling me Porky, short for porcupine.

Sunday, May 4

Last night BD and I parked down by the river. Cars were lined up for a mile, all of them dark, all of them looked empty. Ha-ha. I told BD I felt like I'm part of a factory production make-out line. BD just laughed. He always laughs when he doesn't want to answer. Anyway, he was getting down to business. He's been doing that lately—and we've been fighting about it. A standoff, so far.

"BD, let's kiss," I said. I really like kissing that boy.

"Sure," he said, but he didn't stop what he was doing.

So I said, "Quit that, BD, you're getting friendlier than I want you to be."

"Oh, don't you like that?" he said, sort of sweet and surprised. "It feels nice. You are so nice and soft, Jessie. I bet your sister and Mark do this—"

I gave him a little shove. "What's it to you what Anita and Mark do? That sounds sick to me."

"Porky," he said.

"Don't call me Porky," I said. "I don't like it."

"Seems like there are a lot of things you don't like, Jessie," he said. "Don't you trust me?"

"I don't see what that's got to do with anything, BD," I said. "But come to think of it—if I gave you $100 to keep for me, I guess you wouldn't spend it, but what if I gave you one thousand?"

"Jessie, that's silly, you don't have a thousand dollars."

"Answer the question BD," I said. "If I gave you one thousand dollars to keep for me, and then I went away, would you spend my thousand dollars?"

"No, I wouldn't Jessie. I wouldn't spend one single penny of your money."

"What if I gave you that thousand dollars and then I didn't come back for ten years? What if you were told, by someone you knew was trustable, that I was dead. Would you spend my money?"

"Jessie, is this going to be another Fong Mountain," BD said. "Let's get back to the subject. I said you could trust me, and I meant it. I'll be careful."

"Careful. What does that mean?"

"Well, you know, I won't, uh, hurt you—"

"Hurt me?"

"Well, you know, maybe you're afraid of—"

"I'm not afraid, BD."

"If you're not afraid, then why won't you—?"

"Not being afraid isn't a reason to do something. Just because you're not afraid of heights doesn't mean you're going to take a walk along the edge of the Empire State Building."

"I'm not talking about the Empire State Building, Jessie," he said in his patient voice.

"I know what you're talking about, BD," I said, and suddenly I had the feeling that I was up there on Fong Mountain again. And I was all alone. And I thought, Oh! I wish I had someone to talk to.

Saturday, May 10

I have kind of a problem here. What I want to write about is BD and me, but I keep thinking you'll read this, Miss Durmacher. Your eyes might just slip and catch this or that. And if they do, you're going to just keep reading. That's human nature. So this is going to be my second entry for the week.

Friday, May 16

Oh, BD, you mix me up . . . I love you . . . but . . .

Friday, May 23

BD came over last night. I thought we could just walk around, buy ice cream, and maybe talk. Be restful with each other. It was a nice night, warm, and I didn't feel like doing anything special. Also, BD couldn't get the car, which was a relief to me because we wouldn't have to park and then fight over me.

But the minute we set foot on the sidewalk, BD said, "We're going to the movies," and he starts walking fast, getting ahead of me, like he wanted me to have to run to catch up with him.

So I just kept walking along at my usual pace, and I said to his back, "How do you know that's what I want to do?"

"There's a new movie at the Cinema," he said. "You'll like it."

"How do you know that?"

He turned around, gave me one of his smiles. He really has the nicest smile in the world! But he used it unfairly. "Oh, listen, Jessie, if I like it, you'll like it. Right?"

"Wrong!" I yelled.

"Say it again, Porky. They couldn't hear you in Rochester."

"Very funny, BD. And I told you not to call me Porky!"

"Why don't you smile more? When you frown like that it makes you look like a teacher."

"What's wrong with teachers?" I said.

"Who said anything was wrong with teachers. Don't change the subject, Jessie."

"BD, you said if I frowned that made me look like a teacher. You meant ugly!"

"I didn't mean anything of the sort," he said. "I was just talking, just using a metaphor."

I knew he thought he had me there, but Miss Durmacher you had just reviewed all this stuff. "You mean a simile," I said. "The moon is a balloon is a metaphor. The moon looks like a balloon is a simile."

"Don't act smartass! Come on, walk faster, or we'll miss the opening of the movie."

"What movie?"

"The movie we are going to see." BD wasn't smiling now. Neither was I.

"I don't believe I'm going to any movie," I said. "I haven't made up my mind what I want to do tonight. Nobody asked me what I wanted to do, only told me what they wanted to do."

"They," BD said. "There's only one of me."

"Oh, BD," I said, "no, you're a whole government. You're president, vice-president, and secretary of defense all rolled into one."

"What are you talking about?"

"You know what I'm talking about, BD. How you always have to be Top Banana. The Big Cheese. Always telling me. You're a regular Mao Tze Fong! We're going to do this, we're going to do that, we're going here, we're eating this—don't you think I have a mind of my own? You want your own way all the time. You never ask me anything. You just barrel on ahead. You want to lead me around by the nose!"

"You're being difficult tonight," he said. He was smiling. Only not his usual, regular beautiful smile, more of a toothy mean smile, as if he would like to really bite off my arm instead of talking to me. "You've been difficult just about every time we see each other lately. Now, do you want to see that movie, or don't you?"

"I don't care about the movie," I said. "What I care about is that I have a mind of my own, I am a free person also, and I don't want to be in any dictatorship relationship!"

"Dictatorship relationship," he said. And he laughed. Hee-hee-hee. "You mean a dictatorial relationship. Dictatorial, not dictatorship."

I stared at him. Then I turned around and walked in the other direction. And he didn't come after me, and I didn't go back after him.

Wednesday, May 28

I guess everything really is over with BD and me. We really have broken up. I never would have thought it—breaking up over grammar, not sex.

June 2, Monday

I know I missed making a couple of entries, Miss Durmacher, but I was sort of upset. I'll make some extra ones to make up for it. Anita has a job after school at the telephone company. Mom has been going over every day to help Aunt Peggy, who just had her fifth baby. I don't have anything to do except hang around the house, feeling crummy.

June 4, Wednesday

Sometimes, thinking about BD, which I can't help doing a lot, I think I was the biggest fool in the world, because it's true I never loved a boy the way I loved BD. Then I go over everything in my mind, and I don't see what else I could have done.

June 5, Thursday

Why should I miss someone who all I could do was fight with, anyway.

Friday, June 6

I'm sick of hanging around the house, I'm sick of thinking about BD. Two whole weeks is enough. I'm going to get a job.

Saturday, June 7

Everyone at every place I go says, "Leave your name, we'll call you." Or else, "Fill out this application." Then they ask you a hundred questions about your whole life for a job which they don't mean to give you, anyway.

Sunday, June 8

I got a job!

It happened just by accident, this way. Yesterday, I was really discouraged after spending the whole day looking for work. I stopped into Dippin DoNuts on the Blvd. I ordered coffee and a plain doughnut, and just out of habit told the lady behind the counter I was looking for work.

She looked me over. I sat up straighter. She said, "Are you prepared to start next week, and then work all summer?"

I said, "Sure!"

She looked me over again. She asked me how old I was. She asked me where I lived. She said she was Mrs. Richmondi and she owned the place. Then she said that her regular girl had gotten smashed up in a car accident the day before. She needed someone right away. I start tomorrow afternoon.

Sunday, June 15

I've worked a whole week, every day after school from four to seven. (Then Mrs. Richmondi comes in for the last three hours and to close up.) And I worked all day Saturday. I'm a bit tired today, but I like working. Yesterday morning I got up at five o'clock. Everyone was asleep. I crept around the house and let myself out as quiet as I could. The birds were racketing while I walked to work, but everything else was quiet. The streets were empty. Not even one car. And the houses all quiet. It was nice. I was never out early in the morning like that.

Monday, June 16

I have to wear a horrible uniform, orange with white trim (Mrs. Richmondi is big on orange—all the cups are orange, also the napkins), but other than that, I really like my job. Mrs. Richmondi is nice, too, but she hates bare feet. She's got a sign on the door: NO BARE FEET.

Wednesday, June 18

I see BD every day in school and we never say a word, just look at each other and then keep walking.

Mom came into Dippin DoNuts today and ordered coffee and a jelly doughnut. Then a bunch of kids came pouring in yelling orders, and before I'd really taken in who was there, I thought—BD's here! And my hands got sweaty.

Thursday, June 19

BD came into the doughnut shop today.

It was 6:30. At first I almost didn't recognize him. He was wearing a funny-looking hat that was too big for him, a gray, crumpled fedora with a wide brim like something out of a thirties gangster movie. And a red wool shirt and enormous, huge red-and-white sneakers. And he was smoking a cigarette, had it dragging from his lower lip like Humphrey Bogart or Jimmy Cagney in one of those old-time movies.

He sat down at the counter. I wiped my hands down the sides of my uniform. "Yes?" I said, just like I did to anyone who came in. "Can I help you?"

"Cupacawfee," he said, with the cigarette dangling from his mouth.

I poured him coffee into the orange mug and set it in front of him. "Would you like a doughnut with your coffee?" I said, which is the next thing I always say to regular customers.

"Yup," he said.

I was nervous. Some of the coffee spilled. I wiped it up. "Cinnamon, plain, sugar, jelly, chocolate, banana, peach, orange, cream, or cinnamon-chocolate?"

"What kind would you recommend?"

"Whatever you like."

"What do you think is the best?"

"Depends on your taste."

"What is your favorite?"

"The cinnamon-chocolate."

"Then that's what I'll have," BD said. "Cinnamon-chocolate."

"I thought you didn't like chocolate, BD," I said, putting the doughnut in front of him.

"Everyone needs an open mind in this world," he said.

"I haven't eaten chocolate in quite a few years, so I might just as well try it again, don't you agree, Jessie?"

I stared at him. I wanted to say, BD, is that you?

I went into the kitchen and took a tray of fresh jelly doughnuts back into the shop. With a piece of waxed paper I began arranging them on the shelf.

"You like working here?" BD said to my back.

"Yes."

"I heard from some of the kids you were working here."

"Oh."

"What do you like best about it?"

"The people," I said. I finished arranging the doughnuts.

"You eat a lot of doughnuts?" he said.

I nodded. "Too many."

"I wouldn't mind working in a doughnut shop. They'd lose money on me."

I nodded. I had missed BD an awful lot. I had thought about him nearly every single day. Sometimes I had loved him so much in my thoughts, in my mind, that I could hardly stand it. Sometimes I had hated him just as hard. Now here he was, not more than two feet from me, and all we were talking about was doughnuts.

The door opened and a woman and two little boys came in and sat down. I wiped the counter in front of them. "One coffee, two hot chocolates," the woman said. "And—let's see, oh, let's splurge, three jelly doughnuts." She smiled at me. The little boys were twirling on the stools.

I took care of them. BD was brushing up the last crumbs of his doughnut and eating them. "Anything else?" I said. His cigarette was smoking on the edge of the ashtray I'd put down next to him. "More coffee?" BD nodded. I could feel him watching me as I got the Silex and poured his coffee. I took a creamer out of the refrigerator under the counter and put it next to his cup.

The woman and two boys finished and she paid. She left me a dime tip on the counter. I put it into my apron pocket and wiped up everything.

"This smoke bothering you?" BD pointed to the cigarette.

"Some," I said.

BD dropped the cigarette on the floor and stepped on it, ground it out beneath his foot like it was his worst enemy he was grinding down to shreds.

"Thank you," I said.

"Cooperation, ma'am," he said, putting on a Western accent. "We strive to co-operate. For instance, how do you like my hat?"

"Your hat?"

He took off the hat, twirling it on his fingers. "My hat. This venerable, antique, genuine gangster hat. You don't like it, do you?"

"Well—"

"No, I can tell, you don't have to say anything, you think it's an ancient grungy piece of junk. Okay, Jessie, if that's what you think, then I don't want to wear this hat," BD said. And he opened the door and flipped the hat through. I could see it sailing out into the parking lot. "That's what I mean by cooperation, Jessie."

"You dope, BD," I said. "I liked that hat all right, it's your sneakers I'm not so wild about."

"My sneakers? These genuine red-and-white Converse All-Americans? Jessie! That's all you have to say." He kicked off his sneakers one after the other, and sent them sailing through the door into the parking lot where they joined his hat.

"You're crazy, BD," I said. "You're really impossible." And just then my boss, Mrs. Richmondi, parked her car outside in the lot. I looked down at BD's bare feet and than at the sign Mrs. Richmondi had tacked on the door. NO BARE FEET.

"BD, here comes my boss," I said, sort of fast. "You better leave." I put his bill on the counter. "Eighty-one cents." My voice was froggy. I felt kind of sick. Because BD and I hadn't said anything real.

BD reached in one pocket, then in another pocket, then into both back pockets. His forehead got red. He reached into his shirt pockets. "I don't have any money," he said.

Mrs. Richmondi was opening the trunk of her car and taking out packages.

"I don't have any money!" he said again. "I must have come out without my wallet." He turned his pockets spilling a bunch of stuff on the counter. Movie ticket stubs, keys, his map, a pair of sunglasses.

I pushed his stuff toward him. "Put it away," I said.

"My boss hates bare feet. BD, you better just go. I'll pay for you."

"You will?"

"Yes!" I took eighty-one cents out of my apron pocket and put it in the cash register.

"I'll bring you back the money," he said. "I'll go right home and get it and bring it back."

Mrs. Richmondi was coming to the door now.

"BD, you don't have to do that."

"But, Jessie—"

"BD, she's coming!"

Mrs. Richmondi pushed open the door with her shoulder. And the first thing she saw was BD's feet. "Young man! You have bare feet. You shouldn't have let him in, Jessie. I've told you, no bare feet!" She dropped her packages on the counter with a thud.

"I didn't come in with bare feet," BD said.

Mrs. Richmondi glared at him. "Out!" She pointed to the door.

"I'm going," BD said, "but don't blame—"

"Out!"

BD left. I watched him through the window, cutting across the parking lot. Mrs. Richmondi was talking to me.

"I'm sorry, Mrs. Richmondi," I said. "Excuse me, please." I bolted through the door, snatched up BD's sneakers and hat, and ran after him. "BD! BD!" I thrust the sneakers into his hand and clapped the hat on his head. "Perfectly good sneakers, BD," I said, which wasn't what I wanted to say, at all.

"If you don't like 'em, Jessie, I don't want 'em."

Oh, BD, I thought. Oh, BD! I knew I had to go back in the shop. Mrs. Richmondi was watching us through the window. But we still hadn't said anything. Neither of us. And we were just standing there, looking at each other.

"BD," I said. "BD, do you want to be friends?"

"That's what I mean," he said. And then he gave me a smile, that terrific smile which I'd missed all this time.

"That's what I really mean, Jessie."

Friday, June 20

Today I hand in my journal. When I started writing it back in February, I didn't even know BD. It's funny. Odd, I mean. So much has happened. And now, this is the last time I'm writing here. I'm not going to do it anymore. I don't care about the past that much. Not when there's tomorrow to think about and look forward to! So, Miss Durmacher, this is it. Please remember your promise not to read this journal. I trust you, Miss Durmacher.

*Pass.
Carol Durmacher*

ACTIVITIES

VOCABULARY

slather, v. — to spread on thickly
swagger, v. — to walk in an overbearingly self-confident way, to boast
fanatical, adj. — moved by too great devotion, excessively enthusiastic
revere, v. — to show devotion, to honor and respect
aggressive, adj. — showing readiness to attack, forceful
dictatorship, n. — government in which one person has total power and
    often rules unjustly or cruelly
fedora, n. — a low, soft felt hat with a lengthwise crease

FOR DISCUSSION

The kind of pressure Jessie is feeling in early March is different from the kind of pressure she is feeling two months later. Before she begins dating BD, she confesses to her diary that *"The truth is, I have only been kissed a few times — well, not even a few, three to be exact — at parties."* Then she adds, *"But I'm not going to tell Anita that."* What kind of pressure is Anita, Jessie's older sister, creating when she says, *"At your age, you're not going to tell me you're sweet fifteen and never been kissed?"*

Only two months later, however, the situation had changed. Jessie now feels a different kind of pressure. Why does she feel under attack like one of the survivors on Fong Mountain? How is BD similar to the imaginary Mao Tze Fong?

By June the conflict seems to be resolved, and Jessie seems much happier. No longer is she depressed, angry or confused. Her relationship with BD is more solid. What specific evidence in the story shows that BD has matured? Where would you place each of them on the "Scale of Maturity" (page 152) in April? In June?

WRITING ASSIGNMENT: Friday, June 20

How might the ending have changed if Jessie had given in to BD's sexual pressure? Write an alternative Journal entry dated Friday, June 20, in which you imagine what her thoughts and feelings would be if she had NOT decided that *"At this point in my life, the way I feel is — my body is my body, and I don't care to share it with anyone. I don't know totally why I feel that way, and I don't think I have to know why."* How might the circumstances and emotions be different if she and BD had gotten "carried away" as her mother feared could happen?

CLASS ACTIVITY: Instant Replay

Several times in her journal Jessie mentions that she is lonely, and each time she longs to talk with someone or to have someone listen to her and understand. In February she writes, *"I feel sort of depressed. I wish I had someone I could really talk to."* At the end of March, she complains that BD

> *"is another one whose most favorite subject is — myself. That is — HIM-self. The thing is, I really like to listen to him go on because mainly, I like him. But if he never wants to listen to me, after a while, I get this horrible lonely feeling. I think that's it. A lonely feeling. Sad."*

Later when BD is pressuring her, she feels alone and tells her Journal, *"Oh, I wish I had someone to talk to."*

At some level Jessie knows that our greatest happiness comes from the connections we make with other people, the friendships, the love. And she understands that true intimacy is based upon a profound knowledge of one another, NOT just intimate sexual contact. But for a long time BD's focus is mostly on the sexual part of their relationship, so they fight a lot and eventually break up.

Perhaps Jessie and BD would have had a less stormy romance if they had been better able to talk about their problems and disagreements. Learning to talk — and listen — are skills we often underestimate. Good communication takes considerable effort and a determination to hang in there even at times when it goes badly.

BD eventually learns that communication is poor when it's too one-sided, when one person always feels overpowered by the other. Jessie reports that her mother *"doesn't say boo to Dad, she's always very sweet to him,"* but Jessie is different.

> *"I'm not like her in that way AT ALL. I'M NOT SWEET . . . I became aware of this because of BD. I have been noticing that he likes things his own way. Most of the time he gets it. I have noticed too, that I don't feel very sweet about this at all."*

On the one hand, Jessie would be wrong if she never said "boo" to BD and always lets his needs and desires overpower her own. But is constant fighting necessary? Isn't it possible to be assertive and "sweet" at the same time?

Divide into groups of four or five. The setting is one of those nights down by the river. Jessie and BD are parked in his car, part of the "factory production make-out line" as Jessie calls it. Their kissing is wonderful, but BD starts "getting friendlier" than Jessie wants him to be. Instead of starting a fight, what else could Jessie say? How could Jessie persuade BD in a kind, maybe humorous, but also strong and assertive way that he must respect her wishes and that she thinks it would be a mistake if they got carried away? Write her side of the conversation.

When each group has finished, read the monologues aloud. Is one more persuasive than the others (you may decide to take a vote)? Do some sentences stand out as particularly good?

HOUSEPARTY

by Walter Bernstein

T he small room was crowded, but the boy managed to get through without spilling the drink he held in his hand.

"Hello," he said to the girl on the window seat. "You're late," she said. "Last time you were faster."

"I couldn't help it," the boy said. "The place is filling up."

The girl accepted the glass and took a long drink. She looked up at the boy and took another drink. Then she set the glass down.

"What do you put this Scotch in with—an eyedropper?" she asked.

"I'll get you some more."

"No, never mind." She turned to look out of the window.

"That's the library," the boy said.

"Your friend told me. I guess he wanted me to get the idea. He told me five times. Look," she said, "there's a clock on the other side of that tower, too, isn't there?"

"Sure," said the boy. "Four of them."

"Does it keep the same time as this one?"

"Sure."

The girl looked triumphant. "How do you know?" she asked.

"Well—" the boy said. He was a trifle uneasy. "Well, I guess it does."

"You ought to find out," the girl insisted. "You really ought to find out. That clock on the other side might be slow. If you can see only one clock at a time, how do you know it isn't slow?"

"I guess you don't know," said the boy. "You have to take their word for it."

"I'd find out if I were you," said the girl, shaking her head slowly. She took another drink. "You really ought to know." She looked out of the window, then turned back to the boy. "What do they call this place again?"

"Dartmouth," said the boy.

"That's a silly name," said the girl. She finished her drink. "Do you think you could get me another one of these with some Scotch in it?"

"Sure," said the boy. He took the glass and started through the crowd. The girl put her nose against the pane and looked out of the window.

After a while the boy came back, holding the drink above his head so it wouldn't be spilled. He tapped the girl on the shoulder. "Hello," he said. "I'm back."

The girl looked at him. "Go away," she said; "I never heard of you."

"I'm your date," said the boy. "I'm bringing you another drink." The girl peered at him. "So you are," she said. She took the drink and returned to the window.

"I got a little more Scotch this time," the boy said.

The girl turned around. "You're cute," she said.

The boy blushed. "Look," he said, "are you having a good time?"

"I'm having a wonderful time," the girl said. "I am having a simply wonderful time." Her eyes were very large and bright.

"I'm glad," said the boy. He sat down and took hold of her hand. The girl looked at his hand holding hers and then up at his face. She looked at his hand again and took another drink. The boy held on to her hand and leaned forward. "Do you really dance in a chorus?" he said.

"When I'm working," the girl said. "They call us chorus girls." She put her head next to his. "Who squealed?"

"Oh, no one." The boy was emphatic. "My sister told me. Remember? You know my sister. She introduced us in New York."

The girl nodded. "I know your sister." She hiccupped gently. "Little bitch."

The boy released her hand and sat up straight. Seeing his startled expression, the girl put her fingers to her mouth. "There I go again, always belching in public," she said. She leaned toward the boy. "Pardon me."

"Sure," said the boy. "Sure." He sat up very straight.

The girl was beating out a rhythm on the glass with her fingernails, watching the crowd. "How long do you have to stay in this place?"

"No special time," said the boy. "We can leave now if you want."

"Not here," said the girl. "I mean in college."

"Oh. Four years. I have one to go."

"That's a long run." She drained her glass and looked at the boy. "You're cute," she said. She put down the glass and took up his hands. "You have nice hands."

The boy gave her hands a slight squeeze. "So have you," he said, but the girl turned away.

"You touch that glass," she was saying to a girl about to sit down, "and I'll lay you out like a rug." She retrieved the glass and held it out to the boy. "How about another drink?"

"Sure," said the boy. He took the glass and moved into the crowd. As he was pouring the liquor, another boy came over and put an arm around his shoulders.

"How're you doing?" he asked.

The boy spilled a little soda into the glass and started back toward the window.

"Fine," he called back. "Fine." He dodged someone carrying a tray. "She's a cinch," he said.

ACTIVITIES

CLASS ACTIVITY: Made for Each Other?

Most of this very short story consists of dialogue, a conversation between a boy and girl during a fraternity party at Dartmouth College. A few descriptive statements help fill out the scene. At no point is the reader told directly what either character is thinking, but their words and actions paint a fairly clear picture.

Make two columns on the chalkboard, one for the boy and one for the girl. Go through the story section by section and develop lists of adjectives to describe each character. Try to read between the lines to infer what may not be stated directly. For example, why do you suppose the friend pointed out the library five times? Why couldn't he think of anything else to say?

Might this awkwardness say something about the girl as well as about the friend?

After you have completed the lists, compare them. Is this date likely to lead to a solid, meaningful relationship? Do you think they share similar values? To what extent do you think it is important that people's values match identically? We often hear the remark "opposites attract." Is it likely that this occurs in "Houseparty?" Do the values of these two characters mesh or clash? Do you see respect for each other growing into mature, responsible love? Do you consider this couple a good match? Is it possible for people without identical values to complement each other? How would this work? What about people with the same values, but different habits?

CLASS ACTIVITY: Computer Dating Questionnaire

Boys and girls, men and women, virtually everybody hopes to develop a satisfying relationship with a loving partner sooner or later. Some have dreams of marriage and living more or less happily ever after; others just want to share a few good times. If luck is on your side, you may meet the perfect match in the normal course of events whether at school, at work, or standing in line at McDonald's. You might be introduced by friends or relatives.

Not everyone is so fortunate, however, and that is why dating services have become big business. Matches can be arranged through radio talk shows, computerized questionnaires, videotape exchanges, by telephone, face to face interviews or personal newspaper ads. In many cases customers are willing to pay $1000 and more to have introductory dates arranged.

The questions for you are: What is it that provides the best foundation for a loving relationship? What do people need to know about each other or to have in common for the greatest chance of a successful match? As a class develop a list of questions you would include in a personal interview or on a computerized questionnaire.

WRITING ASSIGNMENT: "Dear Ann . . ."

The boy in the story is using alcohol in his attempt to get his date to go along with his wishes. The use of drugs and alcohol can definitely interfere with clear thinking and responsible behavior; the girl in the story already shows signs of losing whatever self-control she ever had. Clearly he is going to expect more than a good-night kiss before the evening is over.

Unfortunately, thoughtful reasoning and deliberate decision making are not always the reasons why we act the way we do in social settings. What other kinds of manipulation or pressures might come into play in dating situations?

Pretend you are Ann Landers or another author of an advice column. Compose a response to an inexperienced person who finds himself or herself in an uncomfortable party situation. How would you answer the following letter?

Dear Ann,
Saturday night there was a party at my best friend's house. Hey, we hang around together every weekend, but this turned out to be different. His parents were away and the word got out.
Everything was okay for a while. We were dancing and just fooling around. Then somebody turned the music up and the lights down. Somebody else got a case of beer. Kids started daring each other and things got a little heavy, if you know what I mean. They want to do it again next weekend.
Ann, these are my friends, but I'm not ready for this.
Troubled Teen,
Anytown, USA

FOR DISCUSSION

All of the selections in this curriculum deal with the issues of either love or sexuality, often both. Some selections give us glimpses of what it means to love well. Others highlight shortcomings in relationships. "Houseparty" is probably the most clearly negative example.

Here we see a stereotypical Dartmouth fraternity party with a guy "on the make." The implication is that he is not only well-educated but supposedly well-bred, at least in terms of conventional, formal etiquette. His victim is again stereotypical, a chorus girl from New York who has never even heard of Dartmouth and whose social graces leave much to be desired. Though it is not clear that she has much inclination toward self-restraint in the first place, he plies her with Scotch to weaken her self-control further.

His attitude is one of calculated manipulation, but she could possibly be accused of using him as well. Does she see in him a ticket to social circles otherwise beyond her reach? You be the judge. Who is to blame in this story? Is the turn of events totally the boy's responsibility, or is the girl also responsible?

The blame lies at least as much in the attitudes of the characters as in their actions. Neither the boy nor the girl demonstrates any concern, consideration, responsibility or respect for the other; each has entered into the relationship solely for what he or she can get out of it for himself or herself.

This story also provides a good opportunity to discuss the effects of drugs and alcohol. Compare this aspect of the story to the similar situation in the excerpt from *The Heart Is a Lonely Hunter*.

THE ELEPHANT IS SLOW TO MATE

by D.H. Lawrence

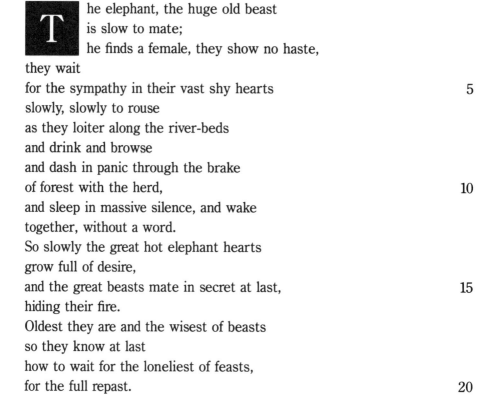

The elephant, the huge old beast
is slow to mate;
he finds a female, they show no haste,
they wait
for the sympathy in their vast shy hearts   5
slowly, slowly to rouse
as they loiter along the river-beds
and drink and browse
and dash in panic through the brake
of forest with the herd,   10
and sleep in massive silence, and wake
together, without a word.
So slowly the great hot elephant hearts
grow full of desire,
and the great beasts mate in secret at last,   15
hiding their fire.
Oldest they are and the wisest of beasts
so they know at last
how to wait for the loneliest of feasts,
for the full repast.   20

REMINDER: Read poetry sentence by sentence, NOT line by line. Pause only where there is punctuation.

They do not snatch, they do not tear;
their massive blood
moves as the moon-tides, near, more near,
till they touch in flood.

ACTIVITIES

VOCABULARY

mate, v. — to pair for breeding, to reproduce sexually
sympathy, n. — emotional and mental compatibility
loiter, v. — to hang around, to linger
brake, n. — a thicket, land overgrown with vegetation
massive, adj. — huge, heavy
repast, n. — meal, feast

QUESTIONS FOR UNDERSTANDING

A. How do the male and female elephants develop "sympathy" for one another?

B. In what way can elephants be considered shy?

C. We usually think of feasting to satisfy the appetite. In this poem, however, the poet is thinking of another basic animal appetite, the sexual appetite. In this context, what is *"the loneliest of feasts . . . the full repast?"*

D. How could this "repast" be other than "full?" Under what circumstances would the poet consider this "feast" less satisfying?

E. What is the lesson that human beings should learn from these wise, old beasts?

ART PROJECT: A Loving Well Mascot

Because of the animal's responsible, delicate approach to lovemaking, the elephant would make a fitting mascot for this curriculum. Using an elephant as part of your design, create a cover for this collection of readings.

FROM A GUY'S POINT OF VIEW

Last year, over one million teenage girls became pregnant. But for each of those girls, there is a guy who was involved too. Strange, but people often forget that. Maybe that's why teenage fathers are somewhat of a mystery. How many of them marry the girls? How many disappear? How many feel guilty about the pregnancy, and how do they handle these feelings? How are a guy's future and education affected? Experts don't know the answers.

But the teenage father is finally coming out of the shadows. Family planning specialists and other organizations are helping both guys and girls to see teenage pregnancy and parenthood as a shared responsibility. More importantly, guys are being helped to consider their sexual activity carefully and make informed decisions beforehand so that unwanted pregnancies don't happen.

Ben (not his real name) found that his girlfriend's pregnancy involved him more deeply than he ever could have imagined. Here is the true story.

BEN'S STORY

Whenever my buddies are sitting around, shooting the breeze about girls, and life in general, I always think of my son Stevie. It makes me sad to remember him. He's almost three years old now and lives far away in another state. I haven't seen him for a year and a half — and probably never will again. A couple of my friends know about him, but with most people, I keep quiet about being a father. I guess I don't want everyone's opinions and advice. When the whole thing happened, I got enough free advice to last a lifetime. It seemed that whatever I did, I ended up feeling guilty.

I go to a large, suburban high school. My life isn't bad at all, but sometimes I feel very inferior. The good news was that our football team was the best in the state, and I was on it. The bad news was that I am not that good and hardly ever get to play. The first-string team is made up of real stars. Some of the guys were shoo-ins for scholarships. I will never get a football scholarship, so I study a lot. I am serious about college. I am under pressure — all the time.

Although I try to act cool, I am plenty confused about girls. My feelings have been hurt in the past. You see, postgame parties are really big events and lots of girls wanted to be a part of them. Sometimes a girl will hang around me and act sweet until I ask her to one of the parties; then she spends the whole evening around the "stars." I hate being used like that.

Right away, Pam seemed different. I am a junior and she is a sophomore and we had a language class together. Sometimes we talked. She had a warm, quiet, ladylike way about her. When she talked to me, I didn't feel she was just hanging around, waiting for me to ask her for a date. With Pam, somehow the pressure was off. Finally, I did call her. That's how it started.

On our first date, Pam and her mother had a screaming fight. Pam was low-key and kind of shy at school, so I never guessed she could get so angry. Pam's mother was divorced. She was just a kind of nervous lady who was only trying to bring Pam up the best she could. But she really seemed like a witch. She was always censoring Pam's clothes and checking out Pam's friends. That night when I arrived, Pam's mother asked me all sorts of questions. She was very suspicious. Pam got fed up and smart-mouthed her a little, and suddenly they were both yelling. I found out that such scenes went on all the time.

Pam's mother worked and didn't get home until 6:30 or 7:00. Sometimes after team practice, I'd go to Pam's house and study with her. Most of the time I'd leave before her mother got home, but once she caught me there. Well, I just barely survived. I told Pam I wouldn't come anymore, but Pam said it was her house too, and we weren't doing anything wrong — just studying or watching TV. She was right — we weren't. So I continued to visit there after school.

We had been dating about three months when sex began to be an issue between us. I was getting really uptight. I had never had sex before, but all the guys on the team talked like they had it every day. (Even then I suspected it might be just talk — but I wasn't sure.) I began to wonder if there was something wrong with me. Sometimes the guys would be talking about some egghead at school and they'd say, "He's a real virgin," or something like that. I'd laugh along with them, but inside I was very scared. I mean, I had my own natural feelings, right? They were enough of a problem. There was the movies. And the magazines guys bought. On top of all this, I was going out with a girl I really liked. After a while, the whole idea of sex really got out of proportion. And I'm ashamed to say a lot of pressure focussed on Pammy.

I have a lot to learn about women, even today, but back then I really was dumb. I truly couldn't understand why Pammy was so reluctant to get physically involved. I knew she really cared for me, and it seemed like such a natural thing to do. I certainly cared for her, so it wouldn't have been cheap or anything. I told her I loved her and really thought I did. After all, I enjoyed being with her, doing things together, talking about things. And I sure was attracted to her. Of course, I didn't think of love in terms of "forever," but I couldn't imagine who did, at my age.

When Pam said she was afraid to have sex because she might get pregnant, I told her I'd be real careful. That's what guys told their girlfriends when the girls worried about pregnancy — but I really wasn't too sure what it meant. Sure, I'd read some books, but I couldn't relate them to myself very well, since I didn't have any experience. Anyway, I really put the pressure on. Once I told her that if she didn't care enough for me, I'd find someone else who did. I know it was a really cheap shot, and I'm ashamed of it even today. But if there's one rule of life, it's that people act like tough guys when they're most insecure. And I was insecure.

Then one day Pam's mother laid down the law. Pam was absolutely forbidden to see me anymore. She'd heard that some guys on the team had gotten out of hand at a party and she associated me with them. I wasn't even there! I never saw Pam so angry. We started to meet in secret. One day it just happened. We began to have sex.

A couple of months went by. I knew deep in my mind that we were playing a dangerous game, tempting fate. It was like roulette. But I didn't want to think about what might happen. And I was too self-centered to consider how Pam felt.

Spring came and Pam's and my romance began to cool down. It wasn't because we were having sex — it was just that I began to notice there were other girls in the world. But on April Fool's Day Pam called and told me she was pregnant. At first I thought it was a joke — then she started to cry. She and I arranged a time to meet. Well, I never moved so fast in all my life. I called hospitals and doctors and got the name of a clinic. Then I called up the clinic and got prices. I even made an appointment for her. I was really proud of myself for taking charge, making decisions.

I told her this the minute we met. "Don't worry," I said. "I'll come with you and I'll pay. It'll be over soon, and no one needs to know."

She stared at me as if I were crazy. "You want me to have an abortion?" she asked. "That's your idea of a solution — just get rid of it?"

"But wouldn't that be the simplest thing?" I asked.

She gave me this strange look. Then she began to cry. "Get away from me," she shouted. She cried and cried.

I was really shocked. In all my talks with the guys about sex, pregnancy was mentioned exactly once. And all I ever heard said was, "Well, you just go to the doctor, and it's all over. There are things you can do." As if it were the easiest thing in the world. They never said what to do if the girl doesn't want to do that. It began to dawn on me that I was in the middle of a giant mess and there was no way to get out of it.

I wanted time. Just a few weeks to figure out what to do. But Pammy told one of her big-mouthed friends and soon it was all over school. I was glad the football season was over. I couldn't have stood the locker room jokes. But one day one of the guys came up to me right after gym class. People who don't think guys gossip have never met Harvey.

"I hear Pam's pregnant," he said.

I didn't answer.

"What are you going to do?"

"I don't know."

"It happened to my brother once."

"What did he do?" I asked.

"Split, of course," Harvey answered. "He made it clear from the beginning that he wanted no part of it. He just told her 'No way, sister.'" This other guy, Eddie, came up and started listening.

"It doesn't seem fair to leave the girl with the whole thing," I said.

"Why not?" asked Eddie. "Girls don't have to have sex. If they don't want to get pregnant, then they shouldn't do it." He spoke as if this was the last word on the subject.

I could have slugged them both. They were the ones who were always bragging. And I had listened to them because I thought they knew so much. They didn't care about anyone or anything either. So they could just walk off scot-free. I mean, I didn't need this problem right now, that's for sure. But I couldn't walk out on Pam, because I knew I was to blame. My father always taught me and my brothers that real men faced up to their mistakes.

Yet when I finally found the courage to tell my dad, he said the same thing as Harvey and Eddie — only in a slightly nicer way. Naturally, he was very upset. First he asked if I was sure the baby was mine.

"Absolutely," I said.

"Well, maybe you ought to leave it to Pam and her family — I mean, let them decide what to do. They love her and know what's best for her. They can't expect much from you — a boy with no money. They can't expect you to give up your future."

"Right," I said. "And what about Pam? What about her future?"

"Well, she doesn't have to have it," my father said. "There are options."

Well, I was shocked at Dad's attitude and I told him so. I reminded him of the values he'd always taught me. He looked a little ashamed.

"Well, of course, Ben, do what you think is right," he said. "But your whole life is ahead of you. I'd hate to see you get emotionally involved with a woman and a baby and give up all that." But I was already emotionally involved. And physically involved. There was no way out that I could see.

For all my big talk, I couldn't bring myself to ask Pam to marry me. I just knew that marriage was not the way. I would be happy with her, help financially — even if it meant giving up certain things. But to give up college and spend the rest of my life with her? I wasn't ready for that. During the next few weeks, Pam avoided me. Maybe she was angry because I didn't suggest we get married — I don't know. But everytime I'd call her she'd hang up. I'd see her at school and she'd head the other way. Finally I pinned her down and she told me her mother thought it was best that she didn't see me.

"We don't want your guilt money. Just get out of my life," was all she could say.

I was so frustrated I could have put my fist through the wall. I was trying to be responsible, but everything I did turned out wrong. My friends thought I was stupid. My father thought I was naive. To Pam and her mother, I was just the creep who got her pregnant. I just felt like saying, "Forget it" and walking away. But I couldn't.

One day Pam came up and told me she was seeing a counselor for advice. "She thinks you ought to come in too," she said. I went gladly.

Pam and I saw the counselor once a week, all summer long. We talked about our relationship and what should be done with the baby. Pam wanted to keep it. I was for adoption. When I gave my opinion, Pam said, "That sure would be easier on you, wouldn't it?" She took a lot of things I said the wrong way, and the counselor pointed this out to her. I hated this position I was in. I had agreed to pay hospital costs, and I felt the baby was as much mine as hers, but I had no real say in what would happen, unless I married her. In the end, Pam could do whatever she wanted; that was the law. But I got to foot the bill.

We talked about marriage. I said it was an unrealistic idea.

"What do you think Pam?" the counselor asked. "Do you really want Ben to marry you?"

Pam thought for a long time. "No," she said. "But I did want him to ask me. I wanted him to prove he cared."

I told Pam I did care, but I didn't think marriage was the answer for us.

She nodded, but I still don't think she quite believed me.

Pam had definitely decided to keep the baby. She planned to live at home with her mother until she had finished school. She had two more years.

My son was born in the late fall. The minute I heard, I cut classes. Pam looked tired but relieved. Both Pam and the baby were fine. She named him Steven. He was amazing — so tiny. I couldn't believe he had anything to do with me. It scared me a little. But I got the bill — over $2,000. I swallowed hard and borrowed the money from my folks. Paying them back would mean extra jobs. I would really have to hustle.

Soon I found out that Pam wasn't living with her mother anymore. She had moved out and gone on welfare. I felt sick when my mom told me. I went to see her right away. She was living in this awful little apartment in a really bad neighborhood.

"I couldn't stand it with Mom a minute longer," Pam told me. "We fought all the time. She wanted to raise Stevie totally her way, and if I disagreed with her, she'd do a guilt trip on me. It wasn't any good for the baby — hearing us fight all the time. And I couldn't get any schoolwork done with all there was to do with the baby. So I just dropped out."

I didn't think that Pam had made the greatest decision. I felt that she should have stuck it out with her mother, so that she could have finished school and given Stevie a nice place to live. But I didn't say anything. I knew Pam would have resented it. I know I would have if somebody dropped into my life every few months and tried to tell me what to do.

Stevie, who had been down for his nap, began to cry, so Pam took me in to see him. As she held him up for me to take, I suddenly noticed how much he looked like my dad — especially around the eyes. It made me so sad, I almost began to cry. I told Pam I could send her $50 a month if that would help. She said it would.

That summer I had an out-of-town job at a resort. But one weekend I came home, and I went to see Pam. When I arrived, there was some guy there. I was a little taken aback. Pam introduced us, but he didn't act too friendly. Well, I could see that I wasn't wanted, so I left. But I went back the next day to find out what was going on.

"I'm going to marry Al," she said. "Then we're going to live out West."

It was as if a train just ran me over. I couldn't say anything. I just sat there and stared. Finally I asked, "Do you love this guy, Pam?"

She looked at me. "He's real good with Stevie, Ben. He plays with him, brings him things. He's willing to give him a name. He can help me finish high school, too. That's part of our plan. He has some money. I can't stay on welfare forever."

"But do you love him?"

"I don't know," she said. "Maybe I could learn to." She looked down at her feet. "To tell you the truth," she added, "I'm not sure I even believe in love anymore. Anyway, Al doesn't want you to come around here now. I'm sure you can understand that."

I walked out of there stunned. It was strange — but I had grown to care for her and Stevie a lot, and the thought that some other guy was going to be my son's father really upset me. I had a million thoughts. Pam was too young to marry. The guy looked like a jerk. Should I try to get visitation rights to my son? How much would legal fees cost?

I was really out of it for a long time. I didn't want to talk with my friends, my parents, anyone. I didn't have any appetite. I wasn't looking forward to going back to school.

Finally, I saw that I'd have to just let the whole thing go. I couldn't be half in, half out forever. I chose not to marry Pam — so what could I say if she wanted to marry someone else? I also felt that Stevie should have one "real" father. It would be better if I didn't make problems. I asked Pam if I could see my son for one more time. And when she said yes, I wept.

It's really weird, being a father when you're a kid. There's no one you can talk to about it. You have to cope with the pain of it all by yourself. No one wants to hear your problems. No one wants to know, cares to know. At times I think I was really responsible about it all, and at other times I feel I totally copped out. I think about Stevie all the time, wonder how he's doing. I probably always will.

ACTIVITIES

FOR DISCUSSION

A. During their first three months of dating, Ben and Pam seemed to have a very good relationship. Find evidence in the story to show that their friendship was a special one before sex complicated it. How did it change after they had sex? After Pam got pregnant?

B. Unfortunately, it is only through hindsight that Ben fully understands why he acted the way he did when he was dating Pam. He admits now that he was "uptight," "insecure," and "self-centered." Explain how each of these adjectives applies to him. What other adjectives would you add to give a fuller description of Ben?

C. Ben expected that having sex would make him feel more mature, but it didn't work out that way in the long run. What other expectations turned out to be false?

WRITING ASSIGNMENT: The Other Sides of the Story

Not surprisingly, Ben is the central character in "Ben's Story." He uses the first person "I" throughout his narration, and we see everything through his eyes. Imagine for a moment that we had met Pam, or her mother, or one of Ben's parents before we met him. How might their version of the same story be different?

Label each of five slips of paper with a different character: Pam, Pam's mother, Ben's father, Ben's friend, and Stevie. Then as a class divide into five groups and draw one of the names out of a hat. Confer for ten or fifteen minutes to share ideas and check the story for clues, then begin to write. The assignment can be done in class if there is time or for homework. Do remember to write as if you are the character telling your own story.

When everyone has finished, gather in the original groups once again. Share each other's stories, and pick one from each group to read aloud to the entire class.

JUDY'S STORY

I t has been almost two years since I had my child, Melodie. The pain has lessened a lot. Still, almost every day, I think of her and all the stuff that happened back then.

I was in the eighth grade when I met Rob. I was really unhappy and confused at the time. My sister, Ginny, had married and was living away, so there were just my parents and me. My parents had never gotten along very well, but now they fought all the time. I felt like my family was breaking up.

I volunteered to help with the school theater productions, that's where I met Rob. He was a ninth grader and was working as backstage manager. He was studious, soft-spoken, and kind of good-looking. He had a really nice way of teaching me what to do. Every time he spoke to me, I felt all warm and shy.

One day I was feeling really rotten. I'd just had a fight with my best friend, Barb. I just wanted to be alone. So I went out on the school lawn and sat down under a tree. Well, who should come down the walk but Rob?

"Say, what's wrong? Are you crying, Judy?" He walked over to me.

Well, I was so touched, that someone was acting sweet to me that I really began to cry. I just couldn't tell him about Barb — it would have sounded silly — so I said I was having family problems. We talked until the final bell rang. That night he called to ask me to a movie on Saturday.

You know how you can get those feelings about destiny? Well, I felt that fate had brought Rob and me together; just when I needed someone most. Having an older boyfriend made me special in the eyes of my friends. It gave me a place in school. And Rob became my best friend in the world. We talked about all our innermost thoughts. He told me his parents didn't get along very well either, and it made him feel guilty.

Rob would talk about how important the theater was to him, and how he really wanted to give it a shot. He talked about a college that has a good theater program. He had it all planned out. I was so proud of him.

On the last day of school Rob came to me with the news that really shook me. His dad had accepted a job in a far away state. I was shattered and I cried. I put my arms around him and hugged him tight, inside I had terrible feelings. I knew it would be over between us when he went away. I suddenly felt I'd been living in a dream for these months, but soon I'd be waking up.

That night we went off to dinner. When he brought me home, no one was there. What happened then should never have happened. And despite the bitter feelings I've had about Rob, I can't say it was his fault. We had been talking about having sex, but decided it wasn't right for us. He never really pushed me. But that night I felt — I don't know — desperate. Reckless. I felt I was losing him and had to do something to make our relationship more real and more lasting. I figured I had nothing to lose. Was I wrong! Was I ever wrong.

After that, things changed between me and Rob. We didn't talk nearly as easily. It was as if we both knew we had done something dangerous, something wrong, so we didn't want to discuss it. But we continued to have sex anyway. It was like we had to make it okay by continuing to do it. But it still didn't feel okay. Of course I knew girls got pregnant that way. But I didn't really think it would happen to me. For one thing, we didn't do it all that often. I felt I could get away with it. My head was in a funny place — I just wasn't using my judgment at all.

The last day of school meant Rob was leaving. After breakfast when I was getting dressed, suddenly the world began to spin. I ran to the bathroom and threw up. I had this awful feeling, a foreboding of doom. I knew that nausea in the morning was an early sign of pregnancy. All through the last day the feeling wouldn't go away. That evening when Rob put his arms around me, I said, "No, Rob, I don't want to anymore. It's wrong for us. It's spoiling things."

"Okay, Judy," he said. "You're right."

I'm being a good girl now, I thought. Now maybe fate will give me a break. Maybe that nausea this morning was only from nervousness.

But I was sick other mornings, too. I was scared and I had no one to talk to. Rob had gone with his family to visit relatives for three weeks. I began to watch for my period. It didn't come. I walked around the house like a zombie. My parents didn't even notice. With all their problems, they were more out of it than I was. Finally, I confided in Barb.

"You've got to go to the doctor, Judy," she said.

"I can't, I just can't." I was too scared.

The next day she came over with one of those pregnancy testers; we followed the directions exactly. Sure enough, the results were positive, and the bottom fell out of my world.

When Rob returned, I told him right away. He acted as if it was the worst thing that ever happened to him. I mean, I didn't expect him to be thrilled, but he acted sort of angry, as if I'd done this thing to us on purpose.

"You can get rid of it, can't you Judy?" he asked.

"Get rid of it?" He was talking as if our baby was some kind of rodent. I panicked. I was beginning to see another side of Rob. He was running scared.

Then we had to tell everyone else, starting with my parents. My mother almost had a heart attack. Half the time she screamed at me, "How could you have done this?" And half the time she hugged me and told me everything would be okay. My father got all red-faced. At one point he was crying! I had never seen my father cry before. It was kind of shocking.

But dealing with Rob's parents was far more humiliating. The six of us got together to "discuss" the situation. Well, Rob's parents did all the talking.

We'll be glad to pay for Judy's abortion, said Rob's mother. When my mother said we didn't believe in abortion, Rob's mother rolled her eyes as if to say, how dumb can you get?

All this time Rob just sat there looking ashamed, never saying a word. He had seemed like such an important person at school. My protector. Now he was just a little boy, going along with whatever his parents said, doing the safe thing.

Then Rob's father gave me the biggest insult of all. "Of course," he said, "there's no assurance that this baby is really Rob's." Well, I'd been trying to keep my cool, but I suddenly blew up. Became hysterical. Never, never had there been anyone but Rob, and he knew it. At that point, Rob said a few nasty words to his father, and came and put his arms around me. But it was too late, as far as I was concerned. My parents took me out to the car and we drove home.

All the way, I cried. I said the whole thing wasn't fair, that I didn't deserve this situation and the treatment I was getting. Mom pulled the car into the drive and took me in her arms. She was real sweet to me for the first time since I got pregnant. She said I was right, life wasn't really fair to women in some ways. She said that it seems so natural and right to have sex with someone you care about, and I hadn't done something unforgivable.

"But," she said, "when you're young, sex doesn't make relationships better (that's for sure, I thought) and the consequences could be enormous. That is why it's better to marry first, and plan for sex, not just let things happen. Now we had the baby's life to think about, and lots more sadness to go through, and some hard decisions to make." No, it wasn't fair, but sex could have huge complications, and that's just the way it was.

I couldn't help wondering why Mom had never said these things to me before. But then I knew that even if she had, I wouldn't have heard them. People had always said things like, "A girl has to look out for herself," and "It's the woman who has the baby," and they sounded like just so many words back then. I saw how really true those words were! When I saw Rob sitting there, I knew that this baby was his problem only if he chose to make it so. It was my problem no matter what. I was the one in the universe who was having this child. That realization made me feel very alone.

I thought maybe being pregnant would make me feel freer and more grown-up. Wrong! Mom watched everything I did, all summer long, especially what I ate. My parents were still having problems, and that made Mom extra cross.

Before he moved, Rob came over a couple of times. He tried to be nice, but I felt he came mostly because he was guilty and not because he cared. He didn't fight for us when he could have, he copped out, and I wouldn't forgive him. It became so awkward between us that he stopped coming over. And I didn't even know when he moved.

When it was time for school in the fall, I wasn't showing yet. The principal said I could come back — as long as I went for special counseling and took a parents' ed class. People say that having a baby without being married isn't as much of a stigma today as it used to be. That's partly true, but not completely. I mean, no one threw rocks at me or anything. But I felt a real difference between me and my friends. They were all nice and all, but they didn't always include me in their conversations the way they used to.

When I began to show, I wasn't asked to parties anymore. One of the girls told me her mother thought it wasn't "appropriate." When I heard my friends talking about who was going with whom, and what clothes they bought, and what the latest records were, I somehow thought all that was silly and unimportant. A real tragedy had gone on in my life, and I felt set apart, old before my time.

Renee, the counselor in my high school, was nice—but tough. She told me there were two alternatives for me—and each would be hard. I could keep my baby, or give it up for adoption. She told me right off the bat that although she knew it wasn't a "fashionable" decision, she favored adoption. She said that because there were so few babies available today, the agency could be assured of getting the finest possible parents—ones who would really want my baby. But, she said, the decision was mine.

I really resisted the idea of giving up my baby. It had already started to become real in my mind. It was mine, and I felt I was entitled to keep it. That's what I told Renee. "Well, if that's the case," she said, "I want you to do a little research. Figure up all your expenses. Do you want to live at home or move out? If you move out, how much will apartments be? What can you get from the government? What kind of job can you get? How much will the hospital cost? Baby clothes? Food? Why don't we meet in three weeks and you can tell me what you've discovered?"

The night before the report was due, I was in my room writing up the results. It amounted to thousands of dollars a year. And what would my earning power be? Practically zero. It was all so depressing. I began to cry. Mom came in and asked what was wrong. I told her.

"Judy, I must tell you something," she said. "Dad and I really don't have the money to raise another child with the economy the way it is. On top of that we may separate—in which case we'll have even less money. So if you have this baby, I'm afraid you'll have to quit school and go to work. I'd give anything for you to finish school and even go to college. That's my heart's desire for you, Judy, to have a good life. But you can't have that with this baby. But, if you're dead set on keeping it, I'll do what I can to help you. Don't expect much though, Judy. I don't have much to give right now."

I cried and cried that night. Then I stopped crying and lay awake for hours. I had some insights as I lay there. A sort of wisdom came to me. I realized that in a way, I had sex with Rob to keep him, even if I didn't really know it at the time. It didn't work; in fact, I didn't even like him anymore. But this baby was the result. I'd also wanted to hurt my parents a little, I think, or at least get their attention. Okay. I'd hurt them. But did I have any right to hurt them for the next 20 years by giving them a burden they didn't ask for? If I thought I wasn't getting enough from my parents, why was I giving them a new baby, who needed so much more?

Right then, it seemed that the simplest, wisest thing to do would be to give the baby up. That way, everyone would be able to start over — the baby, my parents, and me. The next day I gave Renee my report — and my decision.

Melodie (that's what I named her) was born prematurely, two days before Christmas. The first time I saw her, she was in one of those warm boxes. She was tiny. Her legs were like pencils. She had tubes in her nose and mouth. "Preemies are more commonly born to adolescent mothers," I heard the doctor say. I just stared at her. I couldn't even cry. It's all my fault, I thought. What if she turns out to be a vegetable? What if the adoptive parents don't want her? What if no one wants my baby? What would happen to her?

It came time for me to go home. Melodie's condition was still unpredictable. Both Renee and the doctor advised me not see her anymore, but I told them I absolutely had to come and see her every day until she was okay. I couldn't stand having to remember my daughter gasping for air through tubes.

So they agreed that I could come. Every afternoon I came. "Live Melodie," I'd say as I stood at the window. Melodie lived. Finally she was well enough to leave, and people I didn't know came to take her. Six months later, I signed the final adoption papers. It was the saddest thing I'd ever done.

After that I went back to school. I was accepted pretty much by my old friends — but there were differences. I didn't date very much. I didn't really feel like it at first. I had too many painful memories that couldn't be put aside right away. And I never knew what guys thought. Sometimes a guy and I would begin to go out, and he would stop calling. I never knew if it was because he just wasn't that interested, or because he couldn't deal with my past.

I think of Melodie everyday, pray for her, hope she's okay. But every time I visit Ginny and see how much she gives to her kids, how much she worries and cares, I know I did the right thing. I wouldn't have been ready to give that much to Melodie. I was only a kid myself. Someday I will be ready for marriage and children, and when I am, I'll give my husband and kids the best of everything.

ACTIVITIES

FOR DISCUSSION:

A. At the end of her story, Judy says, *"Some day I will be ready for marriage and children, and when I am, I'll give my husband and kids the best of everything."* But how will she know when she's ready? In his story, Ben obviously wasn't ready when Pam got pregnant. Why not? Pam tells Ben, *"I'm not sure I even believe in love anymore."* Isn't love an important part of being ready? What else is important? How do we know when the time is right?

B. What feelings are behind Judy's decision to have sex with Rob? What makes her so "desperate" and "reckless" on that one night? How are the consequences different from her expectations? How do both Judy and Rob "get burned?"

C. Judy has suffered disappointment, loneliness, and loss in her quest for love. Nonetheless she wants to try again some day. What changes will she make to insure that she, her husband, and her children have "the best of everything?"

CLASS ACTIVITY: Learning Lessons the Hard Way

After Judy becomes pregnant, her mother tells her that *"When you're young, sex doesn't make relationships better, and the consequences could be enormous. That's why it's better to marry first, and plan for sex, not just let things happen."*

Judy's reaction is one of frustration. She says, *"I couldn't help wondering why Mom had never said these things to me before. But then I knew that even if she had, I wouldn't have heard them."*

Sadly, at least in this case, experience is truly the best teacher. Many of

Judy's and Ben's ideas and expectations about love and sex turned out not to be true. Though their stories are totally separate, both Ben and Judy learn some of the same painful lessons. For example, they learn that when you're young and unmarried having sex is more likely to cause problems than solve them. What other lessons do Ben and Judy learn through experience? Make a list using direct quotations from the two stories.

HOMEWORK ASSIGNMENT: Parent Survey

Based on Ben's and Judy's experiences, and on your own research, make a list of conditions that would have to be right before you would advise anyone to have a child.

Interview at least two parents who are willing to talk about their experiences. As a class, you may expand or change the following list of questions if you are uncomfortable with these or think of others you'd rather use. They appear here only as suggestions:

1. Were you still in school when you first became a parent?

2. Did you have a job?

3. Was money a problem?

4. How did becoming a parent change your life?

5. Was becoming a parent different from what you expected?

6. What was the best part of becoming a parent?

7. What was the most difficult?

8. Did your parents give you advice about starting a family? What did they say? How did you react?

9. Looking back on it, do you think the timing was good?

10. What would you change if you had it to do over again?

After everyone has completed their interviews, compare answers. Are there similar responses on many of the questionnaires? Can the class draw any clear conclusions about the best circumstances for starting a family?

ROMANCE: *FINALE*

MUSIC PROJECT:

Love has long been a principal source of inspiration for the performing arts as well as for studio arts such as painting, drawing, and sculpture. Dance choreographers, dramatists, and composers have always drawn on themes of love for their productions. These productions reflect changing attitudes over time. For this project, your class will take a look at what twentieth century music says about the values of recent generations.

Part I:
> What songs are at the top of the charts today? Which ones talk about love? Brainstorm as a class, then collect the lyrics from the biggest hits about love. What messages do they give about love? Are the messages similar? Compare these "love" songs to the stories you have been reading.

Part II:
> Choose three or four typical songs and show the lyrics to people of your parents' and grandparents' generations. What do they think about the messages of these popular songs? Have a follow-up discussion to compare their reactions. If you have recordings or can catch the songs on the radio, ask the adults what they think about the musical accompaniment as well as the lyrics.

Part III:

What songs about love do parents and grandparents remember as favorites from their younger years? Collect lyrics they can remember, even if only phrases or small segments from songs. Are the messages different? If so, in what way? Are there "golden oldies" that are popular today? If so, what is it about them that speaks to today's teenagers?

Part IV:

Which songs, old or new, contain the most valuable ideas about loving well? Can your class decide on a theme song for this book?

Section Three:

COMMITMENT

AND

MARRIAGE

BEAUTY AND THE BEAST

by Madame Leprince de Beaumont

O nce upon a time there was a merchant. He had six children, three girls and three boys and, because he was immensely rich as well as sensible, he had given them all the best education possible.

All of his daughters were beautiful, but the youngest was the loveliest of all. When she was little everyone called her Beauty, and somehow that name clung to her, which made her sisters very jealous. What is more, Beauty was not only better looking than her sisters, she was better in every way. Being so rich had made the two eldest girls very proud. They thought themselves great ladies and were far too grand to make friends with other merchants' daughters. They were always going to balls and plays and showing off in fashionable society and they scoffed at their younger sister for spending all her time at home reading books.

Everyone knew that the girls were amazingly rich, and more than one wealthy merchant came to ask for their hands in marriage. But the two eldest answered that they had no mind to marry, unless it might be to a duke or an earl at least. Beauty thanked all her suitors very kindly but said she was too young and wished to stay with her father for a few years yet.

Then, quite suddenly, the merchant's ships were wrecked at sea, all his money was lost. Nothing was left to him but one small house in the country. He wept as he told his children that they would have to go there and make a living by working like the peasants.

His two eldest daughters said at once that they had no intention of living anywhere but in the city and they had young men who would be only too glad to marry them, money or no money.

But in this they were mistaken. Their admirers would not look at them now that they were poor. They were so proud that nobody liked them and people said: "They don't deserve our pity! We're glad to see them humbled. Let them practice their airs and graces on the sheep!"

At the same time, everyone was sorry for Beauty because she was so sweet and gentle and had always been kind to the poor. There were quite a few gentlemen who would have married her, even without a penny to her name. But she told them she could never bring herself to leave the poor father and meant to go with him to the country to comfort him and help him in his trouble.

When they were settled in their new home, the merchant and his sons set to work farming the land. Beauty learned to get up at four in the morning to keep the house clean and cook dinner for the whole family. She found it hard at first, for she was not used to the life of a maid of all work, but after a month or two she grew stronger and the work only made her pleasantly tired. When it was done, she would read or play her lute or sit singing to herself while she sewed.

Her two sisters, on the other hand, were bored to tears. They lay in bed until ten and spent the remainder of the day bewailing their lost friends and their fine clothes.

"Just look at that stupid sister of ours," they would say. "The little idiot actually enjoys this terrible life."

But the good merchant thought differently. He knew that Beauty was more fit than her sisters to shine in the world and he was full of admiration for her patience and good temper. He could see that her sisters, not content with letting her do all the work of the house, were also as rude to her as they knew how to be.

The merchant and his family had been living in this lonely farmhouse for a year when a letter arrived, saying that one ship, which had been given up for lost, had come safely to port. They were all very excited, but the two eldest daughters were especially pleased because they thought it meant a return to their old way of life. They even helped their father pack his bag and saddle his horse, all the time begging him to bring them expensive presents. Beauty said nothing. It seemed to her that her sisters had already spent all the money their father was likely to gain.

It was not until he was almost ready to ride away that the merchant turned to his youngest daughter.

"Well, Beauty," he said, smiling at her. "Your sisters have given me their orders. What would you have?"

Beauty knew she must ask for something if she did not want to hurt his feelings, so she said quickly: "Thank you, Father. Will you bring me a rose? We have none hereabouts."

The merchant rode away, full of hope. But when he came to his ship, he found that he had to go to court for his money, so that in the end there was very little profit from the voyage. He turned homewards, tired and depressed, and very nearly as poor as when he had set out.

The weather turned dark and cold. Night was coming but the merchant pressed on, eager to see his home and children again. He had only thirty miles to go. The road led through a deep forest and soon, as the wind rose and snow began to fall, he knew that he was lost.

The trees closed in on either side and he could hear wolves howling in the distance. Whirling snowflakes clogged his mouth and eyelids and twice his horse stumbled and threw him, so that at last he plodded forward on foot, clinging to the reins.

He was sure that he was going to die of cold and exhaustion when suddenly the wind dropped and he saw an opening in the wood and a light twinkling far away in the distance. Turning towards it he found himself in a great avenue of trees. The snow had ceased and the night was very still. The merchant struggled on through the drifts until he could see that the lights came from a huge, glittering castle. He hastened towards it, thanking heaven for his deliverance. But as he passed through the gatehouse, he was surprised to find the courtyard quite empty. Lights were everywhere, but not a groom or a human being of any kind could he see.

The stable doors stood open and his horse, as tired and hungry as himself, at once scented the warm straw and made its own way to the waiting stall. The merchant followed as if in a dream and saw the animal fed and watered before he himself entered the house. In the great hall lights blazed everywhere and a good fire burned on the hearth, but all was as silent and deserted as outside. A table set for one stood near the fire, with food and wine upon it, as though waiting for a guest.

The merchant went towards it, steam rising from his wet clothes. After a moment, feeling that the master of the house, whoever he was, could not begrudge him a little comfort on this stormy night, he helped himself to a glass of wine. Then he took a seat by the fire and dozed until a clock, striking eleven, startled him awake. The sight of the loaded table before him was too much. He could not stop himself. Beginning with a leg of chicken, he ate ravenously and then, as no one had yet appeared, he set out to explore the castle. Each of the rooms he passed through seemed grander than the last until, coming on one that had a good bed in it, he tumbled into it and instantly fell asleep.

It was ten in the morning when he woke. To his great surprise he found that his old, travel-worn garments had vanished and in their place was a handsome suit of clothes, like those he had worn in days when he was rich. He put them on, convinced that the castle must belong to some good fairy who was taking care of him. When he looked out of the window he saw that last night's snow was all gone and a garden full of flowers met his eyes. In the great hall, where he had eaten the previous night, a small table was laid for breakfast and this time the merchant sat down to it with no qualms, thanking the good fairy aloud as he did so.

When he had drunk his chocolate, he went to find his horse. A rose bush, covered with flowers, reminded him of Beauty and of his promise to her.

Smiling, the merchant drew the knife from his belt, seized hold of one flowering branch and cut it off.

At once he heard a dreadful cry. He looked up and beheld, advancing on him, a monstrous beast, so hideous that the merchant nearly fainted with horror.

"Ungrateful man!" The beast spoke in a voice that struck terror into his heart. "I saved your life by taking you into my castle and this is how you repay me! By stealing my roses which mean more to me than all the world! For that you must pay with your life. You have fifteen minutes to make your peace with God!"

The merchant flung himself on his knees before the beast. "Oh, my lord, forgive me! I meant no harm. I took the roses for my daughter, because she longed for them."

"I am not your lord," the monster growled. "I am the Beast. Do not try to flatter me. Say what you think. I'll like you better for it. You say you have a daughter?"

"Three, sir."

"Then I will spare your life, but on condition that one of them is willing to come here and die for you. No! No argument! Only, if your daughters will not give their lives, swear to me that you will return yourself before three months have passed."

Three months of life seemed to the poor merchant better than none. At least he would have time to say goodbye to his children. For of course he had no intention of allowing any of them to die for him. So he gave his word to the Beast.

"Go then," the Beast said. "And because I would not have you leave empty-handed, return first to the room where you slept and fill the chest which you will find there with whatever takes your fancy. I will see that it is carried to your home."

With that the Beast turned away and the merchant, comforting himself that at least he would not leave his family destitute, did as he was told.

Besides the chest the Beast had mentioned, he found great amounts of gold and jewels in his room. He filled the chest and closed the lid. Then he went thankfully to the stable, saddled his horse and rode out of the castle, a sadder man than he had entered it.

He never knew how long it took him to reach home. His horse seemed to find the way of its own accord. But as his family gathered round him, full of eager welcome, he could not help the tears springing to his eyes as he looked at them. He was still holding the roses he had brought for Beauty and now he gave them to her, saying: "Take them, Beauty. These roses have cost your poor father very dear."

His children stared at him in horror as he told them his sad tale. Then the two eldest girls broke out into such shrieks and cries that they seemed half mad. Both of them turned on Beauty and blamed her bitterly for what had happened.

"It's all your fault," they told her. "You couldn't be like us! You had to ask for something different! You have brought this trouble on our father. And now you can't even shed a tear for him!"

It was true that Beauty was not crying. But she was standing close by her father and holding his hand in a way that gave him more comfort than all her sisters' clamor.

Now she answered them firmly: "Why should I weep for him? My father is not going to die. Since the Beast is willing to take one of us in his place, I shall go. The fault, as you say, is all mine."

At this Beauty's three brothers cried out angrily that she should not sacrifice herself. They would go and slay the Beast.

Their father told them roundly that they were talking nonsense. "I have seen the power of the Beast," he said. "It is so great, we have no hope of destroying him. I am grateful, my dear Beauty," he added fondly, "but what kind of father should I be if I were to let you face death for my sake? I am old. My only sorrow will be in losing you, my children."

"I may be young," Beauty replied, "but I would rather be eaten by the Beast than die of grief at losing you. You shall not leave this house without me."

And that was her last word. Her father and brothers grieved and protested but her sisters were secretly delighted, because they had always been jealous of her.

Meanwhile, the merchant had almost forgotten the Beast's treasure chest. He found it that night, standing at the foot of his bed, but decided to say nothing about it except to Beauty. She told him that while he was away a number of young men had visited the house and two of them seemed to have fallen in love with her sisters. She hoped he would consent to their marriage and provide them with a dowry apiece. Beauty said this, even though she knew her sisters did not love her, because she was a good-hearted girl and she could not bear to think of them unhappy.

They, for their part, could not wait to be rid of her. As the day approached when Beauty and her father must set out for the Beast's castle, the wicked girls took to rubbing their eyes with onions, so that they might seem to be crying. But Beauty's brothers wept in earnest, for they were very fond of her. Beauty did not weep, for she would not add to their grief.

She mounted before her father and once again the horse seemed to find its own way. As night was falling they came in sight of the castle, blazing with lights and yet with no one to be seen. As before, the horse went directly to its stable and the merchant led his daughter into the great hall. Here they found a table spread with great magnificence and places laid for two.

The merchant had no heart for food but Beauty sat down and tried to encourage him by her example. To herself she thought drearily: "I suppose the Beast wants to fatten me up before he eats me."

They finished eating and were sitting quietly, trying to converse in a normal manner, when suddenly they heard a terrible sound, a hoarse yet thunderous roaring, like the sea in a distant cave. The merchant trembled and started to bid his daughter farewell, for he was sure that this was the Beast coming to eat her. Beauty herself could not help flinching when she caught sight of him, but she forced herself to be brave. When the monster asked her if she had come to the castle of her own free will, she answered him in a small voice: "Yes."

"You are good," said the Beast. "I am much obliged to you." He turned to the merchant. "You, sir, leave this place tomorrow and never seek to return. Farewell, Beauty."

"Farewell, Beast," she replied, and with that the Beast left them.

The merchant threw his arms around his daughter. "Oh, my dear child," he cried. "Save yourself! Leave me to my fate!"

"No, Father," Beauty answered him steadfastly. "You must go and leave me to trust in heaven's goodness."

With that they retired to bed, each convinced they would not close their eyes. But to their surprise both fell asleep as soon as their heads touched their pillows. The merchant slept dreamlessly until morning, but Beauty, in her dreams, saw a beautiful lady standing by her bed.

"I thank you for your goodness, Beauty," she said. "What you have done, in gladly offering your own life for your father's shall not go unrewarded."

In the morning Beauty told her father of her dream, hoping to comfort him a little at their parting. But still he was full of grief and her own eyes were full of tears as she watched his bowed figure riding slowly away from the castle.

When he had gone, she ran back to the great hall and gave way to her tears. But she was a brave girl and when grief and terror had worn themselves out she sat up and began to take stock of her situation. It seemed to her unlikely that the Beast meant to devour her before the evening and so she resolved to pass the time exploring the castle.

She found it very beautiful. Each suite of rooms seemed more magnificent than the last and the views from the windows showed a landscape of well-tended woods, lakes and gardens. Then she found herself staring in surprise at a door over which was written, in letters of gold, the words:

THESE ARE BEAUTY'S ROOMS.

Beauty opened it at once and found herself in a chamber which outshone all that she had seen before. But what impressed her most was the sight of the huge bookcase which took up one whole wall and the many musical instruments with which the room was filled.

"I could stay here for a year," she thought, "and never be bored. So how could all this be given to me just for one day?"

With that thought her courage revived and she began to look about her. Going to the bookcase, she saw, inside the first book she opened, the inscription:

ALL THAT YOU SEE HERE IS YOURS.

YOUR WISH IS MY COMMAND.

Beauty sighed. "Alas," she thought to herself. "My only wish is to see what my poor father is doing at this moment."

Just then her eyes fell on a tall mirror by her side and to her astonishment she saw, pictured within it, the door of her old home and her father alighting from his horse. His face was wet with tears and she saw her sisters coming to meet him. But although they tried to hide it, it was not hard for Beauty to see that in their hearts they were overjoyed. Then the scene in the mirror vanished and she saw nothing but her own reflection there. But it left her still more convinced that in this place she had nothing to fear.

At midday she again found the table set for a meal and while she ate, she listened to an admirable consort of musicians, although none was visible. But in the evening, as she took her place, there came instead of music the terrible dragging roar of the Beast's approach.

He came towards her as she sat, rigid and staring. But his voice was unexpectedly gentle.

"Beauty," said the Beast, "may I stay with you awhile?"

"You are the master here," Beauty answered, trembling.

"No," he replied. "You alone are mistress. Bid me go, if I offend you, and I will leave you at once. Do you find me very hideous?"

"I do, of course," Beauty admitted. "I must tell the truth. But I think you are very kind."

"Thank you," said the Beast. "But I fear I am dull as well as ugly. A great, stupid Beast."

"It is not stupid," Beauty said, "to know one's limitations. No fool ever did that."

"Eat your supper, Beauty," said the Beast. "Try to be happy in this place. All you see is yours and I would be sad if it failed to please you."

"You are very kind, Beast," Beauty answered. "Your goodness of heart makes you seem less ugly in my eyes."

"My heart is good, yes," the Beast said bitterly. "But I am a monster for all that."

"There are many with human faces more monstrous than you," Beauty told him. "I prefer you, looking as you do, to those whose handsome looks hide a false and wicked heart."

"If I were clever," the Beast said, "I would make you a graceful compliment for that. But I am too dull. I can only thank you."

Beauty smiled and addressed herself to supper. She had almost lost her fear of the Beast but all at once he startled her dreadfully by saying abruptly: "Beauty, will you be my wife?" She gazed at him, trembling, afraid of arousing his anger. But at last she made herself say quietly: "No, Beast."

For a moment the Beast looked at her mournfully, then he heaved a great sigh, like the wind roaring down the chimney. "Then farewell, Beauty," he said, and with that he went from the room, turning round once in the doorway for a last unhappy look at her.

Left alone, Beauty sat for some time thinking pitifully of the poor Beast. It seemed to her very sad that he should be so kind and look so fearsome.

Three months passed and Beauty lived very pleasantly in the castle. Each evening the Beast came to her at suppertime and the two of them talked comfortably of this and that, like old friends. Beauty thought that although the Beast might not be clever, he spoke with a great good sense and her regard for him grew day by day. She had grown used to his appearance and now, far from dreading the sight of him, she often caught herself glancing at the clock, counting the minutes until he would be with her again. He never failed to appear on the stroke of nine.

The only thing that continued to trouble her peace of mind was his habit of asking every night, before he left her, if she would be his wife and when she refused, as she always did, his seeming so overcome with sadness. One day she could not help telling him so.

"I am sorry, Beast. I wish I could marry you," she said. "But I cannot deceive you. I shall never do so. But I will always be your friend. Can you not be content with that?"

"It seems I must," the Beast replied. "I cannot blame you. I know I am a loathsome monster, but I love you. It is enough for me that you are willing to stay here. Tell me you will never leave me!"

Beauty felt herself blushing guiltily. She had seen in the mirror that her father was very ill, pining for his lost daughter, and she longed above everything to go to him.

"I will gladly promise to remain with you for the whole of my life," she said, "if only I might see my father once again! It is like a knife in my heart that he is ill and I cannot go to him."

"It is a knife in mine," the Beast said instantly, "to see you unhappy. But if I send you to your father, you will surely stay with him, and then your poor Beast will die of grief."

"No, no!" Beauty cried, almost in tears. "I care for you too much to cause your death! I promise to return to you in a week, if you will only let me go. I saw in my mirror that my sisters are married and have left home and my brothers are all away at wars. My father is quite alone. Let me go to him for a week."

"You shall be there when you wake tomorrow," the Beast said. "Only remember your promise. Take this ring. You have only to place it on the table by your bed when you wish to return. Farewell, Beauty."

As he uttered these words, the Beast gave one of his great sighs. Beauty went to her bed, full of sadness for the grief she had caused him.

When she awoke the next morning, all thought of sadness had gone. She was in her own bed, in her father's house, with the sun slanting in her window just as it always had. She lay for a little while, contentedly, then a mischievous smile touched her lips. She reached out to the little bell that stood on her bedside table. Almost at once a maidservant, new since Beauty's leaving home, appeared in the doorway, threw up her arms and shrieked. The sound brought Beauty's father hurrying from his room and the sight of his lost daughter sitting up in bed and laughing at him was almost too much for the poor man's fragile health. He hugged her to him, laughing and crying at once, and it was a long time before either of them had eyes for anything but each other.

At last Beauty said she must get up, only she did not know what to do for clothes, since she had brought none with her. "Oh, but you have, my lady," the maidservant said. "There is that great traveling trunk out in the passage. All blue leather and gold studs, it is!"

The trunk was brought in and proved to be full of wonderful dresses, each one trimmed with gold lace and diamonds. Silently thanking the Beast for his thoughtfulness, Beauty chose the simplest of them to wear that day, telling the maid to set aside some of the most magnificent ones as presents to her sisters. But the instant she said so, the whole trunkful vanished as if it had never been. Beauty stared in amazement but her father began to laugh.

"It seems the Beast has his own ideas about that," he said. "He means you to keep the dresses for yourself."

At once, as if in agreement, the trunk reappeared.

Beauty got dressed and in the meanwhile messages were sent to her sisters, saying that Beauty was home, but only for a week. They soon arrived, bringing their husbands with them. Neither was happy in her marriage. The eldest had wedded a man as handsome as the day, but so in love with his own beauty that he had no eyes for her. The second had married one who was clever but whose chief use for his tongue was to quarrel with everybody, beginning with his wife. Both sisters nearly fainted with jealousy when they saw Beauty, dressed like a queen and looking more radiantly beautiful than ever.

They could hardly contain themselves as they listened to Beauty's description of the Beast's palace and the delights of her life there. As soon as they could, they escaped into the garden to plot how to spoil things for her.

"Why should she be so happy," they said, "when we are quite miserable?"

The eldest said: "Sister, I have an idea. What if we were to keep her here longer than a week? That Beast of hers might be so angry when she breaks her promise to him that he'll turn on her and devour her."

"Sister, I think you have it," said the other. "We'll keep her here at all costs."

With this in mind they began to behave quite differently to Beauty. They sought her company, praised her looks and admired her dresses. They even invited her to their houses. Beauty was touched. She wondered if perhaps they had been sorry after all when they wanted her dead. When the week was over, they wept and wailed and tore their hair, pretending such distress that Beauty was at last compelled to stay another week.

She did promise, but her heart ached when she thought of the pain she would be causing her poor Beast. She found, too, that she was missing him quite badly.

On the tenth night in her father's house, Beauty dreamt that she was back in the castle. She was walking in the gardens, beside the long lake. The Beast was lying on the grass and she knew that he was dying. His eyes reproached her for her broken promise. Beauty woke suddenly and found that her face was wet with tears.

She lay for a long while, thinking of her dream. She recalled that, for all this monstrous form, the Beast's eyes were beautiful and the look of speechless suffering in them was almost more than she could bear. "How could I be so cruel," she asked herself, "when he is so good to me? Is it his fault that he is ugly? He is kind and that is worth more than beauty and cleverness put together. Why shouldn't I marry him? I would be happier than my sisters are with their husbands. Even if I cannot love him, I like and respect him, and gratitude alone should make me hesitate to wound him. I could never forgive myself."

In another moment she was tugging off her ring. No sooner had she placed it on the table by her bed than, with a deep sigh, she fell fast asleep.

She woke to find herself back in the castle. Joyfully she sprang out of bed and only then remembered that the Beast never came to her before the evening. She had no means of knowing where he spent his days. For a long time Beauty wandered about the castle restlessly. She knew that it was no use seeking him, yet still she could not settle to her music or her books. She passed some hours dressing herself in the clothes she knew he liked but soon grew tired of her own face in the mirror, and after that there seemed nothing to do but wait.

Nine o'clock struck. But no familiar sounds echoed through the castle. No Beast entered the hall. Beauty paced the floor uneasily, remembering her dream. Still he did not come and she began to be afraid that she had killed him. Panic seized her. Filled with dread for his sake, she ran wildly through the palace, calling his name. But the fine rooms remained empty and silent. At last, near to despair, she made her way out into the darkening gardens.

Straight for the lake she ran, to the place where she had seen him in her dream. And there he lay, close by the water, just as she had feared she would find him.

With a cry of grief and remorse, Beauty cast herself down upon his body. Sure that he was dead, she clasped him in her arms, oblivious to his monstrous features. But even as she lay there weeping, she felt his heart beat faintly and, in sudden hope, she took out her handkerchief. Dipping water from the lake, she touched it to his dry lips.

Wearily the Beast opened his eyes. "Beauty, is it you? I thought you would not come," he whispered. "You broke your promise and I wanted to die. But I shall die happy now that I can see you again."

"No, no, you shall not die!" Beauty cried fiercely. "You must live and I will marry you! I will! I believed that what I felt for you was no more than friendship but when I saw you there and thought you were dead, I knew I could never live without you."

No sooner had she spoken than lights sprang up all over the castle. Music and fireworks filled the night. But Beauty had no eyes for anything but the beloved Beast. Yet even as she looked at him, she saw that he was changing. The air about him shimmered, the beastly carcass blurred and fell away and he rose to stand before her, a handsome prince, fairer than the day.

"The Beast?" Beauty stammered. "Where is he?"

"Here, at your feet," the prince said, kneeling. "A wicked fairy condemned me to that likeness until a lovely maiden should consent to be my bride. She made me ugly and stupid and you alone were good enough to love me for my heart alone. Now I am free to offer you the man I truly am, and not only my love but my crown."

Gladly Beauty gave him her hand. They walked together to the castle and there, in the hall, she found her whole family assembled, transported there by the lady she had seen in her dream, who was the prince's fairy godmother.

"Welcome, Beauty," said the fairy. "The choice you have made in the wisdom of your heart will bring you happiness as long as you live, and you shall find beauty, wit and kindness united in your future husband. You will become a great queen and I know that power will not mar your goodness. But for you—" Here the fairy turned to Beauty's two sisters. "I know too well what mischief is in your hearts. To prevent it I shall clothe your bodies in stone, though your minds shall remain unchanged. Stand as two statues at your sister's gates and be it your punishment to watch the daily happiness of her life, until such time as you may truly repent. Not," she added sadly, "that I have much hope of repentance. Pride, anger, greed and most other deadly sins may be overcome, but for a really wicked and jealous heart there is no cure in this world."

Thereupon the fairy waved her wand and all those present were instantly transported to the prince's kingdom, where his subjects greeted him with all imaginable joy. Beauty and the prince were married in great state and lived together throughout the length of their lives in the most perfect and deserved happiness.

ACTIVITIES

"Beauty and the Beast" is the most famous of a large group of stories that have come to be called "animal groom stories." You may also know "The Frog King." The key event in each of these stories is the marriage of a young maiden to a rather unusual groom. The groom is trapped in the form of an animal until the maiden's love transforms him into a prince. In all cases, the girl's father is involved as the story unfolds. The large number of these stories indicates that there must be something very "true" about them. Recently a version of "Beauty and the Beast" had a long run on prime time television, so clearly there is something about these animal groom stories that still has great appeal.

FOR DISCUSSION

A. This story makes us think about what's beautiful and what's ugly. Beauty's sisters are so jealous of her that they make themselves miserable. They are also described as beautiful, so why are they jealous? What does Beauty have that they don't? What is beautiful about the Beast? Is he as beautiful as Beauty? Often beautiful or handsome people complain, "Nobody sees *me*. They just look at the outside!" What do they mean? Is there a difference between the way you *actually* feel about physical beauty and the way you think you *should* feel?

B. Another central idea in these stories has to do with the way relationships change over time. For example, when we fall in love and are ready to build our own homes and family, we typically grow away from those who cared for us as children. This process is natural though often painful. In "Beauty and the Beast," the relationship between Beauty and her father undergoes considerable evolution. Trace the changes that occur in the story. Can you find symbols that represent these changes?

C. One way of getting to understand this story and others like it is to reflect on why the male groom is portrayed as a beast. Could it have something to do with the basic idea of this book that sexuality is a big deal and we can make bad mistakes by not taking it very seriously? Is there anything in the story that suggests this possibility? The Beast almost dies because Beauty listens to her sisters, who beg her not to leave them. She tries to please everyone, but she may also be trying to give herself some time to think. Do you think she was trying to sort out her feelings about the Beast when she stayed away so long? Why might Beauty have hesitated to return to the Beast even though she loved him?

D. The Beast is ugly, but he isn't cruel or wicked. What is "beastly" in this story? Can you think of real-life experiences where someone looks beastly but isn't or acts beastly but doesn't look it. Because he is under a spell, the Beast must remain ugly and stupid until somebody loves him for his heart. How can true love actually change people for the better?

APPOINTMENT WITH LOVE

by S. I. Kishor

ix minutes to six, said the clock over the information booth in New York's Grand Central Station. The tall, young Army officer lifted his sunburned face and narrowed his eyes to note the exact time. His heart was pounding with a beat that shocked him. In six minutes he would see the woman who had filled such a special place in his life for the past 13 months, the woman who he had never seen, yet whose written words had sustained him unfailingly.

Lt. Blandford remembered one day in particular, the worst in the fighting, when his plane had been caught in the midst of a pack of enemy planes.

In one of his letters, he had confessed to her that he often felt fear, and only a few days before this battle, he had received her answer: "Of course you feel fear . . . all brave men do. Next time you doubt yourself, I want you to hear my voice reciting to you: 'Yea, though I walk through the valley of the shadow of death, I shall fear no evil, for Thou art with me.'" He had remembered, and it had renewed his strength.

Now he was going to hear her real voice. Four minutes to six.

A girl passed close to him, and Lt. Blandford started. She was wearing a flower, but it was not the little red rose they had agreed upon. Besides, this girl was only about 18, and Hollis had told him she was 30. "What of it?" he had answered. "I'm 32." He was 29.

His mind went back to that book he had read in the training camp. *Of Human Bondage*, it was; and throughout the book were notes in a woman's writing. He had never believed that a woman could see into a man's heart so tenderly, so understandingly. Her name was on the bookplate: Hollis

Maynell. He got hold of a New York City telephone book and found her address. He had written, she had answered. Next day he had been shipped out, but they had gone on writing. For 13 months she had faithfully replied. When his letter did not arrive, she wrote anyway, and now he believed he loved her, and she loved him.

But she had refused all his pleas to send him her photograph. She had explained: "If your feeling for me has any reality, what I look like won't matter. Suppose I'm beautiful. I'd always fear that you were taking a chance on just that, and that kind of love would disgust me. Suppose I'm plain (and you must admit that this is more likely), then I'd always be haunted that you were going on writing because you were lonely and had no one else. No, don't ask for my picture. When you come to New York, you shall see me and then you shall make your own decision."

One minute to six . . . he flipped the pages of the book he held. Then Lt. Blandford's heart leaped.

A young woman was coming toward him. Her figure was long and slim; her blonde hair lay back in curls from her delicate ears. Her eyes were blue as flowers, her lips and chin had a gentle firmness. In her pale-green suit, she was like springtime come alive.

He started toward her, forgetting to notice that she was wearing no rose, and as he moved, a small, provocative smile curved her lips.

"Going my way, soldier?" she murmured.

He made one step closer to her. Then he saw Hollis Maynell.

She was standing almost directly behind the girl, a woman well past 40, her graying hair tucked under a work hat. She was more than plump; her thick-ankled feet were thrust into low-heeled shoes. But she wore a red rose on her rumpled coat. The girl in the green suit was walking quickly away.

Blandford felt as though he were being split in two, so keen was his desire to follow the girl, yet so deep was his longing for the woman whose spirit had truly companioned and upheld his own; and there she stood. He could see that her pale, plump face was gentle and sensible; her gray eyes had a warm twinkle.

Lt. Blandford did not hesitate. His fingers gripped the worn copy of *Of Human Bondage* which was to identify him to her. This would not be love, but it would be something precious, a friendship for which he had been and must ever be grateful. . . .

He squared his shoulders, saluted, and held the book out toward the woman, although even while he spoke he felt the bitterness of his disappointment.

"I'm Lt. Blandford, and you — Miss Maynell. I'm so glad you could meet me. May - may I take you to dinner?"

The woman's face broadened in a tolerant smile. "I don't know what this is all about, son," she answered. "That lady in the green suit begged me to wear this rose on my coat. And she said that if you asked me to go out with you, I should tell you she's waiting for you in that restaurant across the street. She said it was some kind of a test."

ACTIVITIES

FOR DISCUSSION

A. Have you ever had a long term pen pal? How is getting to know someone through letters different from getting to know them in person?

B. It has been said that character is destiny. In other words, the way our lives unfold is determined by those qualities that make each of us unique. Short as this story is, it reveals a great deal about its characters. What adjectives would you choose to describe Lieutenant Blandford? To describe Hollis Maynell? What is at the core of their passionate attraction to one another? Are there signs that this relationship will be a happy and lasting one?

CREATIVE WRITING: Crystal Ball

What happens after this romantic meeting in Grand Central Station? How does this love story play out? Set the scene in a time and place at least 20 years later. Who are your characters? Are Lt. Blandford and Hollis Maynell still together? Have other people come into their lives? Although you are focusing on a future moment, let your story reveal what has gone on in intervening years. Remember that specific details will bring your story to life.

Be prepared to read your narration to the class and explain what led you to predict the destiny you describe.

UNIT ACTIVITY: Your Appointment with Love

Your ideas are likely to change as you grow older, but the stories in this section should help you think about the kind of person you'd like to meet some day under the clock at Grand Central Station.

Think about yourself, your values, the person you hope to become, the life you hope to lead. What is it that excites you? What kind of person do you find most attractive? Try to write descriptions both of yourself and of the person you hope to meet. It might be helpful if your class brainstorms about the qualities that might be included in these descriptions. For example, is a sense of humor more important to you than athletic ability? What about honesty and loyalty? Do you prefer large parties or quiet evenings at home?

OZZIE AND HARRIET

by Irene Wanner

Jessie Foss used to think, when she was awake at night, about a house of her own, a job that paid so well she would not sit awake in bed worrying, and a lover. She would have an old farmhouse, the sort magazines feature with before-and-after pictures, enthusiastically explaining the joys of stripping wood to its basic beauty while neglecting to mention sweat and splinters, scraped knuckles, and toxic fumes. It was a five-acre farm, say, with an orchard of apple trees gone wild that she would coax back to bearing fruit for juice. She would have cats, a barnful, a yellow bitch named Nell, and a dapple-gray horse. Someone would pay her outrageous amounts of money to do something at home in her own spare time. No commuting, no fluorescent-lit offices, no typing. Her lover would be gentle and good at fixing everything. He would bring surprises. These night dreams were so mundane, so storybook, they began to make Jessie anxious about her mind, which, at 25, should have progressed beyond her mother's promises of a prince and a palace.

Later, after her twenty-eighth birthday, Jessie still woke at night. She was settled in a home with a man, David Wainwright, an architect, provided for and safe but "living in sin," as her mother and father called it. Jessie now dreamed of her former freedom.

Awake, with David snoring and mumbling beside her, she thought of those years alone, moving from place to place, when her belongings fit into the back of the car and she was able to make a little money stretch. She was surprised how exotic her old life appeared. Excavating Mexico, hitchhiking around Europe by herself. Those romantic notions left out the heat and dust, fatigue and nausea; they were as superficial as the rosy pictures in travel magazines. Jessie had begun to realize something about the emptiness of her youthful illusions, but also realized she could not continue believing the grass was always greener elsewhere. At night, not worrying about a home or money or loneliness, she thought perhaps if she were smarter, or even a bit more stupid, she might stop dreaming.

Jessie and David were friends for a year, then lovers for a year, and this year David brought her along to look at houses, spoke of marriage and children, plans to remodel, investments, retirement. They had agreed not to marry, she thought, and she had prevented pregnancy as long as she could remember. Remodeling and investments were for the rich, retirement for the old. Jessie wondered who this stranger was. As soon as David's earnest money was accepted, he began to age.

Often, she sat alone at night in the apartment, wondering where they could fit the couch in the new house or how they would ever get their bed through the door and up those stairs. Bookshelves had been emptied. Boxes of records and clothes, pots and pans, towels, tools, camping gear, and tennis racquets lay in piles. Exposed, those things seemed useless. The furniture was out of place, some missing, already moved; stains and faded spots and trails of wear showed in the carpet, revealing unknown routines about their lives. Paintings, ceramics, dishes, and glasses had a new fragility.

Other things Jessie had once paid no attention to became impossibly large and heavy. David had accumulated his own furniture and furniture left by his parents and furniture bought from friends who could not stand the idea of having to move it themselves. A cherry cabinet, four feet high, with double doors and brass handles. A gaming table and dining room table. A low, square coffee table so heavy that it might as well have been ironwood. Several bookshelves, eight feet high and four feet wide and a foot deep. Desks, tables, chairs, a fig tree in an antique stoneware crock.

Against so many things — impedimenta, her college Roman-history professor had called such clutter and baggage — Jessie set out a box for Goodwill. She told David when they began to pack, "Think of moving as our chance to dump this stuff we never use."

He looked up from the boxes he was filling with dusty books and worn out shoes. "What stuff?"

Jessie watched David pack half-filled bottles of dishwashing liquid, almost-empty salt cartons, unused containers of floor wax, and seasonings so old they had solidified in the jars. She thought of her mother's perpetual house-cleaning, that relentless war against junk, and a high school home ec edict: When in doubt, throw it out. Unencumbered by such strictures, compulsive as a crow collecting bottlecaps and tinfoil, David packed bits of string and broken rubber bands, outdated coupons, and keys to locks no longer remembered, checks written years ago, and cookbooks with recipes they would surely never try.

"I don't meant to tell you what to do," Jessie said.

"But?"

"But do we *need* all this stuff?"

David's hair was red and curly. When he fussed, he wound locks of hair around his fingers and tugged; like Orphan Annie or some other cartoon character frozen on a page, David appeared electrified. He sat back on his heels, his freckled hands resting lightly on the box as though it contained relics of the church.

"Someday we might need it," he answered. "You never know."

Jessie stood by his drafting table, thinking about how much paint they would need to buy and how soon they must have a lawn mower. David had swung the black elbow lamp around so its light, aimed before him, cast a slanting amber ray into the box filled with smaller boxes of those things they might someday need. He picked up a slide rule in a faded leather case.

"This belonged to my father."

"I'm not saying you should throw away things that are important."

"Oh."

Jessie could see David did not understand how he was supposed to decide what was important, what might be useful someday, and what she wanted him to throw out. Those days when she spoke to him, his answers — when he answered — came back after a time lag that reminded her of men on the moon speaking to earth: in that thin air and low gravity everything was alien. David's office, where closets were always neatly shut and architectural tools were arranged in patterns exact to the millimeter, looked as though it had been hit by a meteor.

Among his books and boxes were suits and clothes Jessie had never seen, which David must have worn after he finished at Yale, before she met him, when he thought appearances and first impressions might be more important for getting a job than his ability as an architect. Instead of boots and jeans and wrinkled permanent-press, there were tweeds, and cashmere, oxford cloth and silk ties, a tuxedo, ruffled shirt, and patent leather shoes. Jessie had not known the man who wore those clothes. Seeing them was like trying to gauge a stranger's character by the clothes he brought to the laundromat.

"David, a tux?"

"You never know."

Jessie took the yellowed dress shirt from its hanger, the old cotton cool in her hands.

"What are you doing?" David said, brushing the seat of his pants as he stood. "I want that."

"It could use a wash."

David frowned at the shirt. "I had it washed and pressed."

"When?"

"The last time I wore it."

"When was that?"

He patted his pockets and glanced out the window, had cigarettes but no matches. "I can't remember."

Jessie left him to make his own decisions, knowing the only decision David would come to was not to decide anything. He would pack everything. Clearing out the kitchen, she found three bottles of allspice, three of cloves, three of cinnamon, and three of peppercorns. "It makes me think," she called to David, "your last three lovers each came up with a complete set of spices that she left behind when you broke up."

"I've not had three lovers," he said, surprised and puzzled.

"No mysterious dark women who cooked with curry and ginger and hot peppers?"

Nothing was in its place then. Jessie felt uprooted. Her nerves were raw to the air. She and David bumped into each other as they wandered among piles of strange and forgotten things that could have been dropped by a tornado. Have you seen the screwdriver? he might ask. It's in a box somewhere, Jessie would say, which was the same answer he gave to all her questions.

They talked about where things should go in the house, but Jessie could not juggle the size of things against rooms she had seen full of others' belongings. She could hardly remember the house among all the houses they had seen. We'll have so much room, David had been saying before he noticed Jessie's silences. The blueprints in his mind were invisible to her.

At the apartment's kitchen table, Jessie worked on copyediting and proofreading for a university press. Manuscripts and galleys and page proofs and blue lines ended up everywhere. Style manuals and dictionaries, envelopes and papers, letters to authors, queries, corrections, shavings from pencils, all crowded into their lives. Friday night pizza in front of the TV became daily dinner on the coffee table. They were accustomed to small spaces there: David in his leather chair by the books, Jessie at the end of the couch, the cat on her pillow by the windows, like puzzle pieces that fit only one place and, once David made the down payment on the house, the puzzle had been overturned into a senseless heap.

Jessie resisted David's suggestions to clean up her books and papers, to pack so he could take her things by the house on his way to work in the morning. She claimed she was on deadline, but it was the orderliness of rules, the consistency of decisions reinforced with red marks on paper, that made her cling to one spot while David tried to move them. She thought she had known him. Instead, Jessie went to bed with a stranger who muttered about thermal windows and insurance. She watched him sleep. I'm too tired to make love, he said for the first time.

They moved across town in February, carrying load after load in a high-kicking wind that rattled bare bushes and drove dark clouds eastward. David worried about rain, then about snow, tugging at his hair until it stood out like a cap of rusted steel wool. Jessie pictured them that evening in their new home: she would not be in a dress and David would not be freshly shaved. No chilled champagne waited on a polished set with white winter roses. Unlike old movies or romance novels, men no longer carried women over the threshold.

Too tired to shop or cook on their first night, they argued about where to have dinner, then ate silently in a hamburger stand parking lot. Jessie waited for David on the steps at home, holding the gas company Sorry We Missed You card that she found hooked to the front doorknob.

"I thought you left a key under the mat," she said.

David rubbed his eyes and slumped beside her. "I guess I forgot. I'm so tired of forgetting things." He put his arm around her shoulder and Jessie ran her palm up under his pant leg, caressing David's smooth calf. "Make us a fire, Jess? It's getting cold."

Leaning against the couch and surrounded by liquor store boxes used for moving cartons, they huddled in the firelight, wrapped in an afghan. Jessie had split kindling and brought up wood from the small basement room that once served as a coal bin, which they now called the poet's garret and joked about renting to a suffering artist who would thrive in its dismal atmosphere. David's stocking feet protruded from the cover, inches from the flames. He and Jessie shared a pint bottle of brandy.

"Isn't this the life," thought, David. "Our own house."

Jessie rubbed his toes and the fire warmed her fingers. She could still see her breath. "It's strange having a house."

"Why strange?"

"I've dreamed of one," she told him, resting back in his arms, "but in dreams things are perfect. This is more demanding."

"The house?" David flicked his cigarette into the fire, blew into his palms, rubbed them, then touched Jessie's cheek with an icy hand. "How is it demanding?"

"This house was decorated in about 1957," Jessie said, thinking of the work needed. One bedroom was baby blue, another pea green; the living room rug was red and the bathroom was pink. Doors and woodwork painted with indestructible coats of lemon yellow enamel; the wall had cheap plastic fake wood paneling. There were white ruffled curtains in the kitchen and an ancient refrigerator that froze milk but melted ice cream. Doors did not hang true on their hinges and cold wind hissed past the windows that were not painted shut. "Ozzie and Harriet could have lived here."

They discussed things the house needed: a washer and dryer in the basement, a deep freeze, rose bushes for the garden, hedge clippers and hoses and sprinklers and lawn junk for the garage, a trash can.

"It will insist we have two sons," David said, "and that every year on their birthdays we record their heights on the back of our bedroom door."

They went to bed early, cold and exhausted. David drew Jessie close for the first time in weeks. Awake, she felt his body begin to relax beside her warmth. She must try to make the house and all David's worries that had come between them find other places.

Jessie closed her eyes, but she remained awake thinking of fifties cars with tailfins, bulky furniture, Elvis and rock'n'roll, white anklets and full skirts and Peter Pan collars on pastel blouses, all past and now things. We were young then, she thought, and had no responsibilities. Ozzie and Harriet were incredibly old. They were square. The new house demanded they realize that they were becoming Ozzie and Harriet.

After two days David was sent to Washington D.C., on a weeklong business trip. Jessie drove him to the airport, carried his bags to the ticket counter, smiled, and said she would miss him but everything will be all right. The phone man would come later that morning so David could call home tonight. Tomorrow the washer and dryer were scheduled to be delivered, and although they would not be installed, Jessie could stop putting aside change for the Laundromat.

"Your father's an engineer, Jess, right?" David kissed her forehead, held her hands. "I'm sure you'll manage to get everything hooked up."

She stepped back. "I didn't know an understanding of electricity was hereditary."

On the way home she bought a bottle of Scotch and stopped at the hardware store. In only two days David had pulled enough nails from the house and garage to fill a one-pound coffee can. Jessie mixed Spackle and took it from room to room, dragging along a new stepladder, filling holes. The walls are as spotted as an appaloosa's rump, she would tell David when he called.

Mornings, Jessie found herself kneeling on the kitchen floor, pouring Scotch into a coffee mug so the woman next door, whose kitchen overlooked hers with a wide expanse of picture windows, would not be scandalized into starting the neighborhood gossip. With a buzz on, painting did not seem so tedious. Evenings, she pulled the drapes and sat in the dark, a little dizzy, the cat in her lap as she reclined by the fire and dreamed of locking the doors and leaving. Light sparkled on the ceiling that previous owners had sprayed with a lumpy substance resembling rhinestone oatmeal.

She watched men on television explain why women needed cleansers, deodorizers, sprays, waxes, and detergents. The men smiled patiently at housewives whose lifelong pursuit of the ultimately whitened and brightened socks and shorts could not possibly be obtained without new improved bleach. Television's obsession against dirt, smells, and smudges somehow reminded Jessie of a back-alley office in Mexico City, where she had seen a line of tourists waiting politely for their travel agent. He was late, they said, and they were hot and dusty and sweaty. They needed showers. They did not know the agent was sitting next door in a dime cafe, smoking as he drank a cold beer and joked with the waiter about the tourists swatting flies. You can always tell Americans, the agent had said, they're too clean.

While David was away, Jessie received a postcard from a friend digging at an Aztec site. Around the post office's forwarding-address sticker, which had been pasted across the message, she restored her friend's words as though they were fragments of an inscribed stone that would reveal past mysteries. The note mentioned grants, money available for study and travel, and the possibility of a position on that summer's excavation. Jessie set the card on a windowsill and later accidentally dripped paint across the blue sky, palm trees, and glistening water. When David phoned, she would say the right thing, that she missed him.

"I'm lonely," his distant voice told her. "And tired. This trip is a waste of time. I want to come home."

"You come home, then, and I'll do some traveling."

"Sunday, Jess, we can put on a roast and chill a bottle of wine, laze around in our bathrobes all day reading the comics and watching old movies. Get potatoes to bake when you're at the store, too, okay? Can you make gravy?"

"No." She remembered sitting, like a dunce, on the kitchen stool when she was a child. Her mother had said someday she would need to know how to make gravy, so she'd better pay attention and learn. "Can you?"

"Make gravy?"

"Yes."

"Of course not." David laughed, then waited for Jessie to speak. When she did not, he said, "I mean, I never tried. It comes in packages, doesn't it?"

"There was a storm the first night you were gone," Jessie told him. "The back fence blew down."

"You didn't tell me."

"I wanted it to be a surprise. I built a fence. By myself."

When David came home, they stood in the mist looking at the new split-rail fence. The rails were level, the posts solid. David crossed the yard and hitched himself up, hooking his heels over the middle rail.

"So tell me, Jess, when do we get a horse?"

"This is a city fence. For livestock the rails have to go on the insides of the posts, David, or the animals just push them out." She walked through the weeds to his side and put her hands on his knees. 'Why do I know that and not how to make gravy?"

He smiled and smoothed a strand of dark hair from her forehead, tucking it behind her ear, then he leaned down to kiss her, his fingers combing back, loosening her braid. "I've brought you a present."

They exchanged gifts in bed. Wool socks for David; for Jessie a book on how to keep warm using an axe. There was a large woodpile in the yard and that first cold night she had said she could heat the house with an axe and maul and splitting wedge.

"I sound like a hippie or a pioneer, don't I?" she said, stretching close to him. "Next thing you know I'll be spinning wool and putting up peaches."

"You could plant vegetables out back, Jess."

She tried to imagine David mucking out stalls, chopping off chickens' heads, plowing. They lay quietly together, drifting to sleep as rain rustled over the low, muffled moans of foghorns. David's forearm cradled Jessie's neck. She turned and kissed his palm. There was a spot of waterproof ink on his thumb. His hand was white, its fingers smooth, with closely bitten nails.

Closing her eyes, Jessie saw a long dusty road running west toward a late-afternoon sun. In every direction the land was gold with wheat, spreading away in long shadows and gently rising hills gone russet. She stood in the road, the earth hot under her feet, shielding her eyes, listening for David. Bees droned. A yellow hound crossed the fields toward her, its slender tail a flag in the grain. The sweet heavy scent of ripened blackberries lifted on a breeze rich with the smells of dust and grass. Swallows dipped and rose, wheeling above her. Jessie imagined these things, but David always came into her vision in a three-piece gray pinstriped suit, a portfolio under his arm.

"What would you think of having a child?" David said.

Jessie sat up. "I thought you were asleep.'

"I can't decide," he said, drawing her down. "It frightens me."

Jessie rocked him. David's shoulders were as white as porcelain, and faintly freckled. He seemed frail to her then, letting her hold him as he admitted he had fears. She realized he must also have dreams.

"One afternoon back in D.C. I slipped away early," he told her. "I went to see paintings at the National Gallery, left there, too, went to my hotel room and got drunk."

"Thinking about a child?"

"I don't know." He stretched, frowned, raised himself to one elbow and looked at Jessie. "Thinking profound nothings that got forgotten by a blackout."

"Do you ever think you're becoming your father?" Jessie said.

"How?"

"I've begun thinking of new curtains and carpets, of shelves in the kitchen, of dining room chairs and upholstery. Things my mom passed her time with that I never cared about."

"You don't make good apple pie yet."

"Pretty soon, David, I may be trading recipes with the neighbor ladies at Tupperware parties. I'll have a little plastic box stuffed with cards and priceless ratty papers ripped from homemaker magazines."

"In our family no one gets blackout drunk. The women don't chop wood or build fences. I don't think we're turning into them, Jess." David shivered and settled back under the blankets. "Or maybe we are. I don't know."

They rose later and began again "playing house," as one of their old friends from the apartment called life in the suburbs. David pulled nails; Jessie painted. David hung pictures and set up bookshelves; Jessie wrote away for seed catalogues and began pulling weeds. She sent David to work each morning giving him a kiss and a cup of coffee at the back door. He called her every day before lunch, then, after a while, began calling after lunch. Each day he called later. Sometimes he was not in when she phoned to ask him to stop at the grocery on the way home. Jessie wondered if his secretary was pretty; she wondered if David made love to other women; she wondered what had happened to her former ideals, when she had stopped believing in freedom and started expecting faithfulness.

Jessie swung at the earth with a red-tipped hoe she had bought on sale at the hardware store. She turned up dirt, as books recommended, a foot deep. She added manure and peat and vegetable nutrients. In a scratchy Mexican sweater, old jeans, and boots, she dug furrows for seed in trenches that were as straight as a ruler's edge, ten centimeters deep. She sent a postcard to her friend in Mexico, claiming her excavations had brought to light a 1938 dime, a 1939 penny, an aluminum chip with a soft-drink label, nails, and peach pits.

"Hardly remains of the most exciting civilization in world history," she told David one day when he arrived home from work. "What's that?" he said, pointing to two bare trees and a line of brown sticks evenly spaced along the fence.

"Eucalyptus," Jessie said. "Dogwood." She turned. "Raspberries."

"Oh."

Jessie stood beside him. From his vantage behind the car, she saw a lumpy plot of mud, barren except for heaps of dead weeds and grass. He set down his portfolio and rubbed his eyes. Jessie stepped away.

"Look, David."

He faced her, blinking, reaching back to massage his neck. "What?"

"Potatoes, carrots, spinach, onions, tomatoes, broccoli." She took a half-meter pace, indicating each row. "Fresh raspberries. Cornflowers and straw-flowers, daisies and delphiniums."

"Jessie?"

"Yes."

"Are you going to Mexico this summer?"

She had received an invitation to dig and to help with the editing and publication of finds. She left the letter out for David to read, uncertain, hoping somehow the right decision would happen by itself.

"I don't know."

He motioned her to him. "Go if you need to."

"What about you?"

"I'll be all right."

"What about the house?"

David looked up at it, then back to Jessie. "What about it?"

"Who's going to mow the lawn and scrape the windows, fix the antenna, and get the plumbing taken care of?"

"That's beside the point."

"No, it isn't." She slipped her arm around his waist. "All my life I've rented apartments and rooms and condominiums. Other people's places. I need to stop, I guess, David. I've begun feeling the housework changes."

"What changes?"

"I'm learning to cook and I even like it, how to fix things and how to plant things." Jessie turned and moved her arms around his shoulders. "I've gotten worried you have lovers because I'm too fat."

"You're not fat, Jess."

"I even bought a bra. With lace."

He moved his hands up her sides. "Which you're not wearing."

"One thing at a time." Jessie propped the hoe inside the tool shed and walked up the driveway with David. "I'm looking forward to summer here, to barbecuing hamburgers, to playing softball and going to the beach, to getting the house ready for next winter."

"This winter isn't even over yet."

They stopped by the back door, where they had a view across the street to the aluminum-sided house with two trucks and a dented van parked bumper to bumper behind a stained fiberglass speedboat that rested crookedly in high weeds. Jessie and David stood silently, watching a paunchy young man in a yellow baseball cap bump and slam at the blinking pinball machine he kept in his living room. Nearby, a woman in pink foam-rubber curlers pointed a flabby arm at something; her jaw flapped. She pointed again, then stood, wearing sheer shortie nighties that revealed gray doughy thighs and fat rump in pink panties with holes where the elastic had pulled loose. Her voice shrieked about the pinball bells. A child rushed out, slamming the front door. The woman followed, opened the door, planted herself there, and screamed.

"In Mexico," David said, "you might not be able to hear them."

The man and woman were screaming at each other now, a routine they repeated several times each week.

"Do you suppose he *ever* takes off that hat?" Jessie said.

David propped his elbow on the porch railing, running a finger along the white trim that would need paint soon. He looked away, back to the screaming woman. "Jess, *that's* fat. If I were him, I'd get a lover."

"If I were she, I'd leave."

"Will you? Leave?"

She shrugged. They climbed the stairs and shut out the lives of their neighbors. People like that, Jessie thought, shouldn't have kids. Then, wondering what sort of people should have children, she took out a cookbook, propped it open, and started supper. David put away his portfolio, changed clothes, and came back to slice tomatoes. They moved around each other, a silent waltz that had become comfortable.

Jessie realized she was content to stay for now. The work in Mexico would continue for years and she could go any season. For the first time, she wanted to be home. Just as she had learned more about David's past and his methodical nature by seeing things strewn everywhere when they had moved, she came to understand that she had always been moving on, looking elsewhere, thinking her dreams could come true only if she kept trying to get over the next horizon.

"David?"

"Yes."

"What do you dream for?"

"I don't understand."

"When you can't sleep at night," Jessie said, "what do you wish for?"

David hesitated, closed his eyes, and when he opened them again, he seemed to be coming back from someplace far away. He smiled and shook his head slightly.

"It's hard to say."

They stood quietly for a moment, then ate dinner, and gave up working on the house early so they could go to bed. Later that night Jessie knew she could no longer wait for mid-April average frost date for setting seeds. It was almost the end of March. Tomorrow David would go to work; he would grin and give her his parting platitude: Off goes the breadwinner to bring home the bacon. Jessie would stay in, laboring over a dreary biology textbook manuscript whose wages would help pay off more household bills. At noon, when the sun had cleared the fir and cedar trees to the east, she would go out to mark each north-south row in the garden with string pulled taut between stakes. She would set in seeds, putting down roots, as though their lives depended on it.

ACTIVITIES

VOCABULARY

coax, v, — to influence by gentle urging or caressing
mundane, adj. — earthly, pertaining to the world, ordinary
superficial, adj. — on the surface, not profound or thorough, shallow
perpetual, adj. — everlasting, constant
stricture, n. — critical remark
amber, adj. — dark orange, yellow
gauge, v. — to estimate, judge, to determine the capacity of
garret, n. — a room or unfinished part of a house just under the roof
russet, adj. — reddish brown
portfolio, n. — a case for carrying papers or drawings
platitude, n. — a dull, flat or trite remark

FOR DISCUSSION: The Impossible Dream?

The Prince Charming and his lady fair who fall in love at first sight and ride off to live happily ever after in palatial splendor are purely fictional. They are Disney cartoon characters who are two dimensional at best. Real life is never so simple or so perfect, yet we all have our dreams and our fantasies.

The difficulty comes in striking a balance between our dreams and reality. What are reasonable dreams, visions of what our lives could be, actual goals to work toward? And what dreams are too fantastical, so far beyond reason that we are doomed to disillusionment and disappointment if we hold on to them?

A. In "Ozzie and Harriet" Jessie admits that three years ago at the age of 25 she still held on to *"her mother's promises of a prince and a palace."* This promise was translated into an idyllic vision of homemaking lifted straight from the pages of women's magazines. But now that she is 28 she realizes it hasn't worked out quite as it was supposed to. She has come to recognize *"something about the emptiness of her youthful illusions."* What is wrong with the vision that she describes in the first paragraph of the story? She has the house and the man she dreamed of then, so why isn't she as satisfied as she expected to be?

B. Ironically, now that she has settled down with a home and a man who loves her, she longs for the freedom and the excitement of her old life. But she realizes that she cannot *"continue believing the grass (is) always greener elsewhere."* Why does Jessie label the memories of her old life *"romantic notions?"* What does she mean that they are *"as superficial as the rosy pictures in travel magazines?"*

FOR DISCUSSION: The Possible Dream

In "Ozzie and Harriet" Jessie struggles with her own values and comes to a clearer understanding of what it means to live happily ever after. She hints at an earlier, more idealistic stage of her life, an era probably in the late sixties when "freedom" was the cry echoing across the country. Young women burned their bras and kicked off their shoes while young men grew hair to their shoulders and donned ragged jeans in symbolic rejection of middle class values. Both marched with banners that proclaimed "Make Love, Not War." The materialistic and regimented lifestyle of businessmen in three piece suits and their Junior League wives was not for them.

These children of the sixties did not want to be tied down by possessions or responsibilities. They wanted freedom to search for a personal truth, some profound reason for their existence. Jessie, however, finally realizes that she has been searching long enough. *"She comes to understand that she had always been moving on, looking elsewhere, thinking her dreams could come true only if she kept trying to get over the next horizon."*

A. Jessie buys a bottle of Scotch when David goes away, and she drinks it from a coffee mug so the neighbors won't gossip about her. David admits to drinking so much he loses memory. Some people drink to escape their problems rather than trying to solve them. What conflict drives Jessie and David to drink in this part of the story?

B. Why do you suppose David and Jessie have not yet been able to commit to marriage and having a child? Do you suppose they will eventually add children to their family?

C. By the end of the story Jessie finally understands that we all have to make our own happiness. It is not something we can discover like a buried treasure. The opportunities are at hand, and we can take charge. She and David will not lead storybook lives. Their differences will undoubtedly cause friction, and there are already times when sleep has more appeal than making love. The passion of new love has yielded to a less intense but deeper love. Their lives will be richer together than separate. They see the value of commitment, of "putting down roots." They will focus on the immediate pleasures of life, the Sundays reading comics and watching old movies, the dinners of roast beef and a special bottle of wine. They will cope with the problems and savor the joys of today instead of dreaming about a perfect tomorrow. At the end of the story, what is the significance of Jessie's planting seeds?

D. Our ideas about marriage change at different times in our lives. Why do you suppose the divorce rate is higher for teenage marriages than for marriage during later years? Why do you suppose the divorce rate is lower for second marriages?

CLASS ACTIVITY: Television Then and Now

Jessie feels her mother's promise of an enchanted life as a wife and home-maker is misleading, but Jessie has not been able to shed that romantic vision. The Nelson family, Ozzie, Harriet and sons David and Ricky, embodied that ideal for a generation of television viewers in the fifties. Their domestic bliss was never threatened by illness, financial pressures, or any serious conflict. Both parents had infinite time, wisdom, and patience to tend to the demands of their family, and friends. Harriet was the perfect household manager, and Ozzie somehow supported his family without ever revealing what he did for a living.

Have times changed? Are television shows more realistic today? Virtually all families have conflict and problems yet somehow think they are the exception. In fact, it's the couple who lives happily ever after that is the exception to the rule. How do current situation comedies or dramas portray family life? Do these programs set up false expectations?

Interview adults about the family shows they watched at your age. What were the most popular ones? How were they different from today's television shows? Do shows today reflect the same family values as they did 20 or 30 years ago? You might have fun watching reruns or current hits together and discussing them.

BEYOND WHAT

by Alice Walker

We reach for destinies beyond
what we have come to know
and in the romantic hush
of promises
perceive each   5
the other's life
as known mystery.
Shared. But inviolate.
No melting. No squeezing
into One.   10
We swing our eyes around
as well as side to side
to see the world.

To choose, renounce,
this, or that—   15
call it a council between equals call it love.

ACTIVITIES

VOCABULARY

inviolate, adj. — incapable of being harmed or destroyed, sacred
renounce, v. — to give up, abandon

CLASS ACTIVITY: One Plus One = ?

Two souls merging into one may be an appealing poetic image, but it probably is not the wisest model for a happy marriage. "Beyond What" and the following three excerpts all contain thoughts about love and togetherness. Divide the class into four groups, one for each of the readings. Study together for about 20 minutes. Analyze the main ideas and consider how they would translate into practical advice for couples considering marriage. Then use your own words and specific examples to explain your reading to the rest of the class.

A. *"A good relationship has a pattern like a dance and is built on some of the same rules. The partners do not need to hold on tightly because they move confidently in the same pattern, intricate but gay and swift and free, like a country dance of Mozart's. To touch heavily would be to arrest the pattern and freeze the movement, to check the endlessly changing beauty of its unfolding. There is no place here for the possessive clutch, the clinging arm, the heavy hand; only the barest touch in passing. Now arm in arm, now face to face, now back to back — it does not matter which. Because they know they are partners moving to the same rhythm, creating a pattern together, and being invisibly nourished by it."* (From *Gift From the Sea* by Anne Morrow Lindbergh)

B. *"A togetherness between two people is an impossibility, and where it seems, nevertheless, to exist, it is a narrowing, a reciprocal agreement which robs either* *one party or both of his fullest freedom and development. But, once the realization is accepted that even between the closest human beings infinite distances continue to exist, a wonderful living side by side can grow up, if they succeed in loving the distance between them which makes it possible for each to see the other whole and against a wide sky!"* (From *Letters* by Rainer Maria Rilke (tr. J.B. Greene and M.D.H. Norton)

C. *"It takes years to marry completely two hearts, even of the most loving and well-assorted. A happy wedlock is a long falling in love. Young persons think love belongs only to the brown-haired and crimson-cheeked. So it does for its beginning. But the golden marriage is a part of love which the bridal day knows nothing of.*

"A perfect and complete marriage, where wedlock is everything you could ask and the ideal of marriage becomes actual, is not common, perhaps as rare as personal beauty. Men and women are married fractionally, now a small fraction, then a large fraction. Very few are married totally, and then only after some forty or fifty years of gradual approach and experiment.

"Such a large and sweet fruit is a complete marriage that it needs a long summer to ripen in, and then a long winter to mellow and season it. But a real, happy marriage of love and judgment between a noble man and woman is one of the things so very handsome that if the sun were, as the Greek poets fabled, a God, he might stop the world and hold it still now and then in order to look all day long on some example thereof, and feast his eyes on such a spectacle." (From a selection by Theodore Parker)

THE BIRTHDAY PARTY
by Katherine Brush

T hey were a couple in their late thirties, and they looked unmistakably married. They sat on the banquette opposite us in a little narrow restaurant, having dinner. The man had a round, self-satisfied face, with glasses on it; the woman was fadingly pretty, in a big hat. There was nothing conspicuous about them, nothing particularly noticeable, until the end of the meal when it suddenly became obvious that this was an occasion — in fact, the husband's birthday, and the wife had planned a little surprise for him.

It arrived in the form of a small but glossy birthday cake with one pink candle burning in the center. The headwaiter brought it in and placed it before the husband, and meanwhile the violin-and-piano orchestra played "Happy Birthday to You!" and the wife beamed with pride over her little surprise, and such few people as there were in the restaurant tried to help out with a pattering of applause. It became clear at once that help was needed, because the husband was not pleased. Instead he was hotly embarrassed, and indignant at his wife for embarrassing him.

You looked at him and you saw this and thought, "Oh, now, don't be like that!" But he was like that, and as soon as the little cake had been deposited on the table, and the orchestra had finished the birthday piece, and the general attention had shifted from the man and the woman, I saw his movement to say something to her under his breath — some punishing thing, quick and curt and unkind. I couldn't bear to look at the woman then, so I stared at my place and waited for quite a long time. Not long enough though. She was still crying when I finally glanced over there again. Crying quietly and heartbrokenly and hopelessly all to herself under the big brim of her best gay hat.

ACTIVITIES
_____

VOCABULARY:

banquette, n. — a long, upholstered bench
pattering, n. — quick, light, soft clapping
indignant, adj. — angry at being treated badly
curt, adj. — rudely abrupt

FOR DISCUSSION

A. It is the husband's birthday, so they decide to celebrate by going out to dinner. The wife arranges for a special cake, but the husband is not the only one who is surprised when it is delivered. How is the wife also surprised?

We see the story unfold through the eyes of another guest in the restaurant. Does this narrator sympathize with the husband or with the wife? Who do *you* think is to blame for the disaster that results, the husband or the wife? Is he an unappreciative bore, or is she too insensitive to realize that her husband would be embarrassed by the attention?

B. Maybe the husband was just having a bad day. Our physical condition, the events and people in our lives, and perhaps even the weather, can affect our moods. We may be much quicker to snap at a friend on the day our history exam comes back with an "F" than on the day the grade is an "A." On the other hand, it pays to be alert to the moods of those around us. Are there days when it seems wise to stay out of the kitchen at your house or when you decide you'd better be on your best behavior in class?

What are the danger signals? An eagerly anticipated phone call doesn't come? An overdue bill arrives in the mail? A headache? An unexpected visitor? What circumstances tend to make you or those close to you more irritable than usual.

CLASS ACTIVITY: You Finish the Picture

In a well-written story, particularly one this short, every word is chosen carefully. We are not given much specific information about this married couple, just an impression. They are fairly average, neither particularly young nor particularly old but *"in their late thirties.* There is *"nothing particularly noticeable"* about them. He has *"a round face with glasses on it,"* nothing distinctive. She may once have been a beauty; however, she is only *"fadingly pretty"* now. But it is her hat that is important enough to the story to be mentioned twice. What kind of hat is it? What does it tell us about her? Is she perhaps not quite as lackluster and dull as her husband?

The restaurant chosen for this special occasion befits this couple. It is *"little and narrow"* with only a few other guests. It does have an *"orchestra,"* but orchestra usually means more instruments than just a violin and piano. The birthday cake is also small, though admittedly *"glossy,"* and even the applause is just a *"pattering."* What is the author telling us about this couple? From the few details, use your imagination to fill in the picture.

- What kind of job do you think the husband has?
- How does his wife spend her days?
- What kind of car(s) do they drive?
- Do they have children? If so, how many? What are their names?
- How do they spend their leisure time? Where do they go for vacations?
- What are their favorite television programs?
- What did they order from the menu the night of the birthday party?
- How long have they been married?

CLASS ACTIVITY: "For Better, For Worse . . ."

The greatest joys as well as the greatest sorrows in life almost always involve other people. Nothing is more important than the relationships we establish. But as we've seen in so many of the stories in this book, loving and being loved are not always easy. Good relationships take work to establish and to maintain. But the good news is that the payoff is usually well worth the effort.

The author describes the couple as *"unmistakably married."* What does this phrase mean? Obviously it does not mean that they are holding hands and staring passionately into each other's eyes. How does a couple look *"unmistakably married?"* If this incident in the restaurant is typical of exchanges between this husband and wife, their relationship is far from ideal. What do you think has gone wrong? How did they get to this point where they don't communicate well with each other? Something has to be done if they want to rekindle the passion that presumably drew them together many years ago.

CONGRATULATIONS!! After many grueling years of medical school and an internship as a psychiatrist, you have finally opened your own office. Your specialty is marriage counseling, and the husband and wife of "The Birthday Party" are your first clients. What advice would you give them? Since this is your first case, you decide to consult some of the other doctors in your group practice. Break up into discussion groups of five or six and brainstorm. After about ten minutes, come together as a class again. Have one person report on the discussion in each group. Are there suggestions everyone agrees upon? Can you role play their discussion during and after the birthday party to show them how the situation should have been handled?

FUNERAL PLANS

by J. California Cooper from *A Piece of Mine*

I shouldn't be tellin this secret, but you can just call me Ms. Can'thel-pit cause I just can't help it! I got to tell it!

You can say what you willomay but I believe the Lord gives you something every time something else is taken away! If you got half a piece of sense, you will find that to be true. Just call me Ms. Senseless cause it has taken me so many years to truly know what that means and then I learned it from someone else . . . one of my friends, Willetta. I call her "Letta."

Letta and me kinda grew up together in this little one horse town, but I believe no matter how small a town is, it's still got some of every kind of people the whole world got in it.

Letta's people was as good to her as two poor people could be. She was their only child, and the Lord had sure blessed them in that one thing. They both worked hard. The mama sewing and cooking for white folks and the daddy farming his own little piece of land and doing odd jobs and also working at the plant just outside of town there. They must have loved each other too, another blessing of the Lord's, cause they sure needed it. Letta studied hard in school cause they was planning for her to go on to college and she really was smart! Me, myself, I just dreamed of getting married someday. Ms. Dreamy, you could call me.

But when Letta was just past fifteen years, her mama had taken a nice lunch over to her daddy's job at the plant, and as the devil would have it, one of them evil white men who was sitting in his tractor, having only a warm beer for his lunch, decided to "play" a game on Letta's daddy and slowly backed that tractor up and claimed, when he planned to stop, the tractor kept going backward! Well, Letta's mama and papa was crushed up bad! The mother lost her legs, had to have em both cut off! And her daddy's ankles and knees and hips, and shoulders was pushed together and he never could straighten out again. Leastways the doctor didn't think there was no big reason for goin through too much trouble for em cause what was they good for anyway? I heard that myself cause I use to, and still do, kitchen work for some of the best folks here in town, and I hears a lot! You can call me Ms. Goodear, cause I got em! Well, say what you willomay, you got to know what's goin on around you, if for nothin else cept to stay out the way of other folks' tractors!

Well, back to Letta and her troubles! The plant said it wasn't no fault of theirs cause it was all in "fun," not at working, so they didn't have to pay nothin! Nothin! The hospital sent a big bill, and I don't know what for, cause Letta's mama and daddy came out of that hospital just like they went in, bent up and crushed! Ain't no pills in the world worth all the money was on that bill! Letta just put that bill in a drawer and shut it! Was a nice white man and his wife her mama had worked for came over and had the house fixed to Letta's name and the hospital couldn't take that when it tried, so the bill just stayed in that drawer . . . for 25 or 30 years till she threw it out, til her mama and papa died, cause that's how long she taken care of them!

And I mean she took care of them! That's why I said they was blessed! Neither one could move! You had to put them to the pot, put them to bed, get them up, set them up somewhere and feed em, all of it! She did it! I use to feel so sorry for them two people . . . just set and face and stare at each other all day long and sometimes tears comin down one face for a while and then the other, til Letta make them smile bout somethin. She kept them clean and the house clean. I would hear her sigh, them great big tired breaths sometimes but she didn't never act mad cause her life had changed so. Future all gone. Present gonna stay forever, look like.

Oh, people came over at first, preachers and neighbors, to try to run her little house and business but she didn't want none of that, said she wasn't no child. She was proving that! Sho was! I helped her all I could.

Now, Letta had helped her mama work, cookin, sewing and washing, so she just kept doin these things and she took to doin hair in her kitchen for a few friends and so she was able to make it. She sold some of their things what was valuable to them, watches, clothes they was never goin to use again, the piano, things like that. But not her mama's wedding ring. She used to get so mad and frustrated and she would cry! Chile, there wouldn't be nothin to eat! But she never sold that ring, it stayed right on her mother's finger! Said, "my mama got to have something!" Well, they did have something! Her!

I don't have to tell nobody who ever worked for money for a livin, how hard it can get to keep goin on. Letta suffered plenty hardships and went without almost everything! Some days, she didn't eat, but mama and daddy did! Many a night she didn't sleep, just tossed, cried at first, but finally just tossed and thought . . . hard. No candles or electric lights at night . . . save that money! Don't burn that little bit of firewood, go to bed and cover up. She could sew, but couldn't sew for herself, so her clothes got pretty full of thin places and she was still growing. Some of her old friends, the stupid ones, laughed at her when they see her in them clothes, glad to see her not lookin so cute anymore. She would get so disgusted, but I never did see her get mean and bitter. She just try to keep carryin on . . . and she did. Things got better over the years tho. Now I say that and the sayin goes so quick! To say "a year" takes less than a second I bet, and for Letta, a year, each year, took 365, 24-hour days. Long years.

Letta's sewing got mighty fine and the best people used her, and I mean USED her. They paid her half of what it should have cost, but they knew she needed whatever she could get, so that's what they paid her, whatever they could get away with. And her bakin stuff she was turnin out was truly beautiful to see and sho nuff good to taste! She had taken them tools her mama-dear had given her and turned them into blessings and a full way! She was a full provider long before she was 20 years old.

I had done got married bout that time and had two little sweet children I was raisin. They so sweet when they little! Me and my husband bought a little land and we builded a little house with our own hands. I loved my home and, come to think of it, Letta even came over there once to give us a hand on our house! She was somethin! Call me Ms. Admirer cause I sure admired her!

Some mens did too, but when they come over to her house and see those two skeleton-like bodies sittin there all day and fixin for them and them just staring and sometimes droolin, well you can't catch everything right away, you know? Well, they just lost heart or never had it in the first place, I guess. Mens! They want to "fool" around, say that's what she need to relax her body! But she didn't want none of that! She say she did WANT it but not that way, cause one more mouth to feed by herself, and she would kill everything in that house! Letta had to be more tired than even I thought cause Letta had a good heart, not mean at all and wouldn't just ordinary think of killin! Anyway, they never got married to her, so she was alone . . . that kinda alone . . . man and woman kind.

Well about 25 years or so after the "accident," Letta's mama died quiet in her sleep and Letta didn't say it was a relief or not. Just hugged and rocked her mama til they took her away, then she put her mama's wedding ring on a chain and put it around her neck. I said, "Why don't you wear it on your finger?" I didn't add the rest of what I was thinkin bout she wasn't never going to get one of her own, but that's what I thought . . . she was bout 40 then, or more! She told me, "No! I want my own wedding ring on my finger!" Well, you can call me Ms. Hushmouth, cause I sure know when to do that!

My husband had been dead five years or so, then. Worked hisself to death, in the cold and damp, days and nights of our life. Making food, finding food, going for medicine at nights in the rain, walking babies when he needed his sleep and I was sick and couldn't, so many things. He was a good man . . . my good man and my world. But one night my world slipped away from me and I was alone to raise my children. Course, I had my mama's help, but I got to know a little more what Letta was going through, had gone through all her life. You could call me Ms. Tired and Sad, cause that's all I remember bein . . . tired and sad.

Letta's father lived on another four or five years then he passed away too. She buried him lovingly, too. I began to look at Letta kinda funny then. Was somethin wrong with her? I mean, how can one person do everything right? Was she human? This was goin too far! She was too good to be true! I got kinda mad at her . . . not jealous . . . mad! She was my friend, but I didn't like her bein so good! Well, you can just call me Ms. Shamed cause I'm shamed I forgot all she had been through ALL her life. The Lord had to have given her strength and there I was getting mad at her for havin it! Just call me Ms. Shamed! How I know how tight she was holding on? Or how close she was lettin go, losin her hold? Well, I done already told you once, you could call me Ms. Senseless!

Two or three months after the father passed, Letta came by my mama's house. I had done lost mine, my husband built for me. Had taken a few loans out to help my kids in some personal and sickness problems and the kids had done moved away somewhere else and I couldn't pay them notes and so they took my million dollar home for $400, and I moved back to my mama's. She was down and I was taken care of her anyway. I loved her and she had been good to me. She was dying too tho. Well, she was old. Hell, I was old! Seemed like I was always just between life and death, life and death. Scared of life and scared of death. Call me Ms. Scared, cause that's the way I was runnin then.

Anyway, Letta stopped by the house one day and said, "I want you to bring me some of them fancy ladies clothes magazines from your job sometimes, if you will, Ms. Friend." She always call me "Ms. Friend."

I said, "I sho will, Letta. You mean the real fancy ones?"

"Real, real fancy, Ms. Friend."

"You want some of the recipes magazines?"

"Yea" she smiled, "Bring some of them too, I got a plan!"

"You got a plan?" My ears perked up.

"Yes." Her smile was what you would call BRIL-LI-ANT. "Been thinkin about my life . . . now that it's mine to do with whatever I want! All mine!" I looked at her and she did look rested and better and I would say younger except you don't have to be younger to look good! So I asked her, "You ain't gone fly off to no big city and leave me here is you?" I laughed, but I sho didn't want her to go. Misery lovin company I guess, but . . . well, shame, shame, shame. She laughed back, "No, I'm too tired for a big city. I just want a good husband and I got a plan to get the kind of man I want . . . I think!"

"Plenty of these men roun here want to marry you now, Letta!" She frowned up her face "Yea, now that I ain't got any problems! But they the ones with the problem now . . . they are all poor, cept for the ones already married, and I have decided! I do not want a poor man or a poor nothin! I have already done all the poor I can take! Sides, I want to be in love and be loved!" I was gettin excited cause I wanted to talk about things like this and never did know I had anybody to talk bout them with! I said, "I would just like a man of my own!" She answered me right back, "I don't just want a husband, a man, Ms. Friend, they ain't all that hard to get. I want somethin special! Somethin different! Somethin else from all what I know!"

I couldn't say nothin but "YEA!"

She went on, "See, I got this plan. Now I may not win at it, maybe I'll lose at it . . . but one thing, I won't regret tryin it! I want LOVE and I think I know somethin!" She laughed a little girl laugh, "Anyway, I got a plan!"

She left then and I wanted to follow her home and talk some more but I heard my mama callin me. I thought about her plan and love all night. I rushed to work so fast the next day the lady I work for musta thought I was goin crazy and if she hadn't given me them books, I might've gone crazy for real all over her.

I took them magazines over to Letta's soon as I could cause I wanted to hear bout that plan! She was playin her new second-hand piano when I got there. She was takin lessons again for the last year or so and was soundin real good! She was playin a spiritual, with great big dips and curves and deep bass bumps in it! You can just call me Ms. Spiritual, cause I loves them! The house was beginning to look different. Not new but with more life in it. New curtains, slip covers and things like that. Say what you willomay, hope shows! Anyway, we got together over them books and this is what Letta told me. She say, "See, I been close to death for years and years. It don't scare me none. I've even seen some beauty in it. Death is mighty powerful but it can be kind and gentle too. And I done been to a lot of funerals, too many maybe, but I plan to go to a lot more fore its over."

Now, I lowered my voice to the correct funeral tone and said, "Oh, I hope not Letta."

But she said, "Oh I hope so! Not wishin nobody to die, still they gone do it whether I want them to or not! And I been noticing . . . if a woman die, a man is left alone! If a man die, his friends come to the final hours and some of them is single and good men!" Well, right there I began to see. You can call me Ms. Quicksee now! She went on, "Well, I can sew and now I got a little extra money to spend on myself, I been makin me some beautiful clothes, bettern any I ever seen anyone wear round here!"

Well, she sure was right about that! That sewin can sure help your closet!

She went on, "Only chance I get to dress is for a funeral! And I'm the best dressed thing there! And everybody brings food and my cakes are the best lookin and best tastin, except for the real old ladies been bakin a long time, cause I been makin them for a livin! Now, I'm learning plenty new ways to make a cake look like a angel baked it!"

Well, she was talking to her friend so a little braggin didn't hurt nothin!

On she went. "I'm playin the piano better and better, so now is my time to stretch out! There is funerals around here up to 20 or 30 miles away I can go to, and even further out where I have some relatives! Why, Ms. Friend, I can find a good husband if I just make the best funerals!!"

Well, she looked so happy and hopeful I didn't have the heart to say how terrible it all sounded to me. She saw my look tho and said, "You better quit frowning and try to get you own self together! You too young to be alone the rest of your life less you want to be! Do you want to grow old all by yourself?"

I shook my head "No" cause what she said was true, I was too young! I also didn't want to keep runnin behind some bush with a man what wasn't mine, every now and then only, you know?

"Well," she said, "this can work for you too! Start doing somethin with yourself! Do you feel old?"

"No!" I shook my head again.

"Well, you better get on the ball and bounce up and do some planning of your own!"

"Yes!" I nodded, my head like to flew off, and you can call me Ms. Grinning cause it suddenly seemed alright! I grinned my butt off all the way home cause I had a plan too! That's the first day I really cleaned that house up and cooked a full, delicious meal for me and mama in a long time, since my husband died almost, cept for holidays!

Letta was ahead of me tho, she was still slim from all that work she used to have to do and she could really do her hair. And she really read them books and could copy a pattern down to the ace degree! Me, I decided I would settle for a medium kind of man. Well, facts about it, I had to! I had let some things go down I never would get up no more!

Letta started going to them funerals and taking cakes to the wakes and things. She would play the piano AFTER the funeral. She said, "No jobs, just sit and cross them clean pretty legs and look around."

Sometimes Letta went 30 miles or so . . . on the bus! She had to win! She had what it took! Bout four months later, a very well to do mortician asked her to play chamber music sometimes before the funeral. Like, you see, come early. He was single and bout her age. His business was about 35 miles away and he took to sending a car for her. A big, long black Cadillac. She was in style! Chile! Other mens came to see her but she wouldn't carry on with none of them. She said, "I might like somethin they do and end up in love with a poor man and I don't want to, so if I am not around them, I can't grow to like them!" That was that!

She always came home on that same day she left at first, but pretty soon, she didn't come home the same day! Her and that mortician was getting pretty close. Then one day, she stayed home three weeks without going anywhere. Told me, "I like that man and I could love him, but I don't want no job. I want love and a husband and that's what I know I can get! Hope it's him, but if he ain't right, he can do it with them dead folks for all I care! I sure could love him though!"

I was so busy going to funerals and learnin how to sew I didn't see her for a little while, a week or two, but when I did see her she flashed a smile and an engagement ring on me and you couldn't tell which one was the brightest! She began to drive her own big car, I don't know what it was, but it was not black! Well, Letta married that mortician and it's like her life just started! I been over there to see them, at the funerals, you know! They both look like they in love. He watch her with such pride, she watch him like to say "I'm glad I'm where you are." Funeral long gone out of their minds and they right there in the middle of it! "I understand," she tells all the bereaved.

Me, I'm still working the plan, for real now, sho nuff! Cause the other day at a funeral, a man got up to say something bout the deceased. I'm learning all the words now, I used to say, dead or passed on. Anyway, he happened to say he wasn't married. He just bout my size too. I like his looks. After the funeral, when he was blowin his nose and wiping his eyes, I walked over, patted him on the back and said, "I understand." He looked at me real bright and reached out to shake my hand and hug me. I paid good attention to how it felt to be in his arms, had to do it real quick but I liked it. I invited him to a good ole-fashion, home-cooked meal. I didn't take time to be smart like Letta. When he accepted and we was on our way to my house I wondered if he had a plan too! But I don't care. I'll tell you somethin, they say a good man is hard to find, well, a good woman is too! Anything good is hard to find and if you got any sense you don't want nobody else's. Like me, I want mine! So, when we was walkin along and talkin you could just call me Ms. Happy Hopeful cause I was!

So, now I am cuttin him a piece of dessert cake I just made this morning from a new recipe. See, I got a lot to share and you can catch more bees with honey than you can with butter, so now I'm goin on in my fresh clean livin room where this new man friend of mine is helpin my mama get comfortable and take him some of this delicious cake! You can just call me Ms. Honeybunch, cause I'm on my way!

ACTIVITIES

FOR REVIEW

Though we never learn the narrator's real name in "Funeral Plans," she does give herself a series of nicknames as she tells us about her own life and about her friend Letta. Use the following list of these nicknames to trace both the events of the story and the development of the narrator's character:

    Ms. Can'thelpit
    Ms. Senseless
    Ms. Dreamy
    Ms. Goodear
    Ms. Admirer
    Ms. Hushmouth
    Ms. Tired and Sad
    Ms. Shamed
    Ms. Scared
    Ms. Friend
    Ms. Spiritual
    Ms. Quicksee
    Ms. Grinning
    Ms. Happy Hopeful
    Ms. Honeybunch

FOR DISCUSSION: "Life Begins at Forty!"

Although the title might seem a bit inappropriate at first, "Funeral Plans" is a story about two women who want to live life to the fullest. These women have done a lot of living and a lot of thinking and a lot of talking. Though both are strong and independent, they do not want to live alone. They are convinced that life's greatest joy is to be found in a good marriage. They know what they want in a partner, and they go for it.

What does the story tell us about the need for physical and emotional intimacy? About what makes a good relationship? About letting fate take its course or trying to shape it? About passion and joy as one becomes older? Find specific quotations to support your answers.

These would be good topics to write about in your journal.

A RESEARCH PROJECT: "With this ring, . . ."

The narrator talks about a wedding or engagement ring three separate times. Locate those three times and discuss the significance of each. Both her mother's wedding ring and her own engagement ring are very important to Letta, but they mean different things to her. How do these rings reflect the different kinds of loving well we see in the story?

Some couples consider rings to be a very important part of their engagement, wedding ceremony, and marriage. Ask married friends and relatives to tell you the stories of their rings, and find out all you can about the tradition of wedding rings. You might go to the library or to a jeweler for answers to some of the following questions. Do people of all cultures wear engagement and wedding rings? Why is it tradition that women wear engagement rings but men don't? Are there new trends that reflect changing relationships between the sexes? What do wedding rings symbolize? (Can you think of anything in "Cinderella" that is comparable to a wedding ring ceremony?)

ALONE

by Maya Angelou

L ying, thinking
Last night
How to find my soul a home
Where water is not thirsty
And bread loaf is not stone   5
I came up with one thing
And I don't believe I'm wrong
That nobody,
But nobody
Can make it out here alone.   10

Alone, all alone
Nobody, but nobody
Can make it out here alone.

There are some millionaires
With money they can't use   15
Their wives run round like banshees
Their children sing the blues
They've got expensive doctors
To cure their hearts of stone.
But nobody   20
No nobody
Can make it out here alone.
Alone, all alone

Nobody, but nobody
Can make it out here alone.   25
Now if you listen closely
I'll tell you what I know
Storm clouds are gathering
The wind is gonna blow
The race of man is suffering   30
And I can hear the moan,
Cause nobody,
But nobody
Can make it out here alone.
Alone, all alone   35
Nobody, but nobody
Can make it out here alone.

ACTIVITIES

VOCABULARY

banshee, n. — a female spirit whose wailing warns of approaching death

FOR DISCUSSION

The main idea of Maya Angelou's poem is repeated six times over in very simple words. But the simple words of her poetry raise some complicated questions:

Is being alone the same as being lonely?

How is it possible to feel alone even in a crowd of people?

How is it possible to be alone without feeling lonely?

What does it mean that "nobody, but nobody can make it out here alone?"

How is it that "the race of man is suffering?"

What might the "storm clouds" be?

In which other *Loving Well* selections is loneliness an important theme? What attempts to overcome loneliness turn out badly? What are good solutions?

WRITING ASSIGNMENT: Imitations of Intimacy

The physical and emotional intimacy between a husband and wife who are deeply in love and who are committed to sharing their lives "so long as they both shall live" is unquestionably an achievement of the highest order and the best possible hedge against loneliness.

But we learn about intimacy long before we are mature enough to marry. When four year olds share a special secret, their friendship grows. If a confidence is violated, however, the friendship suffers. At this age a child may even invent an imaginary friend for company all day long and into the scary darkness of night. At times it feels safer to trust someone who can't let us down. An imaginary friend, a doll, or a pet can sometimes provide the comfort we need. To reveal ourselves to another person involves much more risk, but what an accomplishment it is to build a friendship based on intimacy and trust, to have someone with whom we can share our deepest thoughts, our hopes and fears!

Write a one page description of the best friend you have ever had. (You don't need to name names!) What was special about the two of you? Were there shortcomings in your friendship? Are you still friends? What did you learn from this experience that might help others be better friends?

LET ME NOT TO THE MARRIAGE OF TRUE MINDS

by William Shakespeare

L et me not to the marriage of true minds
Admit impediments. Love is not love
Which alters when it alterations finds,
Or bends with the remover to remove.
O no! it is an ever-fixed mark   5
That looks on tempests and is never shaken;
It is the star to every wandering bark,
Whose worth's unknown, although his height be taken.
Love's not Time's fool, though rosy lips and cheeks
Within his bending sickle's compass come;   10
Love alters not with his brief hours and weeks,
But bears it out even to the edge of doom.
If this be error and upon me proved,
I never writ, nor no man ever loved.

ACTIVITIES

VOCABULARY

impediment, n. — an obstruction, something that gets in the way
tempest, n. — storm
bark, n. — a ship
compass, n. — sweep, range
writ, v. — wrote

This famous Shakespearean sonnet consists of three quatrains, which are four line units of verse, and a concluding couplet of two rhyming lines. The poem's meaning follows its form; each quatrain and the couplet are separate sentences and separate thoughts.

FOR DISCUSSION:

1. The first quatrain states that true love remains constant in spite of any obstacle or assault. What kind of obstacles or assaults might threaten a less pure love?

2. What word in the first line indicates that the poet is describing a bond between lovers that goes far beyond infatuation or simple physical passion?

3. What comparison does the second quatrain make between true love and the North Star?

4. The third quatrain describes an image we often associate with New Year's Eve. What is this image?

5. What power does the "bending sickle" have? What are the limits of its power?

6. In the couplet the poet asserts the truth of his ideas by the use of paradox, a seemingly contradictory statement. What two contradictions can you find in the couplet?

RESEARCH PROJECT: "Till Death Do Us Part"

History and literature have produced many legendary lovers. Briefly investigate the lives and loves of any famous couple. What impediments did their love encounter? Prepare a two or three minute oral report to give to the class. Be sure to distinguish between fiction and fact. Some possibilities include:

King Edward and Wallis Simpson
Antony and Cleopatra
Robert Browning and Elizabeth Barrett
Romeo and Juliet
John and Priscilla Alden
Sir Lancelot and Queen Gwynevere
Dante and Beatrice
Troilus and Cressida
Helen of Troy and Paris
Cyrano de Bergerac and Roxanne
Henry VIII and Anne Boleyn

EXPERIENCES IN A CONCENTRATION CAMP

from *Man's Search for Meaning* by Victor Frankl

In spite of all the enforced physical and mental primitiveness of the life in a concentration camp, it was possible for spiritual life to deepen. Sensitive people who were used to rich intellectual life may have suffered much pain (they were often of a delicate constitution), but the damage to their inner selves was less. They were able to retreat from their terrible surroundings to a life of inner riches and spiritual freedom. Only in this way can one explain the apparent paradox that some prisoners of a less hardy make-up often seemed to survive camp life better than did those of a robust nature. In order to make myself clear, I am forced to fall back on personal experience. Let me tell what happened on those early mornings when we had to march to our work site.

There were shouted commands: "Detachment, forward march! Left-2-3-4! Left-2-3-4! First man about, left and left and left and left! Caps off!" These words sound in my ears even now. At the order "Caps off!" we passed the gate of the camp, and searchlights were trained upon us. Whoever did not march smartly got a kick. And worse off was the man who, because of the cold, had pulled his cap back over his ears before permission was given.

We stumbled on in the darkness over big stones and through large puddles, along the one road leading from the camp. The accompanying guards kept shouting at us and driving us with the butts of their rifles. Anyone with very sore feet supported himself on his neighbor's arm. Hardly a word was spoken; the icy wind did not encourage talk. Hiding his mouth behind his

THE ART OF LOVING WELL

upturned collar, the man marching next to me whispered suddenly: "If our wives could see us now! I do hope they are better off in their camps and don't know what is happening to us."

That brought thoughts of my own wife to mind. And as we stumbled on for miles, slipping on icy spots, supporting each other time and again, dragging one another up and onward, nothing was said, but we both knew; each of us was thinking of his wife. Occasionally I looked at the sky, where the stars were fading and the pink light of the morning was beginning to spread behind a dark bank of clouds. But my mind clung to my wife's image, imagining it with an uncanny acuteness. I heard her answering me, saw her smile, her frank and encouraging look. Real or not, her look was then more luminous than the sun which was beginning to rise.

A thought transfixed me: for the first time in my life I saw the truth as it is set into song by so many poets, proclaimed as the final wisdom by so many thinkers. The truth—that love is the ultimate and the highest goal to which man can aspire. Then I grasped the meaning of the greatest secret that human poetry and human thought and belief have to impart: *The salvation of man is through love and in love.* I understood how a man who has nothing left in this world still may know bliss, be it only for a brief moment, in the contemplation of his beloved. In a position of utter desolation, when man cannot express himself in positive action, when his only achievement may consist in enduring his sufferings in the right way—an honorable way—in such a position man can, through loving contemplation of the image he carries of his beloved, achieve fulfillment. For the first time in my life I was able to understand the meaning of the words, *"The angels are lost in perpetual contemplation of an infinite glory."*

In front of me a man stumbled and those following him fell on top of him. The guard rushed over and used his whip on them all. Thus my thoughts were interrupted for a few minutes. But soon my soul found its way back from the prisoner's existence to another world, and I resumed talk with my loved one: I asked her questions, and she answered; she questioned me in return, and I answered.

"Stop!" We had arrived at our work site. Everybody rushed into the dark hut in the hope of getting a fairly decent tool. Each prisoner got a spade or a pickax.

"Can't you hurry up, you pigs?!" Soon we had resumed the previous day's positions in the ditch. The frozen ground cracked under the point of the pickaxes, and sparks flew. The men were silent, their brains numb.

My mind still clung to the image of my wife. A thought crossed my mind: I didn't even know if she were still alive. I knew only one thing—which I have learned well by now: Love goes very far beyond the physical person of the beloved. It finds its deepest meaning in his spiritual being, his inner self. Whether or not he is actually present, whether or not he is still alive at all, ceases somehow to be of importance.

I did not know whether my wife was alive, and I had no means of finding out (during all my prison life there was no outgoing or incoming mail); but at that moment it ceased to matter. There was no need for me to know; nothing could touch the strength of my love, my thoughts, and the image of my beloved. Had I known then that my wife was dead, I think that I would still have given myself, undisturbed by that knowledge, to the contemplation of her image, and that my mental conversation with her would have been just as vivid and just as satisfying. *"Set me like a seal upon thy heart, love is as strong as death."*

ACTIVITIES

VOCABULARY

constitution, n. — physical makeup of the individual, physique

paradox, n. — a seemingly contradictory statement or situation

uncanny, adj. — mysterious beyond what is normal or expected

acuteness, n. — keen perception, sharpness

luminous, adj. — lighted, shining

transfix, v. — to hold motionless

aspire, v. — to seek to achieve something great

salvation, n. — something that saves, saving from danger, evil or sin

contemplation, n. — the act of looking at or thinking about something steadily

desolation, n. — grief, sadness, loneliness, devastation, ruin

perpetual, adj. — lasting, constant

FOR DISCUSSION

A. How does Frankl explain the fact that often physically feeble or weak prisoners in concentration camps survived better than some of the stronger, healthier prisoners?

B. Can you think of situations other than a concentration camp when the life of the mind might help sustain the life of the body?

C. Frankl uses religious imagery to reflect the supernatural or spiritual power of love. And love is often described as a special "magic" between two people. What are the special powers of love as we see them in the relationship of Frankl and his wife?

D. How would Victor Frankl define love?

CLASS ACTIVITY: The Secret to Our Success

The form of this questionnaire is by way of suggestion only. Adapt it to suit the particular interests of your class by adding or changing the questions. It can be handed out as the format for an in-class panel or as a survey. In any case, go to the experts. Interview the married couples (husband, wife or both) who seem to have a happy relationship, one you hope to emulate later in life. For this assignment, do not interview your own parents.

1. How old were you when you were married?

2. At that time, what image did you have of married life?

3. Has it turned out as you expected? What has been different?

4. What is the most difficult part of being married?

5. What is the best part?

6. Do you have any advice about loving well?

7. Can you recommend any books, poems, plays, movies or songs that you believe are especially valuable in understanding love?

CUPID AND PSYCHE
by Apuleius

P syche was the youngest daughter of a king and queen. She had two elder sisters both of whom were remarkably beautiful. Their beauty, however, might be described in words. But the beauty of Psyche herself was past all description, as was the majesty of her bearing and her sweet and gracious disposition. So from all over the world people came to the country where she lived merely to look at her. They looked at her with wonder and adoration, believing her to be either the goddess Venus herself, who was born from the foam of the sea, or else a new Venus, no less divine than the goddess of beauty and love.

Thus the temples and ceremonies of Venus were neglected. People no longer offered sacrifices and prayed to her. Instead, they thronged to visit Psyche, worshiping her as soon as she left her home in the morning, and laying garlands before her feet.

The true Venus was greatly angered by the neglect shown to her by men. "It is I," she said to herself, "to whom, on Mount Ida, Paris gave the prize of beauty. And am I to share my honours with a mere mortal girl? She will soon be sorry for being more beautiful than is allowed."

Then Venus called for her winged son, Cupid, the god of love, who with his arrows can conquer the gods themselves, who ranges over the earth like a bee, the brilliant and mischievous youth. "Now, my dear son," she said to him, "you must revenge the injury done to your mother. Mortals are worshiping this girl Psyche instead of me. I want you to make her fall in love with some wretched creature, poor and abject, the ugliest in the world. You with your bow and arrows can do this."

She took him then to the city where Psyche lived and pointed her out to him. Then she herself, after kissing her son, went to the shore nearby, planted her rosy feet on the sea-water, making it calm, and took her way over the sea to her sacred island of Cyprus. Around her played the dolphins and sea gods rose from the waves to make music for her on their horns of shell; nymphs of the sea came to shade her from the sun with their veils of silk or to hold before her eyes her golden mirror.

Meanwhile Psyche received no advantages from the adoration which was given everywhere to her extraordinary beauty. She was praised and worshiped, but no king or noble or even any common person came to woo her to be his wife. All wondered at her, but only as one might wonder at a picture or exquisite statue. Her two sisters, though less beautiful than she, had married kings. Psyche sat alone at home, hating the beauty which delighted everyone except herself.

In the end her father, suspecting that the gods must be envious of his youngest daughter, sent messengers to the oracle of Apollo to inquire what he should do. The reply of the oracle was: "Let Psyche be dressed in black, as for a funeral, and let her be placed on the top of the mountain that rises above your city. Her husband is no mortal being. He is like a dragon that flies in the night. The gods of heaven and earth, even the darkness of Styx, fear his powers."

Psyche's father and mother, who had been so proud of their daughter's beauty, now wept and lamented the sad fate that was in store for her. What the oracle commanded seemed more like death than a wedding. As they prepared to carry out the will of the oracle not only they, but all the people, wept continuously in mourning for the unhappy event. But Psyche said: "You should have wept before, in the time when everyone worshiped me and gave me the name of Venus on earth. Now you see what has come of my beauty. I am overtaken by the jealousy of the gods. Come now, lead me to the dreaded place. I myself long for this marriage I have been promised. At least it will end my unhappiness."

Then, in a great procession, most unlike a wedding procession, they took her to the wild rocky summit of the mountain. There were no glad songs or bright lights. Tears put out the torches. The people went back to their houses with bowed heads, and Psyche's wretched parents shut themselves for days in their palace, mourning for her fate.

Meanwhile Psyche was left alone, trembling and weeping, on the high rock. But there came a mild gentle breeze which softly lifted her from the ground and carried her, with her clothes lightly fluttering, gradually past the precipices and forests till it brought her to a deep and sheltered valley where she was laid down on a bed of grassy turf among the most beautiful and sweet-smelling flowers. This soft bed and the fragrance of the flowers calmed Psyche's restless and astonished mind. Soon she rose to her feet and saw in front of her a fine and pleasant wood with, in the middle of it, a running river as bright as crystal. And there among the trees stood a palace so beautiful that you would think it to be a mansion for one of the gods. The roof was made of citron and ivory. It was supported by pillars of gold. The pavements were of precious stones arranged by some great artist in the form of splendid pictures of animals, birds and flowers. The walls were built of great blocks of gold, and each door and porchway seemed to give out its own light.

The wonder of the place so enchanted Psyche that she boldly went inside and here again found everything magnificent and looked lovingly at everything. There were fine store rooms full of rich dresses and all kinds of wealth. What greatly surprised her was that in all the palace nothing was barred or bolted, nor was there anyone there to guard all these immense riches. While she stood still, half in amazement and half in delight at what she saw, she heard a voice, though no body was to be seen. "Why do you wonder, my lady, at all this wealth? It is yours to command. We, whose voices you hear, are your servants and are ready to do anything you desire. Go therefore to your room and rest on your bed. Then tell us which kind of bath you wish to have prepared for you. Then, when you have refreshed your body, a royal dinner will be served."

Psyche, wondering still more, went to her room and rested. After a perfumed bath, she found the table all set for her convenience. Invisible hands brought her rare wines and delicious dishes of food. After dinner, another unseen servant came and sang; yet another played on the harp. Then it seemed that she was in the middle of a great choir of voices singing most perfectly to the sound of all kinds of instruments. Yet singers and instruments alike were invisible.

As night approached the concert of music ended and Psyche went to bed. Now she became frightened at the thought of the terrible husband promised her by the oracle; but again invisible voices assured her that her husband was one to be loved and not feared. When it was dark, he came and lay down beside her. Though she never saw his face, she heard his voice and felt his body. In the morning he left before dawn, after telling her of his love and promising to return to her each night. So, though she was lonely in the day, she passed each day in great pleasure, being most pleased with the beautiful singing voices that surrounded her; and each night she spent with her husband whom she loved more and more.

Meanwhile her father and mother did nothing but weep and lament for their daughter whom they thought must certainly be lost forever, either devoured by wild beasts or by the terrible dragon. The news of her fate spread far and wide, and Psyche's two sisters came to visit their parents and to mourn with them. That night Psyche's husband spoke to her. He said: "My sweet love and dear wife, a cruel fortune is bringing you into terrible danger, and I wish you to be greatly careful. Your sisters, thinking that you are dead, will come to the mountain in order to mourn for you. If you hear their voices, do not answer them, for, if you do, you will bring me great sorrow and bring yourself absolute ruin."

Psyche listened to him and promised that she would do as he said; but, when he went away next day, she passed all her time in weeping, and began to think that her fine house was really no better than a prison, if she was allowed to see no one and not even able to console her dear sisters who were mourning for her. She ate nothing that day and took no pleasure in her music. Red-eyed with crying, she went to bed early. Her husband also returned earlier than usual and at once he said to her: "Is this the way you keep your promise, my sweet wife? Crying all day and not even now comforted in your husband's arms? Do what you want to do. You may remember my words too late, if you bring on yourself your own ruin."

Then Psyche begged him more and more urgently to give her what she wanted, that she might see her sisters and speak with them. In the end he was won over by her entreaties and told her that she should give her sisters all the gold and jewels that she wished, but he earnestly entreated her never to be led by her sisters' advice into a longing to see his own face. If she did so, he said, she would lose the good life she had now, and would never feel his arms about her again.

Psyche was now full of gratitude and love for him. "I would die a hundred times," she said, "rather than be separated from you, my sweet husband. Whoever you are, I love you and keep you in my heart as though you were my own life. I could not love you more if you were Cupid himself. Now I beg you to let your servant the West Wind bring my sisters down to me here to-morrow, as he brought me." Then she kissed him and called him her sweet soul, her husband and her darling. He, such was the power of her love, agreed to do as she desired.

Next day her sisters came to the rock where Psyche had been seen last, and there they cried and lamented for her, so that the rock rang with their cries. The sound came to Psyche's ears and she called back to them, "I whom you weep for am here, alive and happy." Then she called to the West Wind who gently carried her two sisters down to the valley where she lived. For long there was nothing but embracing and tears of joy. Then Psyche showed her sisters her gorgeous house with its store of treasure. She ordered the unseen musicians to sing; she feasted them with fine food and wine, and they (shameful creatures that they were) became filled with envy of her and determined in some way to ruin her happiness. Often they asked her about her husband, and Psyche, remembering the warning that she had had, pre-tended that she knew him by sight. He was a handsome young man, she said, with the down just growing on his chin, and his chief pleasure in the day was to go hunting in the mountains. Then, since she feared that she might make some mistake in her speech, she gave them all the gold and jewels that they could carry and ordered the West Wind to take them back to the mountain.

No sooner were they alone together than they each began bitterly and enviously to complain of Psyche's good fortune. "She is the youngest one of us three," said the older sister. "Why should she have a palace and stores of wealth? Why should she have those miraculous servants and be able to give orders to the West Wind? Indeed her husband may end by making her into a goddess. Even now she has every happiness. As for me, my husband is old enough to be my father. He is as bald as a coot and he keeps all his riches under lock and key."

The second sister was just as jealous as the first. "My husband," she said, "is always ill and I have to waste my time nursing him as though I were a doctor's assistant. I certainly cannot bear to see my younger sister so happy. Let us therefore tell no one of what we have seen; and let us try to think of some way in which we can do her harm."

So these unnatural sisters hid the gold and jewels which Psyche had given them. Instead of consoling their parents with the news of her safety and happiness, they pretended that they had searched the mountains for her in vain and that they were, with their sad faces, still mourning for her loss.

Afterwards, they went back to their own homes, and there began to think out plans by which they could somehow injure the sister whom they pretended to love.

Meanwhile Psyche's husband again spoke to her in the night. "My sweet wife," he said to her, "those wicked sisters of yours are threatening you with great evil. I think that they will come to see you again. Now I beg you either not to talk with them at all (which would be the best thing) or at least not to talk to them about me. If you obey me, we shall still be happy. Already you have in your body a child of yours and mine. If you conceal my secret, the child, when it is born, will be a god; if you do not, then it will be a mortal."

Psyche was very glad to know that she would have a divine child and was more pleased with her husband than ever. But her sisters hastened on with their wicked plots and, as they had arranged, came once more to the country where Psyche was. Once again her husband warned her: "Now is the last and final day," he said. "Now I beg you, sweet Psyche, to have pity on yourself, on me and on our unborn child. Do not see these wicked women who do not deserve to be called your sisters."

But Psyche said, "Dear husband, you know that you can trust me. Did I not keep silent before? Let me at least see my sisters, since I cannot see you. Not that I blame you for this, and indeed darkness is like day to me when I hold you, who are my light, within my arms."

With such words she persuaded him once more to order the West Wind to carry her sisters to her. Before dawn he left her, and early in the day her sisters were brought to the soft and fragrant valley and to her palace. They were gladly welcomed as before by Psyche, who told them proudly that before many months she would become a mother. This made the sisters more jealous than ever, but they hid their feelings beneath smiling faces and began to ask her once more about her husband. Psyche, forgetting that before she had told them that he was a young man, now said that he was a great merchant from a nearby province, and that among his brown hair he had a few hairs of grey. Instantly the two sisters, when Psyche had left them for a moment alone, began to say she must be lying. "Perhaps," said one of them, "she has never seen her husband. If so, then he must be one of the gods and she will have a child who will be more than mortal. How can we bear this, that our youngest sister should have everything? Let us at once think out some lies by which we may destroy her."

So they spoke together, and when Psyche returned to them she found that they were both weeping. Not knowing that their tears were pretended, she asked them in surprise what had happened. "Poor Psyche," they said, "you who do not know the face of your husband, it is terrible for us to tell you the truth, but we must do so to save your life and the life of the child who will be born to you. The real shape of your husband is not what you think at all. No, it is a great and savage snake that comes to you every night. Remember the oracle that said you would be married to a fierce dragon. The country people have often seen him, swimming through the rivers as he returns at evening. They say that he will wait a little longer and then eat both you and your child. We have done our sad duty in telling you of this. If you are wise, you will take our loving advice and escape from your danger while you still may."

Poor Psyche in her simplicity believed in the false story and in her sisters' love. "It is true," she said, "that I have never seen my husband's face, and he tells me that something dreadful will happen to me if I try to see it. Oh, what am I to do?"

Then her sisters began to work still more upon her fears. "We will help you in this, as in everything," they said. "What you must do is to take a knife as sharp as a razor and hide it under your pillow. You must have hidden also in your bedroom a lamp with oil ready for burning. When he comes to bed and his limbs are all relaxed in sleep, you must get up quietly, on your bare feet, light the lamp, and holding the knife firmly, cut off the head of that poisonous serpent just where it joins the neck. If you do this, we will come back to you next day. We will take all the riches out of his house and marry you to some real man who is not a monster."

Then these wicked women left her, and Psyche, trembling and shrinking from the thought of it, still prepared to do what her sisters had advised. Night came, and her husband, after he had kissed her and taken her in his arms, soon fell asleep. Psyche, made bold by fear, yet still scarcely able to believe that what her sisters had told her was true, slipped from the bed, grasped the knife firmly in her right hand and took the lamp, hardly daring to wonder what she would see when the lamp was lit. What she saw was no monster, but the sweetest of all things, Cupid himself, at whose sight even the lamp burned more brightly. His hair was gold and seemed itself to shine; his neck was whiter than milk; the tender down on the feathers of his wings trembled with the light movement of his breathing and of the air. For long Psyche gazed in love and wonder at the beauty of his divine face, his smooth and soft body. In shame at what she had thought of doing she turned the knife against herself, but the knife shrunk from such a dreadful act and slipped from her hands. At the foot of the bed were Cupid's bow and arrows, small weapons for so great a god. Psyche took them up and, as she tried the sharpness of an arrow on her finger, she pricked herself. Then of her own accord she fell in love with Love and she bent over the bed, kissing him with joy and thankfulness as he slept.

As she was doing so a drop of burning oil fell on the white shoulder of the sleeping god. He woke and saw that she had broken her promise and her faith. Without uttering a word he fled away from her kisses and her embraces; but she clung to him, following him out of the great palace and crying to him.

Then he alighted on the top of a cypress-tree and spoke angrily to her: "Oh foolish Psyche, think how I disobeyed the orders of my mother, who told me that you should be married to some base and worthless man, and instead of this I came myself to be your husband. Did I seem a monster to you that you should try to cut off my head with its eyes that love you so much? Did I not warn you often of this? Your sisters will suffer for what they have done. You too will suffer from not having me with you."

He fled away through the air and Psyche, as long as she could see him, kept her eyes fixed on him as he went, weeping and crying for him. When he had gone beyond her sight, in her despair she threw herself into the running river; but the gentle stream would not take her life; instead it set her on the bank, where again she lamented what she had lost.

The sun rose in the sky and Psyche, weary and wretched, turned away from the palace where she had lived, and wandered through forests and rocky ways aimlessly, except that her aim was to find somehow, if it might be possible, her husband. In her wanderings she came to the city where the husband of her eldest sister was king. She could not forgive her sister's treachery, and now she pretended to be more simple than she really was. To her sister's questions she replied, "I took your advice, my dear sister, but when I raised the lamp, I saw no monster but Cupid himself. Because of my disobedience he has left me, and he said that instead of me he would have you as his wife."

No sooner had Psyche spoken these words than her sister, without offering Psyche herself any help in her distress, hurried away from her home and came to the mountain as she had done before. There was no West Wind blowing, but in spite of this the greedy and deceitful creature threw herself down, crying out: "Now Cupid, I come to you. Take me to yourself as a more worthy wife." Instead of the gentle passage through the air which she had expected, her body was torn and broken on the rocks. Wild beasts and birds tore it limb from limb and devoured it. The other sister suffered the same fate, for Psyche in her wanderings came also to her city and told her the same story that she had told to the elder of the two. Her greed and folly were the same, and she had the punishment that she deserved.

So Psyche went through country after country looking for her husband Cupid. He, however was resting in his mother's house, ill and suffering from the wound in his shoulder which had been made by the burning oil. Nor did his mother Venus yet know anything of what had happened. But a talkative white gull came to her as she was bathing on the sea-shore and told her of how Cupid was wounded and how he had lived in marriage with her enemy Psyche. At this news the anger of Venus grew greater than ever it had been. "Will he," she said, "not only disobey his own mother, but actually fall in love with this wicked girl whose beauty was said to be equal to mine? I shall lock him in the house and make him suffer for it. As for the girl, I shall find her and make her wish she had never set eyes upon my son."

Then she mounted her glorious chariot of gold, thick set with precious stones. Four white doves drew the chariot lightly through the air; sparrows chirped merrily around it, and there followed flocks of all kinds of singing birds, who, being in the choir of Venus, had no fear of hawks, eagles or other fierce birds of prey. So, as the clouds yielded before her, Venus went on her way to heaven and there she complained to all the gods and goddesses of her son Cupid and of his love for Psyche. The others, and especially Juno and Ceres, tried to soothe her anger, partly because they were afraid of Cupid themselves; but Venus refused to be comforted, and ordered her servants to search for Psyche throughout the world.

Meanwhile Psyche, tired out with her wandering and with the weight of her child that had not yet been born, visited the temples of all the gods, asking them for their help. Juno and Ceres indeed would have wished to help her, but they did not dare to offend Venus. Though all pitied her, none would give her rest and sanctuary, so that in the end Psyche decided, in her despair, that she would go to the house of Venus herself. "Perhaps," she thought, "my mother-in-law will forgive me and have pity on me. Perhaps I shall see my husband. Then at least I shall die happy. And in any case my life is now unbearable."

Venus, when she saw the girl for whom she had been so long searching, laughed cruelly at her. "So you have at last decided to come and call on me, have you?" she said. "I suppose you are thinking that, just because you are going to have a baby, I shall be glad to be called a grandmother! You wicked immoral girl, I shall soon show you what I think of you."

Then she leapt on Psyche, tearing her clothes and pulling her hair and knocking her head upon the ground. Afterwards, with her fierce cruel anger satisfied, she put in front of her a great pile of wheat, barley, millet, poppy-seed, peas, lentils and beans. She said, "You are so ugly that no one could want you for your face. Possibly you might find a husband by being a good housewife. Let me see what you can do. I order you to separate all these different grains from each other, before I come back from dinner." Then Venus, putting garlands on her bright gold hair, went away to a great banquet and Psyche sat in front of the heap of grain, weeping to herself since she knew that her task was impossible.

But a little ant took pity on her. He went out and spoke to all the other ants, saying, "My friends, let us help this poor girl who is the wife of Cupid and in great danger of her life." So the ants came and with their quick careful labour soon neatly separated the grains each in its own pile.

At midnight Venus returned, all fragrant with perfumes and well warmed with wine. When she saw how the work was done, she said: "This is not your doing, you vile wicked thing. It must be the work of he who loves you." Then she threw Psyche a crust of brown bread and she saw that Cupid was locked in the most secure room of the house. So these two, who loved each other, spent separate and sad hours in the same house.

In the morning Venus came to Psyche and said, "You see that river over there, with reeds and bushes along the banks? By the river is a flock of sheep which have fleeces gleaming with gold. Go and bring me back some of their wool."

Psyche rose from the hard floor and went out. Her real wish now was to throw herself in the river and die; but when she reached the river a tall green reed, by divine inspiration, spoke to her and said; "Poor innocent Psyche, do not stain my holy water by your death. But do not go near those terrible wild sheep until after the middle of the day. Till noon they are fierce and will kill anyone who comes near them. Afterwards they will rest in the shade and you may easily go up to them and take the wool you will find hanging on the briars."

Warned by this gentle reed, Psyche did as she was advised and in the afternoon came back to Venus with her apron full of the wool from the golden fleeces. Venus still frowned at her in anger. "This again," she said, "is no work of your own. Now I will prove whether you have the courage that you pretend to have. Do you see that overhanging rock at the top of the great mountain over there? From that rock gushes out a stream of black and freezing water that feeds the rivers of Hell, Styx, and Cocytus. Go to the very summit and bring me a bottle of water from the middle of the source of the stream."

Psyche climbed the mountain, but when she drew near the summit she thought indeed that it would be better to hurl herself down on the rocks than to proceed any further with her task. The black stream ran in great foaming cataracts, and slid over slippery stones. Even the force of water and the rugged steep slopes were enough to make her journey impossible. Then on each side of the stream she saw great dragons creeping over the hollow rocks and stretching out their long necks. Their sleepless eyes never ceased to watch the sacred water, and the water itself foamed and bubbled with voices all saying, "Go away! Go away! Fly or you will die."

Psyche therefore stood still, weeping at the hopelessness of what lay before her. But Jupiter's royal eagle saw her and wished to do good to the wife of Cupid. He flew past her face and said to her, "Poor simple girl, do you think that you can even approach these terrible waters that are feared even by the gods? Give me your bottle." Then, taking her bottle in his beak, he flew past the darting tongues and flashing teeth of the dragons, plunged the bottle in the stream and brought it back filled with the water of Styx. Psyche took it back to Venus who again looked angrily at her and spoke harshly. "You must be," she said, "some sort of witch or enchantress to carry out my orders so quickly. Well, there is one more thing that I want you to do. Take this box and go down to hell, to the dwellings of the dead. There you are to ask Proserpine, the Queen of Hell, to send me a little of her beauty, just enough to last for a day. Tell her that I have lost some of mine in looking after my son who is wounded. But you must return quickly, as I have to go to the theatre of the gods."

Now poor Psyche felt that all pretense was over and she was surely doomed to die. She knew of no way of going to the House of the Dead except by killing herself, and so she climbed in a high tower, resolved to throw herself down from the top. But the tower spoke to her and said: "Do not yield, Psyche, to this last and final danger. If you kill yourself, you will indeed visit the world of the dead, but you will never come back to this world. Listen to my words and do as I say. Not far from here is Taenarum where you will find a great hole in the ground. Go down the path bravely and it will lead you to the very palace of Pluto. But you must not go empty-handed. In your hands you must carry two cakes of barley and honey mixed. In your mouth you must have two halfpennies. When you have gone some way on your journey you will see a lame donkey carrying wood and a lame man driving him. The man will ask you to help him pick up some of the sticks that have fallen, but you must go on without a word, and do no such thing. Then you will come to the river of the dead where the foul old man Charon with his leaking boat ferries the souls between the banks. He will do nothing unless he is paid, and you must let him take from your mouth one of your two halfpennies. When you are on the black and deathly river you will see an old man swimming there who will beg and pray you to help him into the boat. You must not listen to him, since this is not allowed. When you have crossed the river you will pass by some old women weaving. They will ask you to help them, but you must not listen to them. These are all traps which Venus will set for you so as to make you drop one of the cakes from your hands. Yet without these cakes you can never make the journey or return again; for you will come to the great three-headed watchdog Cerberus, whose barking rings for ever through this desolate plain. He will never let you pass till you have given him one of your cakes to eat. Once you have passed him you will come into the presence of Proserpine and she will offer you a fine chair on which to sit and fine food to eat. But you must sit upon the ground and ask only for a crust of bread. Above all, do not look inside the box that Proserpine will give you. There is no need for you to have any curiosity about the treasure of heavenly beauty."

So the tower advised Psyche, and she took the two halfpennies and the two cakes and then made her way to Taenarum. She descended the dreadful path to Hell, passed by the lame donkey in silence, paid her halfpenny to Charon, gave no attention either to the man swimming in the river or to the women weaving, gave one of her cakes to the terrible watchdog and came finally into the presence of Proserpine. Here she refused the fine food that was set before her and sat humbly on the ground, asking only for a crust of bread. Then she gave Venus' message and received the secret gift in the closed box. On her way back she gave the cake to Cerberus and her last halfpenny to Charon. So she reached the upper air in safety, but then she said to herself, "What a fool I am to be carrying in this box the divine beauty and not to take a little of it for myself. If I take some I may please my husband in the end."

She opened the box but could see no beauty in it at all. Instead a deadly sleep came over her like a cloud and she fell fainting to the ground, lying where she fell like a dead body.

But Cupid was now cured of his wound, and, in longing for his wife, had climbed out of an upper window. He flew straight to her and, when he had wiped away the deadly sleep from her face and put it back in the box, he woke her by gently pricking her hand with one of his arrows. "Poor creature," he said, "again you were nearly ruined by your excess curiosity. Now go back to my mother and leave me to arrange the rest." Then he flew into the air and Psyche brought the box to Venus. Cupid meanwhile flew up to heaven and begged Jupiter, the father of the gods to help him in his faithful love. Jupiter called all the gods and goddesses to council and said to them, "It is not good that Cupid should always be loose and wandering about the earth. He has chosen a wife and it is right that he should enjoy her company and her love. In order that the marriage shall not be an unequal one I shall make Psyche immortal, and she and Cupid will live together in happiness for ever. This is my will and, since Psyche will be a real goddess, even Venus must be glad of the marriage."

Then he sent Mercury to bring Psyche up to heaven and, when she had come there, he said, "Take this cup of immortality, Psyche, and drink it to the end, so that you may live forever and that Cupid may never leave you again, but be your everlasting husband."

Then the great feast and wedding banquet was prepared. Cupid and Psyche sat in the places of honour and by them were Jupiter and Juno and all the gods in order. Bacchus filled their glasses with nectar, the wine of the gods. Vulcan prepared the supper. The Hours and Graces adorned the house with roses and other sweet smelling flowers. Apollo and the Muses sang together and Venus danced with divine grace to the music. So Psyche was married to Cupid and in time she bore a child whom we call Pleasure.

ACTIVITIES

FOR DISCUSSION

A. The symbolism of the story will probably be clearer if you understand the origins of the names Psyche and Cupid. Cupid is the Roman god of love, often pictured in art as a chubby, rosy-faced child armed with bow and arrow. In Greek mythology, however, the name for the god of love is Eros. Eros refers to sexual desire or the physical side of love. Which image, Cupid or Eros, seems more appropriate for Psyche's husband and lover as you know him in the story? Why? In the Greek language, Psyche means mind or soul. What does the marriage of Psyche and Eros represent symbolically?

B. There are two wedding ceremonies in the story of Cupid (Eros) and Psyche. Compare the two. Why does the first wedding begin with a funeral ceremony? What might that symbolize? Why do you think there is a second wedding ceremony? How is the relationship between Psyche and Cupid different by the time the second ceremony takes place?

C. After the second wedding ceremony we are told that Psyche and Cupid (Eros) "in time" give birth to a child named Pleasure. What does this birth symbolize? Why would the child named Pleasure be born only after the second ceremony? What does this tell us about the author's thoughts on the right time for having children?

D. Cupid forbids Psyche to look at him, but she lights a lamp while he is asleep and bends over him. Some hot oil falls on his shoulder. The pain wakens him, and he leaves wounded and angry. What do you make of Cupid's instruction to Psyche not to look at him? Did Cupid make a mistake by not telling Psyche the reason why she shouldn't look at him? How would you depict their relationship at that stage? What could the burning of Cupid symbolize? How can people in love "burn" each other? How did Cupid respond to being burned? Does his response remind you of anything that typically happens when people get burned? How do you evaluate Psyche's reaction? What would you do?

E. Psyche goes through terrible trials to regain her husband and to establish a relationship of genuine intimacy and trust. What could those trials symbolize? What kinds of "trials" confront lovers today? Do you think it worth while that people undergo trials to achieve genuine intimacy? This story uses a common plot for love stories: love meets love, love loses love, love finds love. Why do you think this theme is so popular? Why do lovers have to separate and suffer so?

F. At long last Psyche and Eros achieve pure joy in love and marriage. Psyche's sisters were never so fortunate. Why do they fail to find happiness? What do they value most highly? What does this story tell us about the source of greatest happiness in life?

COMMITMENT AND MARRIAGE: *FINALE*

The two activities below are for use with "The Order of the Marriage Service," "The Ceremony of Marriage," and the poem, "I Love You."

A. Divide the class into groups of five or six. Each group is to read and study one of the three following selections about the commitment a man and woman make to each other when they marry. Make a list from each reading of the specific responsibilities a bride and groom accept in marriage. What promises do they make to each other? After each group is finished, compare the lists.

B. Marriage ceremonies can be very traditional or highly individualized depending upon the wishes of the couple. It is a matter of personal preference. Though your ideas may change in the years ahead, at this point which of these three statements of commitment appeals to you most? Why? Are there other ideas you would like to include in your own wedding? You may want to try your hand at writing your own future marriage ceremony, deciding on what promises you intend to keep, and what promises you are asking of your future spouse.

FINAL CLASS ACTIVITY: Here Comes the Bride . . . and Groom!

Stage a wedding ceremony as the culmination of your *Loving Well* unit. You can make it as simple or elaborate as you wish. In order to explore all the possibilities, talk to married friends and family about their weddings. If some have particularly interesting stories, invite them to visit your class. Ask ministers, priests, rabbis, or other religious leaders as well as justices of the peace about traditional and non-traditional services. Collect ceremonies from as many religions and cultures as you can, and find out about wedding etiquette and customs. Then as a class decide how to celebrate this most joyous of occasions, the commitment of man and woman to love and live together forevermore as husband and wife.

As a wedding present for the newlyweds and as a memento for everyone who attends the ceremony, create *Love's Little Instruction Book*. Either individually or as a group, review all that you have learned about what it means to love well, and compile a manual for living as happily ever after as is humanly possible. Your publication might become a best seller!

THE ORDER FOR THE MARRIAGE SERVICE

T he Address

The persons to be married shall present themselves before the Minister, the Woman standing at the left hand of the Man. The Minister shall then say,

Dearly beloved, we are gathered together here in the presence of God, and in the face of this congregation, to join together this Man and this Woman in Holy Matrimony; which is an honorable estate, instituted of God, and therefore is not by any to be enterprised or taken in hand lightly or unadvisedly; but reverently, discreetly, soberly, and in the fear of God.

If any man can show just cause why they may not lawfully be joined together, let him now speak, or else hereafter forever hold his peace.

The Charge

And then, speaking to the persons who are to be married, the Minister shall say,

I require and charge you both, that if either of you know any impediment why ye may not be lawfully united in Matrimony, ye do now confess it. For be ye well assured that so many as are joined together, otherwise than God's word doth allow, are not joined together by God, nor is their union blessed by him.

The Vows

There being no impediment, the Minister shall then say to the Man,

_____, Wilt thou have this Woman to thy wedded Wife, to live together after God's ordinance in the holy estate of Matrimony? Wilt thou love her, comfort her, honor and keep her, in sickness and in health, in sorrow and in joy; and forsaking all others, keep thee only unto her so long as ye both shall live?

The Man shall answer I will

The Minister shall then say to the Woman

_____, Wilt thou have this Man to thy wedded Husband to live together after God's ordinance in the holy estate of Matrimony? Wilt thou love him, comfort him, honor and keep him, in sickness and in health, in sorrow and in joy; and, forsaking all others, keep thee only unto him so long as ye both shall live?

The Woman shall answer I will

Then the Minister shall say,

Who giveth this Woman to be married to this Man?

The Minister, receiving the Woman, at her Father's or Friend's hand, shall cause the Man with his right hand to take the Woman by her right hand, and to say after him,

I, _____, take thee, _____, to my wedded Wife, to have and to hold from this day forward, for better, for worse, for richer, for poorer, in sickness and in health, to love and to cherish, till death do us part, according to God's holy ordinance, and thereto I give thee my troth.

Then the Woman shall likewise say after the Minister,

I, _____, take thee, _____, to my wedded Husband, to have and to hold, from this day forward, for better, for worse, for richer or for poorer, in sickness and in health, to love and to cherish, till death do us part, according to God's holy ordinance, and thereto I give thee my troth.

The Man and the Woman shall then loose hands. The Minister, receiving a Ring from the Best Man, shall give it to the Man, who shall in turn place it on the fourth finger of the Woman's left hand. The Man, holding the ring there, shall say after the Minister,

With this Ring I thee wed; and to thee only do I promise to keep myself, so long as we both shall live. Amen.

If there are to be double Rings used at the service, the Minister shall receive a Ring from the Maid of Honor, and give it to the Woman, who shall place it upon the fourth finger of the Man's left hand and say after the Minister,

With this Ring I thee wed; and to thee only do I promise to keep myself, so long as we both shall lived. Amen.

The Prayer
The Minister shall then say,
Let us pray

Eternal God, creator and preserver of all mankind, send thy blessing upon these thy servants, whom we bless in thy name. Enable them to perform through all their years the vows which they have made in thy presence.

May they seriously attend to the duties of the new relation into which they have now entered; that it may not be to them a state of temptation and discord, but of mutual love and peace. Grant them the virtues of trust and patience and undying affection. May they be blessings and comforts to each other, sharers of each other's joys and sorrows, loyal companions in the life and work of every day, and helpers, each to the other, in all the chances and changes of this mortal life.

Hallow to them the home which they are to make and share together. Give them a wise love for all who may be committed to their care, keeping them always mindful that in thee we live and move and have our being, and that thou art our dwelling place in all generations. Through Jesus Christ our Lord. Amen.

The Pronouncement of the Marriage

The Minister shall then say,

Forasmuch as ＿＿＿＿＿ and ＿＿＿＿＿ have consented together in holy wedlock, and have witnessed the same before God and this company, and thereto have engaged and pledged themselves to each other, and have declared the same by joining hands and by giving and receiving a ring (rings), I pronounce that they are Man and Wife; and those whom God hath joined together, let no man put asunder.

CEREMONY OF MARRIAGE

Generations of men and women have reaffirmed in their works the knowledge that love, of all human qualities and feelings, will triumph over our failures and fears with beauty and with strength. Taught by our own lives, we know that love which brings two people together in marriage may so triumph if it will preserve its initial joy and add to that joy with faith and with resolution. Such a love belongs to those who will take a part in creating and preserving it.

We rejoice with these two people that out of all the world they have found each other. Out of our love we have come to witness and to honor the gift which they give to each other and to share in this moment of their joy. Let us find strength in their giving. Let us be renewed by their hopes and their dreams. And let us give to them from our own strength and our own dreams, today and always.

_____ and _____ , in presenting yourselves here today and before this gathering of your family and friends, you are demonstrating your love for each other. The love which now binds you together makes your lives broader and fuller than they could be alone. The strength of your love now is that it is vibrant and new, but its triumph must be in its endurance over many years. Love is a gift of men and women which they must nurture constantly and steadily to make it greater than the vicissitudes of time or chance.

Preserve the joy that now unites you. Add to it with your dreams. Strengthen it with determination, faith in one another and with forgiveness. And you will be a blessing each to the other and to all of us.

May the home you establish be an island where the pressures of a cluttered world may be sorted out and brought into focus; where accumulated tensions can be released and understood; where personal needs do not tower over concern for others and where the immediate does not blur a more distant goal; where the warmth of humor and of love puts both crisis and dullness into perspective.

Who gives this woman to be married? (optional)

Now I ask you to join hands, and I remind you that the hand offered by each of you is an extension of your whole self. Cherish the touch, for you give now your whole self and you receive another. Be sensitive to the pulse. Seek always to understand and to respect its rhythm.

What follows is a question and a vow. You may choose either one set or the other, or you may substitute your own question and vow.

A. Do you _____ take _____ to be your wife (husband) and will you love her (him), comfort her (him), honor her (his) life and keep her (him) for as long as you both shall live? I do.

Vow: I _____ take you _____ to be my wife (husband) to have and to hold from this day forward; for better, for worse; for richer, for poorer; in sickness and in health; to love and to cherish for as long as we both shall live.

B. Do you _____ take _____ to be your wife (husband) to live together with constancy and devotion. Will you love her (him), comfort her (him), honor and keep her (him) for as long as you both shall live? I do.

Vow: I _____ take _____ to be the wife (husband) of my days, to be the mother (father) of my children, to be my companion in our house. We shall keep together what share of trouble and sorrow our lives may lay upon us. And we shall share together our store of goodness and plenty of love.

Exchange of Rings
May the rings which you are about to exchange be forever the symbol of

the unbroken circle of love. Love freely given has no beginning and no end. Love freely given has no giver and no receiver, for each is the giver and each is the receiver. May these rings remind you always of the vows you have taken today.

Vow with the ring. *Here again there is a choice of A or B.*

A. This ring symbolizes two lives brought into one. With it we create life together.
(OR)
B. With this ring I thee wed.

May you find life's joys heightened, its bitterness sweetened and all things hallowed by true companionship and love.

Meditation by the minister.
Declaration by the minister.

I LOVE YOU

by Elmo Robinson

I love you. It is my deepest desire that we spend our days and years together. Our love shall unite us in a genuine union of hearts and lives, in which I shall cherish and care for you; and not merely materially, for I shall honor you for what you intrinsically are, for the richness and promise of your personality.

I love you. I love you unconditionally, hoping for your love freely given in return. My love is not demanding love, nor does it find room for resentments and hostilities. I will seek ever to understand you, to admire you for what you are, to recognize your potentialities, and to help you attain them. I have faith in you and in our future together, a future in which we may ever become persons more completely loving.

I love you. I love you now because I cannot help it, but I know there is more to love than I now feel. I promise to make the continuing effort to purge all feelings of boredom, guilt, or being threatened, and to learn to love more maturely. I will share with you my hopes, my dreams, my aspirations, and strive to make myself a sensitive receiver for your hopes, your dreams, your aspirations. And all this shall not be a grim and solemn task, but we shall be gay and laugh together through it all.

I love you. I say this freely, without any sense of being trapped or being under a compulsion which I resent. The togetherness for which I hope is one in which the strength in each of us will complement the weakness of the other. My love is the beginning of a great project, a new creation. Already the two of us constitute a family, united by an invisible bond, and providing a soil in which love can flourish, increase, and mature. To this bond, as well as to you, I pledge my devotion.

I love you. I shall become part of your clan, and you shall become part of mine. Your responsibilities shall be my responsibilities. If there be children, they shall draw us closer together. In the community in which we all live we will seek the companionship and fellowship of those who will enhance our love rather than endanger it. As the years bring their relentless changes, we will enrich the later years with memories of the earlier days. If together we live out the full span of our years, we will be able to look back over them rejoicing that our love has indeed bestowed upon us the blessings of a union which has led us out of the realm of law and convention into the realm of the spirit.

This statement of commitment could be used instead of more traditional marriage vows.